ANCIENT GREEK LAW
IN THE 21ST CENTURY

EDITED BY PAULA PERLMAN

University of Texas Press

AUSTIN

Requests for permission to reproduce material
from this work should be sent to:
Permissions
University of Texas Press
P.O. Box 7819
Austin, TX 78713-7819
http://utpress.utexas.edu/rp-form

♾ The paper used in this book meets the minimum requirements of
ANSI/NISO Z39.48-1992 (R1997) (Permanence of Paper).

LIBRARY OF CONGRESS CATALOGING-IN-PUBLICATION DATA

Names: Greek law in the 21st century (Conference)
(2011 : University of Texas at Austin) | Perlman, Paula Jean, editor.
Title: Ancient Greek law in the 21st century / edited by Paula Perlman.
Description: First edition. | Austin : University of Texas Press, 2018. |
"The genesis of the papers presented in this volume was a conference
held March 31 to April 2, 2011, at the University of Texas at Austin,
titled Greek Law in the 21st Century."—ECIP acknowledgments. |
Includes bibliographical references and index.
Identifiers: LCCN 2017038783
ISBN 978-1-4773-1521-7 (cloth : alk. paper)
ISBN 978-1-4773-1571-2 (library e-book)
ISBN 978-1-4773-1572-9 (non-library e-book)
Subjects: LCSH: Law, Greek. | Law, Greek—Influence. |
Public law (Greek law) | Greece—Civilization—History.
Classification: LCC KL4106.5 .G74 2018 | DDC 340.5/38—dc23
LC record available at https://lccn.loc.gov/2017038783

doi:10.7560/315217

CONTENTS

ABBREVIATIONS

For abbreviations of literary sources, authors follow H. G. Liddell and R. Scott, *A Greek-English Lexicon*, 9th ed., revised by H. Stuart Jones and R. McKenzie. Oxford, 1996.

CID = *Corpus des Inscriptions de Délos*.
Corinth 8.1 = B. D. Meritt, *Corinth VIII.1. Greek Inscriptions, 1896–1927*. Princeton, 1931.
DK = H. Diels and W. Kranz, *Die Fragmente der Vorsokratiker*. Zurich, 1985.
EKM 1.Beroia = L. Gounaropoulou and M. Hatzopoulos, Ἐπιγραφὲς Κάτω Μακεδονίας. Α᾽ Ἐπιγραφὲς Βεροίας. Athens, 1998.
FD = *Fouilles de Delphes*.
IC = M. Guarducci, *Inscriptiones Creticae*. Rome, 1935–1950.
ID = F. Durrbach, *Inscriptions de Délos*. Paris, 1926–1937.
IG = *Inscriptiones Graecae*.
IK Adramytteion = J. Stauber, *Die Inschriften von Adramytteion. IGSK* 50–51. Bonn, 1996.
IK Byzantion = A. Lajtar, *Die Inschriften von Byzantion. IGSK* 58. Bonn, 2000.
IK Erythrai und Klazomenai = H. Engelmann and R. Merkelbach, *Die Inschriften von Erythrai und Klazomenai. IGSK* 1–2. Bonn, 1972–1973.
IK Iasos = W. Blümel, *Die Inschriften von Iasos. IGSK* 28. Bonn, 1985.
IK Ilion = P. Frisch, *Die Inschriften von Ilion. IGSK* 3. Bonn, 1975.
IK Rhod. Peraia = W. von Blümel, *Die Inschriften der rhodischen Peraia. IGSK* 38. Bonn, 1991.
IPArk = G. Thür and H. Taeuber, *Prozessrechtliche Inschriften der griechischen Poleis: Arkadien*. Vienna, 1994.
I.Oropos = B. Petrakos, Οἱ ἐπιγραφὲς τοῦ Ὠρωποῦ. Athens, 1997.
I.Scythiae Minoris = E. Popescu, *Inscriptiones Daciae et Scythiae Minoris antiquae*. Bucharest, 1976.

I.Thespies = P. Roesch, *Les inscriptions de Thespies*, 2. Lyons, 2009.

IvEphesos = H. Wankel, *Die Inschriften von Ephesos*. Bonn, 1979–1984.

IvO = W. Dittenberger and K. Purgold, *Die Inschriften von Olympia*. Berlin, 1896.

IvP = M. Fraenkel, *Die Inschriften von Pergamon*. Berlin, 1890–1895.

McCabe *Teos* = D. F. McCabe and M. A. Plunkett, *Teos Inscriptions: Texts and List*. Princeton, 1985.

Milet = *Milet: Ergebnisse der Ausgrabungen und Untersuchungen seit dem Jahre 1899*.

ML = R. Meiggs and D. Lewis, *A Selection of Greek Historical Inscriptions*, rev. ed. Oxford, 1988.

LSAM = F. Sokolowski, *Lois sacrées de l'Asie Mineure*. Paris, 1955.

LSCG = K. Sokolowski, *Lois sacrées des cités grecques*. Paris, 1969.

LSCG Suppl. = F. Sokolowski, *Lois sacrées des cités grecques*. Paris, 1962.

Migeotte = L. Migeotte, *L'emprunt public dans les cités grecques: recueil des documents et analyse critique*. Paris, 1984.

OGIS = W. Dittenberger, *Orientis Graeci Inscriptiones Selectae*. Leipzig, 1903–1905.

P. Gurob = J. G. Smyly, *Greek papyri from Gurob*. Dublin and London, 1921.

RO = P. Rhodes and R. Osborne, *Greek Historical Inscriptions, 404–323 B.C.* Oxford, 2003.

Rusch. = E. Ruschenbusch, *Solonos* nomoi. *Die Fragmente des solonischen Gesetzeswerkes*. Wiesbaden, 1966.

Syll.[3] = W. Dittenberger, *Sylloge Inscriptionum Graecarum*, 3rd ed. Leipzig, 1915–1924.

SEG = *Supplementum Epigraphicum Graecum*.

West = M. West, *Iambi et elegi Graeci ante Alexandrum cantati*. Oxford, 1971–1972.

Wilcken 1912 = U. Wilcken, *Grundzüge und Chrestomathie der Papyruskunde* 1.2. Leipzig and Berlin, 1912.

ACKNOWLEDGMENTS

THE GENESIS OF THE PAPERS PRESENTED IN THIS VOLUME was a conference held March 31 to April 2, 2011, at the University of Texas at Austin, titled "Greek Law in the 21st Century." The objective of the conference was to bring together leading authorities in the study of ancient Greek law in order to assess the current state of the field and to explore its future. The decision to publish the proceedings of the conference was based in part on the consensus of the participants that research in ancient Greek law would greatly benefit from a broader perspective that nonspecialists could bring to the field. To assist such readers, care has been taken to provide translations of the Greek and to gloss all technical vocabulary.

Funding for the conference was contributed by the College of Liberal Arts, under the leadership of its dean, Randy Diehl, and by the Department of Classics and its chair, Stephen A. White. I am grateful to both for their generous support. I owe additional thanks to Adriaan Lanni and Robert Wallace for their introduction to this volume and to all of the contributors for their efforts in revising their papers with a broader audience in mind. Stephanie Craven assisted in proofreading and in creating the indices. At University of Texas Press, Senior Editor Jim Burr, Assistant Manuscript Editor Amanda Frost, and Copy Editor Suzanne Abrams Rebillard provided invaluable assistance in producing this volume.

June 2017
Paula Perlman

ANCIENT GREEK LAW IN THE 21ST CENTURY

INTRODUCTION

Adriaan Lanni and Robert W. Wallace

WHILE MAJOR SCHOLARS, INCLUDING LIPSIUS, BONNER AND Smith, and Harrison, had published important studies of Greek law in earlier decades of the twentieth century,[1] Greek law was established as an independent field in the 1970s, in Continental law schools. This development was marked by the 1971 foundation of the Symposion Society for the History of Greek and Hellenistic Law, by Hans Julius Wolff, professor of Greek law, Roman law, and civil law at Freiburg. From its inception the Symposion has ensured that following a conference every three years, and since 1993, every two years, some twenty to thirty papers on Greek law are published in a readily accessible series, which since 1990 has also included critical responses. These conferences have fostered many other collaborative efforts among Symposiasts and other interested scholars, including visiting lectures and more extended teaching at participants' universities; the advent of *Dike*, a journal of ancient Greek law founded by Eva Cantarella in 1998 and edited by Alberto Maffi; the publication in 2005 of *The Cambridge Companion to Ancient Greek Law*, including twenty-two essays, edited by Michael Gagarin and David Cohen; and the appearance in 2011 of the 657-page *New Working Bibliography of Ancient Greek Law: 7th–4th Centuries BC*, by Symposiasts Mark Sundahl, David Mirhady, and Ilias Arnaoutoglou. Seven of the eight members of the Symposion's steering committee have contributed to the current volume (the eighth, Joseph Mélèze Modrzejewski, was prevented from doing so by ill health). All of its contributors, as well as thirteen contributors to Gagarin and Cohen's *The Cambridge Companion to Ancient Greek Law*, have participated in many Symposion conferences.

While Wolff himself was fully cognizant of the differences between Greek, Roman, and modern law, the early Symposia reflected to a notable degree the influence of Continental law professors, not ancient historians.[2] Many early

Symposiasts were Europeans with law degrees and trained in Roman law, the basis of Continental legal systems. They taught modern and Roman law in law schools, and Greek law when they could, although Greek law had no professional significance for their students. The only native Anglophone scholar working in Greek law in the 1960s and 1970s was Douglas MacDowell at Glasgow. He was primarily a classicist and, as he has said,[3] began to study Greek law in order better to understand Greek forensic oratory. The focus of many Symposion essays on what were called Greek procedural and substantive laws, and on the corpus of laws from Ptolemaic and Roman Egypt, reflected the Roman and modern European legal training of many participants.

Scholars from Britain and the United States started attending the Symposion beginning with MacDowell in 1982, then Michael Gagarin and David Cohen in 1985, followed by Gagarin, David Cohen, and Edward Cohen in 1988, and then in greater numbers from 1990, when Gagarin organized the first US Symposion at Pacific Grove, California. Although American Symposiasts David Cohen, Edward Cohen, and, more recently, Adriaan Lanni all hold US law degrees and Gagarin has taught law courses at the University of Texas, common law is profoundly different from Continental law (for one, like Greek law it has no jurists). Moreover, Anglo-American students of Greek law were not practicing lawyers but students of classical texts and ancient history, cognizant, as was Wolff, that for the ancient Greeks, laws and legal procedures were not the subjects of self-standing professional disciplines but best understood as functioning within—as embedded within—the societies of which they were a part. Greek laws and legal procedures were components of social and political history, reflecting not formal legalisms but the daily realities of managing society.

For classicists studying the Greek world, and Greek historians interested in law, interdisciplinary legal sociology and comparative anthropology were not alien disciplines. Though trained as a lawyer and spending most of her career as a professor of law at Milan, Eva Cantarella is also a historian and sociologist of the ancient world. She once observed to one of the current volume's contributors that without anthropology and sociology, "in Greek law we have nothing." The Greeks invented written law in the West, and laws were important to them, but other things were important too, and these things jostled together in legislation, in court cases, and in literary texts, each with its own set of perspectives and complications. Because the Greek society that we know best is classical Athens, and most extant legal, forensic, and historical texts are Athenian (with honorable mention to "the world of Homer"), it is mainly here that we can witness what Robin Osborne has called "law in action."[4] Archaic and classical Crete and Ptolemaic and Roman Egypt offer rich legal documentation, but until recently these societies held little interest for

many classicists and ancient historians, especially as major historical and forensic texts that bring their laws alive are lacking.

THE ELEVEN ESSAYS IN THE CURRENT VOLUME REFLECT
these and other developments in the field of Greek law, crossing the traditional divisions set by Roman law and Continental jurisprudence that have
demarcated this subject from its inception. These papers chart new directions
for the study of Greek law in the twenty-first century by reassessing some of
the central debates in the field (Chapters 1–4); by exploring historical periods
and legal topics that have been comparatively neglected in recent scholarship
(Chapters 5–7); by suggesting new methodological approaches, often drawn
from modern legal theory (Chapters 8–10); and by demonstrating the contemporary relevance of teaching ancient Greek law in the twenty-first century (Chapter 11). They are the product of a conference held at the University of Texas at Austin in honor of Michael Gagarin, the James R. Dougherty,
Jr. Centennial Professor Emeritus of Classics there, and organized by Paula
Perlman. Its contributors are pleased to dedicate this book to Michael, to cel-
ebrate his more than forty years' work on the history of Greek law and rhetoric, as well as philosophy and Greek tragedy.

THE OPENING CHAPTERS OF THIS BOOK ADDRESS ISSUES
that have been the subject of significant debate in recent scholarship and are
central to our understanding of the Athenian legal system. How valid for
Greek law is the traditional Roman and later division between procedural and
substantive law, and what role did laws play in regulating Greek societies?
What role did feuding and revenge play in Athenian courts? Did the Athenians have a notion of "contract"? What was the legal framework for slaves
who engaged in commercial activity?

In "Administering Justice in Ancient Athens: Framework and Core Principles," Robert Wallace first critiques the common view that Greek law was primarily concerned with judicial procedures, not with defining and punishing
offenses (i.e., substantive law). This view derives from the brief, unspecific
way many laws mention crimes and punishments, in contrast to their typically
elaborate details regarding the procedures each type of case should follow. As
Wallace argues here, two reasons for this disparity in laws are that the notion
of defining terms emerged only in the later fourth century, and that, as several Athenian writers state, Greeks knew that any such effort in drafting laws
could rarely be sufficiently inclusive. Details of offenses were set out in indictments—for example, the indictment of Socrates as reported in Plato's *Apology*
and other texts. Second, Wallace contends that each Athenian law carefully
detailed the procedures to be followed in the area it regulated, because Ath-

ens had no general procedural laws. Each law specified the procedures to be used, as otherwise cases could not be brought to court or adjudicated. Third, Wallace argues that the administration of justice at Athens was even systematically organized ("shaped") not by procedural or substantive law, but in accordance with democratic principles and community interests. Many scholars have posited problems with Athens's administration of justice, including sycophancy, appeals to jurors' emotions, and irrelevant material in court speeches. Many such "problems" were a consequence of the system's democratic principles and community orientation, and were not always construed as problems.

In "Revenge and Punishment," Eva Cantarella addresses an important issue raised by the recent work of Symposiasts Danielle Allen and then David Phillips, who develop claims partly derived from David Cohen's view that law courts were agonistic loci of personal feuding (although Cohen did not go as far as they do). Allen and Phillips question the traditional sharp division between the prelegal world of revenge, governed by passions including anger, and the supposedly dispassionate rule of law. For Allen, anger was prevalent in Athens's courts, regulated (like sexuality) primarily by self-control. For Phillips, courts served as a principal locus for pursuing enmity (*echthra*). Cantarella points out that the Athenians did in fact regulate sexuality, by law and also by various forms of social pressure. As for the courts, they were concerned with discovering guilt or innocence according to established laws. There was a role for anger in Athenian justice, but not primarily among the jurors. Literary texts, including Aeschylus's *Eumenides*, stress that vengeance is not the court's function. Litigants also stress that, though angry, they seek to follow the law. Courts inflicted punishment, not revenge or "honor reassessment."

In "Hyperides's *Against Athenogenes* and the Athenian Law on Agreements," Michael Gagarin discusses the well-known, though still vigorously debated, question whether agreements at Athens were legally binding.[5] He argues that the Athenians did indeed have a law stipulating that agreements—for example, in commerce—were binding, while he rejects for Greece the Roman and modern legal term "contract" and the use of Roman and modern legal terminology generally (including, in this case, "real" vs. "consensual" contracts). He further concludes that Athenian law did not specify that agreements had to be witnessed or even be legal or voluntary, although these latter two qualities reflected its intent. He closes with general reflections on how the Athenians understood their laws not as loose texts with imprecise language, but as relying on commonsense understandings of ordinary language. Were unjust agreements enforceable? Although Athens's law on agreements did not mention it, the court would understand that unjust agreements were not enforceable.

In previous work, Edward Cohen has sparked controversy by challenging the traditional view that slaves were largely outside the ambit of legal regulation. In response to recent critiques, in particular by Maffi,[6] Cohen's "Slaves Operating Businesses: Legal Ramifications for Ancient Athens—and for Modern Scholarship" addresses the "paradox" that slaves played a major role in running Athens's economy but seemingly had no legal rights or capacities. Cohen studies various mechanisms to close these gaps, ensuring that slaves bore legal responsibility for their business obligations although such responsibilities would apparently seem inconsistent with the letter of the law. As Cohen indicates, legalistic approaches to these problems were also opposed by the sometime Symposiast Mario Talamanca, who stressed the differences between Greek and Roman law;[7] by David Cohen;[8] and, as Edward Cohen has noted in earlier essays, by a major student of Greek slavery, Yvon Garlan.[9]

Several of the chapters in the volume break new ground by examining substantive areas of law, such as administrative law and sacred law, or sources from historical periods, such as Hellenistic inscriptions, that have been comparatively neglected in recent scholarship.

Despite the many recent studies of Athenian law and Athenian democracy, there has been no attempt to provide an overarching account of the law of the Athenian state, that is, what moderns would call "administrative law." Alberto Maffi's "Toward a New Shape of the Relationship between Public and Private Law in Ancient Greece" begins that important project. For Maffi, ancient Greek administrative law must not be limited to an examination of the powers and discipline of magistrates. Because executive functions could be delegated to private citizens—for example, in the institution of the volunteer public prosecutor—any account of administrative law must incorporate an analysis of private governance as well. Maffi explores several examples in which private citizens were called upon to manage public interests in Athens. As he points out, this examination of a society that combined public and private governance is of particular interest now that modern states are increasingly recognizing the role played by private actors—financial institutions, charitable and other nongovernmental organizations, and even corporations—in advancing the public interest.

Martin Dreher's "'*Heiliges Recht*' and '*Heilige Gesetze*': Law, Religion, and Magic in Ancient Greece" similarly addresses a fairly neglected area in ancient Greek law: sacred law. Aside from the prosecution of *asebeia* ("impiety") in Athenian courts, in recent years legal historians have rarely studied questions of sacred law in depth, while historians of Greek religion tend not to focus on the juridical questions raised in their sources. For this reason, basic questions—such as when legal issues related to sacred law were decided by priests rather than by polis institutions, and what legal powers, if any, did cultic personnel wield to punish religious offenders—remain understudied. Dreher describes the wide range of topics and sources that should be covered to gain an understanding of Greek sacred law, including not just religious offenses, but also the regulation of cult practices and festivals, sacred laws relating to inter-poleis relations and institutions, and curse tablets.

Lene Rubinstein's "Summary Fines in Greek Inscriptions and the Question of 'Greek Law'" shifts the focus from classical Athenian court speeches to inscriptions from non-Athenian communities in the Hellenistic period. This turn to non-Athenian, nonclassical sources is likely to intensify in future research as epigraphical sources become more readily available in digital formats over the web. Rubinstein's contribution illustrates the potential of research that traces a particular legal institution through inscriptions from communities throughout the Greek world. Rubinstein explores the evidence for the imposition of summary fines by public officials in the absence of prior authorization by a court. Her findings suggest that the use of summary fines (as well as other institutions, such as the volunteer prosecutor) was not associated with democratic or oligarchic regimes specifically, but was characteristic of Greek law enforcement more generally. The use of summary fines appears to reflect the practical difficulties of enforcement through court procedures, particularly in maintaining order at mass public gatherings, protecting the infrastructure of the polis and its sanctuaries, and regulating some aspects of the market.

Other contributions in the volume focus attention not on new topics but on the use of new methodologies, including modern legal theory and comparative law.

In "Soft Law in Ancient Greece?," Julie Velissaropoulos-Karakostas draws on concepts in modern legal theory to illuminate aspects of ancient Greek law. She examines the potential application of the concept of "soft law"—that is, quasi-legal regulatory instruments that do not rely on binding rules or formal sanctions—to legal studies of the Hellenistic period. She finds that while forms of "hard law" like statutes and decrees remained the primary mode of regulating relations between citizens, the "globalization" of the eastern Mediterranean in the Hellenistic period led to the emergence of what may be recognized as forms of soft law: international treaties, decisions rendered by foreign judges and arbitrators, notarial practice, and customary law. The use of these tools, she argues, resulted in the "creation of the Hellenistic legal *koinē*, the common private law of the Eastern Mediterranean" that was never codified and only partially converted into forms of hard law.

Adriaan Lanni's "From Anthropology to Sociology: New Directions in

Ancient Greek Law Research" argues for a sociological rather than anthropological approach to Greek law that focuses on the incentives created by legal rules and institutions. She explores two potentially fruitful methods in current legal sociology—law and economics and social norms theory—and provides examples applying each of these methods to explain aspects of Athenian legal enforcement. Lanni's approach seeks to reorient ancient Greek law research from a focus on rhetoric, procedure, and informal dispute resolution, to substantive law and the operation of formal legal institutions.

Mogens Herman Hansen's "Oral Law in Ancient Greece?" calls for the comparative study of the use of oral law in preliterate societies to shed light on the period before written laws in ancient Greece. He asks: "Did [the Greeks] have laws passed by the community and remembered by its members? Or did they just have some customs and traditions that cannot be considered a body of laws in the proper sense?" Hansen provides a survey of several societies—from medieval Iceland and the Incan empire to twentieth-century village communities in Eritrea and Albania—that appear to have had "oral law" in the sense of binding unwritten rules passed by a legislative body or official, and orally transmitted to future generations. Although there is no direct evidence of oral legislation in early Greece, Hansen argues that the comparative evidence, along with suggestive features of early written laws in Greece, indicate that the early Greeks did have orally transmitted legislation, particularly concerning constitutional and religious matters.

The final contribution to the volume reflects not on scholarly methodology but on pedagogy and the relevance of teaching ancient Greek law in the twenty-first century. While here calling himself a "jurist" of the traditional stamp (he is one of the Symposion's finest), in "The Future of Classical Oratory" Gerhard Thür focuses on the continuing importance of rhetoric and the value of teaching our students rhetoric—the art of convincing that is so important to us all. In legal contexts, he argues, one of the tasks of rhetoric is to manipulate the facts, both by selecting which facts to present and in which contexts and by attributing psychological motivations that cannot be proved, but which may be effective in different mass contexts. Thür identifies these principles at work in speeches by Hyperides and Demosthenes. His final point concerns the division between narrow scholarly and popular appeal, which Thür bridges by stressing the importance of teaching rhetoric both by practice and by research into the speeches of antiquity, the reconstruction of opposing arguments (which for ancient speeches rarely survive), and the delivery of these speeches before live audiences who vote. Should we teach students to lie, for example, by manipulating the facts? No, but understanding such techniques helps to penetrate political propaganda and commercial advertising.

NOTES

1. Lipsius 1905–1915; Bonner and Smith 1930–1938; Harrison 1968–1971.
2. See especially Maffi 2001.
3. MacDowell 1997: 384.
4. Osborne 1985.
5. See Gagliardi 2014; Wallace 2014.
6. Maffi 2008.
7. Talamanca 2008.
8. Cohen 2005.
9. Cohen 1992: 94; 1998; 2007; Garlan 1982.

REFERENCES

Bonner, Robert J., and Gertrude Smith. 1930–1938. *The Administration of Justice from Homer to Aristotle*. 2 vols. Chicago: University of Chicago Press.
Cohen, David. 2005. "Crime, Punishment, and the Rule of Law in Classical Athens." In *The Cambridge Companion to Ancient Greek Law*, edited by Michael Gagarin and David Cohen, 211–235. Cambridge: Cambridge University Press.
Cohen, Edward E. 1992. *Athenian Economy and Society: A Banking Perspective*. Princeton: Princeton University Press.
———. 1998. "The Wealthy Slaves of Athens: Legal Rights, Economic Obligations." In *Le monde antique et les droits de l'homme*, edited by Huguette Jones, 105–129. Brussels: Université libre de Bruxelles.
———. 2007. "Slave Power at Athens: Juridical Theory and Economic Reality." In *Individus, groupes et politique à Athènes de Solon à Mithridate*, edited by Jean-Christophe Couvenhes and Silvia Milanezi, 155–170. Tours: Presses universitaires François-Rabelais.
Gagarin, Michael, and David Cohen, eds. 2005. *The Cambridge Companion to Ancient Greek Law*. Cambridge: Cambridge University Press.
Gagliardi, Lorenzo. 2014. "La legge sulla *homologia* e i vizi della volontà nei contratti in diritto ateniese." In *Symposion 2013: Vorträge zur griechischen und hellenistischen Rechtsgeschichte*, edited by Michael Gagarin and Adriaan Lanni, 177–214. Vienna: Verlag der Österreichischen Akademie der Wissenschaften.
Garlan, Yvon. 1982. *Les esclaves en Grèce ancienne*. Paris: Maspero.
Harrison, A. R. W. 1968–1971. *The Law of Athens*. 2 vols. Oxford: Clarendon Press.
Lipsius, Justus Hermann. 1905–1915. *Das attische Recht und Rechtsverfahren: Mit Benutzung des Attischen Processes*. 3 vols. Leipzig: Reisland.
MacDowell, Douglas M. 1997. Review of *Dike Phonou: The Right of Prosecution in Attic Homicide Procedure*, by Alexander Tulin. *Classical Review* 47: 384.
Maffi, Alberto. 2001. "Hans Julius Wolff e gli studi di diritto greco a trent'anni dal I Symposion." *Dike* 4: 269–291.
———. 2008. "Economia e diritto nell'Atene del IV secolo." In *Symposion 2007:*

Vorträge zur griechischen und hellenistischen Rechtsgeschichte, edited by Edward M. Harris and Gerhard Thür, 203–222. Vienna: Verlag der Österreichischen Akademie der Wissenschaften.

Osborne, Robin. 1985. "Law in Action in Classical Athens." *The Journal of Hellenic Studies* 105: 40–58.

Sundahl, Mark, David Mirhady, and Ilias Arnaoutoglou. 2011. *A New Working Bibliography of Ancient Greek Law: 7th–4th centuries BC*. Athens: Academy of Athens.

Talamanca, Mario. 2008. "Risposta a Alberto Maffi." In *Symposion 2007: Vorträge zur griechischen und hellenistischen Rechtsgeschichte*, edited by Edward M. Harris and Gerhard Thür, 223–228. Vienna: Verlag der Österreichischen Akademie der Wissenschaften.

Wallace, Robert W. 2014. "Did Athens have Consensual Contracts? A Response to Lorenzo Gagliardi." In *Symposion 2013: Vorträge zur griechischen und hellenistischen Rechtsgeschichte*, edited by Michael Gagarin and Adriaan Lanni, 215–221. Vienna: Verlag der Österreichischen Akademie der Wissenschaften.

1 / ADMINISTERING JUSTICE IN ANCIENT ATHENS: FRAMEWORK AND CORE PRINCIPLES

Robert W. Wallace

IN 2011 GREEK LEGAL HISTORIANS CELEBRATED TWO FINE achievements: the many contributions of Michael Gagarin to Greek law, rhetoric, and tragedy, on the occasion of his formal retirement from the University of Texas, and the sesquicentennial of Sir Henry Sumner Maine's *Ancient Law*.[1] Since Maine, most legal historians have concluded that Greek law was primarily concerned with fixing the procedures for administering justice, rather than with demarcating crimes and punishments, that is, with procedural rather than substantive law. Many, including Stephen Todd in his impressive effort to understand Athenian law as a system, have defended for Greece Maine's famous pronouncement: "In the infancy of courts of justice, substantive law has at first the look of being gradually secreted in the interstices of procedure."[2] As Mogens Herman Hansen has noted, "In the forensic speeches we hear of innumerable procedures and types of process whereas the substantive rules concerning offenses, obligations, property, etc., are vague and often obscure."[3] Todd writes that Greek law's "primary concern is to enable a case to be heard," and "the priority of procedure underlies the whole structure of this book."[4] Such conceptions have produced some striking formulations. For example, according to Paul Millett, "The unspoken aim of the legal process in Athens was not primarily enforcement of the laws or even securing justice for the individual; rather, it was the settlement of disputes."[5] While most legal historians distinguish between the substantive and procedural components of individual Greek laws,[6] others speak more boldly, seeming to imply that some or even many laws are mostly or only procedural. Robin Osborne writes that early laws "frequently do not decree what may or may not be done—they only decree who is to regulate what may or may not be done."[7] Far from remedying injustice, for Osborne early laws mainly regulated relations between elites.[8] Todd himself states that "procedural gives rise to substantive law," seeming to imply that in ancient Greece, procedural law might be distinct from substantive law.[9] These assessments have also included an important evaluative component, that especially as compared with Roman law, Greek law was "primitive"—Maine's word, which Todd and others repeat—producing uneven justice.[10]

Why do historians think that "the Athenians took much more interest in procedural than in substantive law"?[11] Some of the reasons adduced for this hypothesis, including the nonbinding status of substantive laws in Athenian courts, the absence of jurists, and the weak force of legal precedent, I shall discuss in different contexts later in this essay. Here I begin with the "shape" of Athenian laws, whether and why laws focused more on procedures than offenses. For these questions Draco's homicide law—the subject of an important book by Gagarin—is often exhibit A.[12] That law begins: "and (or, for Gagarin, 'even') if someone kills another without *pronoia* ('premeditation'), he is to be exiled; the *basileis* are to pronounce responsible [. . .]; the *ephetai* are to *diagnōnai* [. . .]; pardon is to be given if there is a father or brother or sons [. . .]" (*IG* I³ 104).[13] As others, too, have noted, Chris Carey—although partly an important heretic, as we shall see—mentions this measure's "lack of concern for definition: the law appears to take for granted one of the fundamental distinctions between categories of homicide (intentional versus unintentional), and concentrates instead on the minutiae of procedure for dealing with the offense."[14] Osborne writes, "The opening of the law . . . makes it look as if it is the killing that is regulated, but in fact the emphasis is not on the killing (there is no further definition of 'without premeditation' . . .), it is on who has the right to grant pardon. . . . This is not a law about homicide as such."[15] Osborne suggests that Draco's law was probably mostly directed toward people returning "to a position of some authority," that is, the elite.

Later laws are similar. They do not define offenses such as *hubris* or *asebeia* ("impiety") but name them and move on. In his pellucid handbook on Athenian law, Douglas MacDowell worried about "the legal definition of impiety" relative to, for example, "the question of intention: was a person guilty of impiety if he accidentally or in ignorance contravened a sacred law?"[16] A story in Aristotle (*Eth. Nic.* IIIIa) about Aeschylus argues no, but an accusation against Andocides (Andoc. 1.113) suggests yes, and MacDowell prefers Andocides. However, he surely points to the truth when he then observes that no law could be complete, and guesses that the law against impiety "said something like, 'If anyone commits impiety, let anyone who wishes submit a *graphē* ("public lawsuit"). . . .'" Even Carey is "inclined to accept the assumption" that "the majority of Athenian legislation was procedural in emphasis."[17]

How do we explain Greek laws' elaboration of procedure but not substance? Outside the texts of these laws, our sources invariably stress the importance of substantive justice, of crimes and punishments, not procedures.

Points of concern are identifying crimes and punishing lawbreakers, and punishing similar offenses equally. The Athenian orator Lycurgus proclaimed, "The law exists to state what should not be done" (1.4). Theseus famously states in Euripides's *Suppliants*, "When laws are written down, the weak and the wealthy have equal justice" (433–434). Supplying evidence for fourth-century Athenian thought (rather than Zaleucus's sixth-century Locri), Strabo records:

> Ephorus says that Zaleucus was among the first to make the following innovation, that whereas before his time it had been left to the judges to determine the penalties for each of the crimes, he defined (*diōrisen*) them in the laws, thinking that the opinions of the judges about the same crimes would not be the same, although they ought to be. (6.1.8; trans. Jones 1924, adapted)[18]

What concerned seventh-century Athenians was the severity of Draco's punishments. When Solon proclaimed that he drafted laws that were "equal for *kakos* and *agathos* ('base' and 'elite') alike, fitting straight justice to each" (fr. 36 W. = [Arist.] *Ath. Pol.* 12.4), and legislated that officials' verdicts could be appealed to the demos ([Arist.] *Ath. Pol.* 9.1), we cannot think he meant that the procedures should be equal. Rather, the guilty should receive even-handed punishment. This point is reiterated in stories of early lawgivers and tyrants, as when Charondas inadvertently broke his own law against carrying a knife into the assembly and was punished (Diod. Sic. 12.19). Charged with homicide, the tyrant Peisistratus showed up in the Areopagus court, although his accuser did not ([Arist.] *Ath. Pol.* 16.8). In classical Athens, courtroom speakers typically care very much whether defendants have broken the law and were guilty as charged. The presentation and interpretation of substantive laws are a major component of forensic speeches, for example, in Lysias 1.30–34 and 49, where Euphiletus's discussion of Athenian law focuses on the punishments for rape and adultery.[19] When the dicasts (lay-judges) swore "I shall vote according to the laws of the Athenian demos" (Dem. 24.149), that oath referred to laws' substantive components.

In his article "The Shape of Athenian Laws," the only major challenge to standard opinions on these issues, Carey observes that many Athenian laws were either largely or entirely substantive, especially laws that empower rather than prohibit, for example, laws on funerals ([Dem.] 43.62) and wills,[20] laws specifying the conditions for legally binding contracts, laws about fulfilling obligations (for example, the stipulation that the husband of an *epiklēros* ["heiress"] must sleep with her three times each month [Plut. *Sol.* 20.3]), or laws regulating religion and cult or the transfer of property.[21] Athens's many constitutional laws, such as those specifying the duties of public officials,[22] will all have been substantive. Carey remarks, "Constitutional law will inevitably have made up a substantial proportion of the lawcode and will have had a profound impact on the Athenians' own perception of their laws."[23] He observes, "Substantive regulations are not always secreted in the interstices; sometimes they are highly visible."[24]

These observations also apply to Solon's laws. For Solon, the detailed substantive measures authentic to his law code promoted social order and reflected systematic thought. In fact, it remains unclear how far his laws included enforcement provisions. One law specified the minimum distance from a neighbor's property to a house, wall, ditch, well, beehive, or certain kinds of trees (frs. 60–2 Rusch. = 60a–c Rhodes/Leão). Another forbade speaking ill of the dead (fr. 32a Rusch. = 32a–c Rhodes/Leão), arguably to curtail violence at elite funerals. His first *axōn* ("rotating board") included a law that if anyone exported any agricultural product except olive oil, "the archon ('chief magistrate') was to pronounce curses upon him, or else himself pay a hundred drachmas into the public treasury" (Plut. *Sol.* 24.1).

As has often been said, many Athenian and other laws state an offense in the conditional form, identify the officials responsible for handling the case, and state the punishment: "If someone does x [a bad thing], his case is adjudicated by y and the penalty is z." Athens's law on *hubris* runs: "If anyone treats with *hubris* any person . . . , let *ho boulomenos* ('volunteer prosecutor') submit a *graphē* to the *thesmothetai* (judicial officials)," who introduce the case into court. "Whomever the Heliaea (the Assembly) finds guilty, let it immediately assess whatever penalty it thinks right" (Dem. 21.47). Other examples include: "If an alien lives in marriage with an Athenian woman, . . ." ([Dem.] 59.16); "If someone catches a *moichos* ('adulterer'), let him treat him as he wishes" (Lys. 1.49); and "If anyone digs up an olive tree . . . he is to owe one hundred drachmas" ([Dem.] 43.71). Already the earliest written laws specify crimes and punishments according to such formulas: "If someone commits fornication in the sacred precinct, one shall make him expiate it by the sacrifice of an ox and by complete purification" (*IvO* 7; Olympia, sixth century BCE); and "If someone commits unintentional homicide, he is exiled" (Draco's law = *IG* I³ 104). Such laws are both substantive and procedural— and as Peter Rhodes and others have noted, the crime is typically mentioned first.[25]

Why do private and criminal laws not define the offenses they proscribe, as has been emphasized by Osborne, Carey, and MacDowell, mentioned at the start of this essay? Although a poet as early as Hesiod thought to distinguish the meanings of words ("there are two kinds of *eris* ("strife")" [*Op.* 11–12]), defining terms was largely a philosophical project that began in the second half of the fifth century. Then Prodicus sought to distinguish similar concepts, such as "bravery" and "courage," Prodicus's colleague Damon sought to distinguish and name different meters (Pl. *Resp.* 400a), and Plato's Socrates asks his interlocutors to define words like "piety" and "justice," although they offer nothing that he does not cut to ribbons. Especially for drafting laws, the interlocutors' "particulars" (e.g., "beauty" is some beautiful thing which they name) could never be sufficiently inclusive,[26] while Socrates himself offers no definitions—the "Socratic fallacy."[27] Plato made progress in defining, while recognizing that "a legislator who has to give orders to whole communities . . . will never be able to give every individual his due. . . . How could any lawgiver be capable of prescribing every act of a particular individual and sit at his side all through his life and tell him what to do?" (*Plt.* 295a–b, so also Arist. *Pol.* 1282b). Aristotle made further progress in defining.[28] As for laws, he observes that they are "not particular but prospective and general," while recommending that "well-drawn laws should themselves define all the points they possibly can and leave as few as may be to the decision of the judges" (*Rh.* 1354a-b; trans. Roberts 1984). If already in the late fifth century Athenians noticed the "ambiguities" of some of Solon's laws ([Arist.] *Ath. Pol.* 35.2), the *Athēnaiōn politeia*—written in the 320s in Aristotle's school—explains the difficulty: "because it is impossible to define what is best in general terms" (9.2). As we have seen, in the mid-fourth century Ephorus stresses that legislators should define legal penalties (Str. 6.1.8). If archaic and classical Greek legislators did not define offenses, that omission does not imply that they thought offenses less significant than the procedures specified to deal with them. Crimes and punishments were the reason why these laws were enacted. Defining was hard, field specific, and comparatively late, in relation to legislation.

Two positive factors compensated for the imprecisions of substantive law. First, the indictment (the charge) supplied a more detailed formulation of the offense. "The following *graphē* was brought by Meletus . . . Socrates does wrong in refusing to recognize the gods whom the city recognizes, but introducing other new spiritual beings. He also does wrong in corrupting the youth. The penalty demanded is death" (Diog. Laert. 2.40; cf. Pl. *Ap.* 24b; Xen. *Ap.* 10–12, *Mem.* 1.1.1). Aristophanes also supplies an indictment, all the more important because it is fictional: "Cyon from Cydathenaeum indicts Labes [a dog] from Aexone for wrongdoing (*adikein*) in that he alone ate up the Sicilian cheese" (*Vesp.* 894–897). The indictment may or may not have named the category of offense (such as *hubris*, or impiety [omitted by Meletus], or the very general *adikia* ["wrongdoing"]), but it always detailed the crime, whether or not in statute language. Some scholars complain that in Socrates's case, "corrupting the youth" cannot be statute language. Precisely so: statutes did not detail the specifics of offenses—that was the function of indictments. Carey will search in vain for "not only fully substantive laws but also laws with a procedural cast and a significant substantive component (by which is meant a fuller definition beyond the act of naming the delict)."[29] That fuller definition was included in the indictment.

A second positive factor also compensated for the imprecision of substantive law. As *Athēnaiōn politeia* 9.2 notes, it was the job of courtroom judges—in Athens, hundreds of lay citizens—to decide whether a defendant's behavior was impiety, *hubris*, or some other offense. I shall return to this point.

One consequence of laws' not defining offenses was that some cases might be brought into court under a variety of possible rubrics. In a well-known example, because the Athenians had no express statute against (or word for) rape, rape had to be prosecuted under some more general statute, such as violence or *hubris*; and of course, those statutes might stipulate different punishments. On the other hand, the competent official had to agree to accept a case as so designated.[30]

Why, by contrast, do Athens's penal laws typically describe in detail the procedures to be followed in adjudicating cases? While all Athenian laws had a substantive component, none was purely procedural, only setting out one or more procedures for administering justice. And because the Athenians had no general procedural laws, each substantive law had to set out the procedures to follow in its case, or else actions brought under that law could not be adjudicated. Different laws typically contained their own, sometimes idiosyncratic, procedural provisions. If individual Athenian laws look procedural, that reflects the absence of general procedural laws, not the greater importance of legal procedures.

The failure to see that many Athenian legal procedures were not fixed but ad hoc and necessarily specified in every statute has created many problems regarding procedures. I give three examples that I have written about before: *phainein*, *mē epexelthein*, and the slightly different *apophainein*.[31]

In judicial contexts *phainein* meant "showing" something to an official. Scholars have long wrestled with the problem of determining the nature and scope of what MacDowell and others call "*the* [my emphasis] Athenian procedure of *phasis*."[32] A standard view is that what was shown to an official was typically contraband goods or other objects, of which the shower received half as a reward.[33] However, our sources document many other instances of "showing": for example, that someone had shipped grain elsewhere than to Athens in contravention of a law (the plaintiff showed the vessel; MacDowell calls this "a natural extension" of *phasis*'s "original use");[34] or that an orphan's estate had not been properly leased (for MacDowell, "a more difficult extension"; also, all agree that the shower cannot have received half an orphan's estate);[35] or in a case of impiety (MacDowell finds this "even more difficult" to explain).[36] The various attested kinds of "showing" are best explained if no general statute defined this procedure. The different statutes that mention "showing" themselves specified the procedure to be followed in their particular case, and procedures differed from statute to statute.

In my second example, most scholars believe that a plaintiff who did not "follow through" (*epexelthein*) a prosecution to trial was subject to two punishments: a 1,000-drachma fine and some permanent restriction of his ability to prosecute future cases, a form of partial *atimia* ("disenfranchisement"). I argued that both the case evidence and contemporary descriptions of Athenian laws (for example, the law against *hubris* at Dem. 21.47) nowhere indicate that those who did not "follow through" a public suit were subject to any form of partial *atimia*, except in suits for battlefield desertion, *lipotaxion* (Dem. 21.103).[37] I concluded that Athens had no general procedural or substantive law regarding *mē epexelthein*; the law against *lipotaxion* included its own substantive sanction.

Finally, *apophainein* ("report"), or *zētein* ("investigate") and *apophainein*, also illustrates the absence of purely procedural laws. Many have thought *apophainein* a particular procedure, established in the mid-350s[38] or 340s. However, attested instances by the Areopagus Council in that period do not presuppose any new procedural law or decree, or any extension of the Areopagus's legal competence. The Areopagus exercised final authority in none of the cases outside its normal jurisdiction, and earlier texts refer to *apophainein* procedures by the *boulē* ("Council of 500") in 409 (*IG* I³ 102 = *ML* 85) and by the *stratēgoi* ("military commanders") in 411 ([Plut.] *X orat.* 833e).

To sum up the first section of this essay, the reasons why Athenian laws typically say little about offenses are that explaining the offense was the function of the indictment, few laws could be inclusive, and even philosophers could not adequately define concepts until the later fourth century. Athenian laws say much about procedures because in the absence of general procedural laws, each law had to set out the procedures to be followed in its case, if the offense it regulated was to be adjudicated. These differences do not imply that the Athenians thought procedures more important than punishing offenses. Other evidence implies the opposite.

IF MAINE WAS RIGHT TO CALL LEGAL SYSTEMS BASED ON procedures "primitive," may we then conclude that Athens's legal system was not? In the second section of this essay I shall begin to outline a case that the administration of justice at Athens, so far from "primitive," was deliberately and even systematically organized, shaped not by procedural or substantive law but in accordance with democratic principles and the welfare of the community—central goals of Athens's legal system, as many courtroom speakers say.[39] Many scholars have mentioned problems with Athens's administration of justice, including the merely persuasive, nonbinding status of laws in Athens's courts; sycophancy; appeals to the dicasts' emotions; and irrelevant material in forensic speeches. All such problems, I shall argue, reflect the system's principles and community orientation. Most were not problems but the point.

To start with the laws, as we have noted, Solon's laws were carefully elaborated and reflect considerable deliberation. These laws remained at the core of Athens's law code (and a code it certainly was). Key provisions included the right of all citizens to prosecute public offenses, and to appeal officials' verdicts to the people, both measures interpreted as highly democratic in the fourth century ([Arist.] *Ath. Pol.* 9.1) and as furthering the Athenians' sense of community (Plut. *Sol.* 18). The laws of classical Athens were organized according to the officials who administered them, as different officials brought different types of cases into court and needed to know their responsibilities: the *basileus* especially for religious cases, the eponymous *archon* especially for family cases, the *polemarch* especially for cases involving foreigners, and so forth.[40] Laws set out offenses, procedures, and punishments. Gagarin rightly adds, "Greek legislation regularly includes information about procedure so that those involved in litigation could learn for themselves, without professional help, how they needed to proceed."[41] Plaintiffs sought out a law and consulted the relevant official, a citizen chosen by lot. That official held a preliminary hearing (*anakrisis*), and if he agreed that the charge suited the offense and met other criteria,[42] he sent the case on to arbitration (if private) or straight to a *dikastērion* ("popular court") (if public). Athens's critics argue that statute law had only persuasive, not binding, force in Athenian courts.[43] This argument certainly has merit, but litigants cited and argued about the meaning of laws frequently, showing that they took laws seriously. The practice of having the city clerk read out the texts of laws made clear the distinction between law and rhetoric. It was a capital offense to cite a nonexistent law ([Dem.] 26.24). The extent to which laws lacked binding force in Athenian courts correlated with democratic concerns. Athenian courts had no presiding judges to declare which laws were relevant or what laws meant, or to compel dicasts to follow any particular law, because the Athenians refused to entrust so much power to any individual. In consequence, each side read out laws and each dicast had to decide himself their force or relevance—no talking was permitted in court; voting took place immediately after the speeches. For this same reason, the Athenians had no jurists; they produced no legal textbooks (a point Todd uses to show their legal primitiveness);[44] and they had no state prosecutor or district attorney to exercise "prosecutorial discretion" (in the US a practice prone to abuse). Instead, they instructed any citizen "who wanted" (*ho boulomenos*) to prosecute cases of public interest. Sycophants (blackmailers threatening legal action) were an unintended consequence of the democratic *ho boulomenos* procedure, and the Athenians struggled hard to suppress them (see, e.g., Isoc. 15.314; [Arist.] *Ath. Pol.* 35.3, 43.5). Also, while showing great respect for the law, Athenian prosecutors should not show too keen an interest in it, as that might smack of the sycophant. This same problem explains some litigants' eagerness to assert that their motivation for prosecuting was private enmity, which clashed with the community orientation of Athenian courts. However, the principle that any citizen was free to prosecute public crimes was too important to sacrifice. Justice should reflect the concerns of the demos, in accordance with the laws and community sentiment.

Once in court, litigants spoke for themselves. For no obvious reason, except perhaps the difficulty of stopping it, the Athenians tolerated logography, buying a speech from a professional speechwriter, an antidemocratic practice that favored the rich. However, not all who bought speeches were rich (Lys. 24), and *ēthopoiia* ("character-representation") helped conceal that the speaker's words were not his own.

Ignoring their own laws about "speaking to the issue" (e.g., Antiphon 6.9; Dem. 57.7, 59, 60; [Arist.] *Ath. Pol.* 67.1), dicasts sometimes listened to material not directly pertinent to the charge or the terms of the law, especially regarding an individual's civic or family standing. That is because, while in the United States what trumps law is fear of the abusive power of the state, so that every day guilty criminals walk free if the state has committed even some minor procedural error, what trumped law in Athens was concern for the community. Lysias says that often "defendants make no defense against the charges, but sometimes deceive you with irrelevant statements about themselves, showing that they are fine soldiers, or have captured many enemy ships" (12.38; trans. Todd 2000). In 30.1 he says that even if a defendant seems guilty, he can be acquitted if he mentions valiant deeds by ancestors and proves that he has served the city well. In [Demosthenes] 25.76 the speaker states, "Before now I have seen some men on trial, who were being convicted by the actual facts . . . , take refuge in the moderation and self-control of their lives, others in the achievements and public services of their ancestors, or in similar pleas, through which they induced their judges to pity and goodwill." Isocrates, a wealthy man, says that in early Athens judges enforced the laws on moneylending instead of considering *epieikeia*, "decency" or "equity" (7.33–34). Such statements can be multiplied. Against these passages David Cohen rightly quotes Demosthenes 20.219–225, that no public service should stand in the way of the law.[45] Both law and public service mattered and could be deployed depending on the contours of one's case, not least because law was intended to serve and protect the community. Similarly, bringing children into court showed that a defendant was a good family man, an important consideration for the Athenians even if antidemocratic Plato has antidemocratic Socrates make fun of the practice (Pl. *Ap.* 34c). Prosecutors in assault cases often sought to assimilate their private suits (*dikai*) to the public crime (*graphē*) of *hubris* because of the greater importance given to crimes against the community (e.g., Isoc. 20; Dem. 54). Cohen contends that the plaintiffs' point was to find a community value for what was actually private vengeance in ongoing feuds.[46] In my opinion, more simply, plaintiffs represented assaults as offenses against the community because the community came first in the minds of the dicasts.

As for the *dikastēria*, 6,000 lay judges (dicasts) were chosen each year; they were paid so that all citizens over thirty could participate regardless of economic circumstances, and they were assigned to the courts by lot. *Thorubos* ("hubbub") may have been formally outlawed (Aeschin. 3.2) but was tolerated as the collective voice of the community.[47] As I have noted, dicasts were forbidden to talk to each other during trials (cf. Aeschin. 2.24—this law was often broken) and while voting (Arist. *Pol.* 1268b7–11—this law was not). The point was that each citizen should follow his own judgment. According to the dicasts' oath, verdicts were to reflect the law, which they considered *kurios* ("authoritative"), and the collective judgment of individual citizens (Dem. 24.149). As Todd observes:

> The terms of the dikastic oath could indeed indicate an awareness that whatever the ideal, the law could not in reality be expected to be coherent and comprehensive: "in cases where no *nomoi* exist, you have sworn to judge according to what in your opinion is most just," as one of Demosthenes's clients tells the *dikastai*. (Dem. 39.40)[48]

Already in Solon's time, officials' verdicts could be appealed to the community, and the community's verdict was final. Similarly, Athens's democracy severely curtailed the Areopagus's powers in 462/1, in the interests of the popular *dikastēria*, the Council of 500, and the democratic assembly ([Arist.] *Ath. Pol.* 25).

How far was Athenian justice arbitrary? True, different avenues to prosecuting an offense (*locus classicus*: Dem. 22.25–26) meant that sometimes convictions for similar offenses received different punishments. Todd claims that this "can only be explained by giving priority to procedure over substance."[49] Others argue that Athens's judicial system was calibrated to different social statuses.[50] However, in my view the Athenians did not create different avenues to prosecution because of relative social status. They did provide a series of general rubrics under which people could prosecute, provided an official accepted the case. Plaintiffs weighed various advantages and disadvantages in deciding which rubric to choose. Similar offenses brought under the same statute were penalized by a fixed penalty or else according to the community court's judgment of an offense's gravity or other circumstances.

The community orientation of Athens's legal system can also mislead. According to Gabriel Herman in another striking formulation, "it was not the [Athenian] jurors' concern to find out the truth. Theirs was the task of weighing the relative merits of the arguments they heard with an eye to the city's best interests. . . . Any idea of ascertaining the 'facts,' and then testing them against the letter of the law, was given short shrift."[51] Dicasts did weigh the arguments in the light of the city's best interests. They also took into consideration substantive law, the truth as best they could see it, and above all, justice.

I therefore propose a different "shape" to Athenian law (*droit*) than one based on substance or procedure. Far from primitive, the administration of justice at Athens was carefully, intelligently, and ever more systematically shaped in accordance both with the law and with the interests and perspectives of the democratic community, not least because Athens's system of justice developed in response not to the "heavy state" (in pointed contrast with common law) or abuses by the majority population, but to abuses by powerful individuals such as "gift-devouring princes" (Hes. *Op.* 38–39). A principal goal of both legal and constitutional reform was to protect and empower the citizen community against abusive elites.[52] To cite two testimonia among many, the orator Aeschines excoriates contemporary *rhētores* (politicians) for making illegal motions: "If the laws are faithfully upheld for the polis, the democracy also is saved" (3.6). [Andocides] 4.19 echoes standard sentiment: "Obeying the officials and the laws is *sōtēria* ['safety'] for all. Whoever ignores these has destroyed the greatest protection of the city." For different historical reasons, Western societies are sometimes willing to tolerate illegal actions (civil disobedience) by individuals acting against the public or the state for reasons of personal conscience, as against the Vietnam War or in support of Greenpeace. The Athenians would have rejected any such conception. Spared the modern state (compare Creon in Sophocles's *Antigone*), their legal system reflects a fundamental belief in the prior importance of the community, everyone together, over any individual.

NOTES

In 2010 and 2014, I presented a first and then more developed version of this essay at the Law School of the University of Athens, at the kind invitation of Julie

Velissaropoulos-Karakostas. On both occasions, as also at Austin in 2011, I profited from many helpful comments.

1. Maine 1861.

2. Maine 1883: 389.

3. Hansen 1975: 10.

4. Todd 1993: 65, 67.

5. Millet 1990: 179; see also Todd 1993: 59.

6. In a fine article, Gerhard Thür writes, "As everywhere else in the Greek world, so also in Athens, there are no inscriptions confined strictly to legal proceedings. Everywhere, substantive and adjective laws, statutes on concrete issues and on judicial enforcement, are mixed up in one and the same text" (Thür 2004: 35).

7. Osborne 1996: 187.

8. Osborne 1996: 187–188.

9. Todd 1993: 70. See also Gagarin 1986: 12–13: "It is easy to see how procedures for settling disputes might arise without any reference to or dependence on substantive rules. Thus it may be more accurate to view procedural law as primary and substantive law as a later development." So also Grethlein 2004: 118: "Firstly, it must be recognized that Athenian law is procedural, not substantial."

10. Maine 1861: e.g., 328, 339; Todd 1993: 64–69.

11. Hansen 1975: 10.

12. Gagarin 1981.

13. Unless otherwise indicated, all translations are the author's. The meanings of *basileis*, *ephetai*, and *diagnōnai* are uncertain. For discussion, see Wallace 1989: 7–22.

14. Carey 1998: 97; see, more generally, Cohen 1995: 190.

15. Osborne 1996: 188.

16. MacDowell 1978: 198–199.

17. Carey 1998: 101.

18. Similarly, in *Pol.* 1272a 36–39, Aristotle criticizes Cretan leaders because "their arbitrary power of acting on their own judgment and dispensing with written law is dangerous" (trans. Jowett 1984). Legal penalties, not procedures, are at issue.

19. Carey (1998: 98) notes that when Athenians talk about law, they often mention its substantive dimension.

20. Carey 1998: 102.

21. Carey 1998: 105, 104.

22. Carey 1998: 105–107.

23. Carey 1998: 107.

24. Carey 1998: 100.

25. Rhodes 1979: 106–107.

26. Nehamas 1999.

27. I.e., if one does not define x, one cannot know that anything is an x. On a legal point, Carey (1998: 100) suggests that by mentioning the *aporrhēta*—five things that "were not to be said"—Athens's law of slander "in effect" defined slander. I consider this suggestion incorrect. The slander law regulated the use of five terms that, if applied to any citizen, disqualified him from public service (Wallace 1994). It did not

take the form "slander consists of the following five terms." It also did not deal with synonyms. (I am grateful to A. Mourelatos for advice on these questions.)

28. Deslauriers 2007.

29. Carey 1998: 109.

30. See Isae. 10.2, and Todd 1993: 126–127.

31. See, respectively, Wallace 2003, 2006, and 2000.

32. MacDowell 1991, in its title and elsewhere.

33. So, following Lipsius (1908: 315) and Harrison (1971: 220), Osborne (1985: 47) says that in "the" *phasis* procedure "the prosecutor was rewarded with one half of the proceeds of the case."

34. MacDowell 1991: 196.

35. Ibid.

36. MacDowell 1991: 197.

37. See Wallace 2006: 65–66.

38. Hansen 1975: 52–57.

39. See Cohen 2005: 224–226 (I need not repeat this material). Lanni (2010: 236) argues that the use of the *graphē paranomōn* ("indictment for an illegal proposal") "was understood as a means of preserving popular decision making structures . . . : the citizenry's lawmaking power, and the jury's wide power to adjudicate disputes."

40. Once the dominant officials of Athens, in the classical period the *basileus*, eponymous archon, and polemarch exercised especially judicial functions, in the areas of religion, the family, and foreigners, respectively.

41. Gagarin 2008: 243.

42. See again Isae. 10.2, and Todd 1993: 126–127.

43. E.g., Todd 1993: 59.

44. Todd 1993: 14.

45. Cohen 2005: 219.

46. Cohen 2005: 216.

47. Bers 1985.

48. Todd 1993: 58.

49. Todd 1993: 66. Such discrepancies also occur in the United States, as when a defendant acquitted of homicide is tried again for violating the plaintiff's civil rights, an offense subject to only civil, not criminal, penalties.

50. See, e.g., Osborne 1985: 43.

51. Herman 1996: 12–13.

52. Wallace 2009.

REFERENCES

Bers, Victor. 1985. "Dikastic *Thorubos*." In *Crux: Essays in Greek History Presented to G. E. M. de Ste. Croix on His 75th Birthday*, edited by Paul Cartledge and F. D. Harvey, 1–15. Exeter: Imprint Academic.

Carey, Chris. 1998. "The Shape of Athenian Laws." *Classical Quarterly* 48: 93–109.

Cohen, David. 1995. *Law, Violence, and Community in Classical Athens*. Cambridge: Cambridge University Press.

———. 2005. "Crime, Punishment, and the Rule of Law in Classical Athens." In *The Cambridge Companion to Ancient Greek Law*, edited by Michael Gagarin and David Cohen, 211–235. Cambridge: Cambridge University Press.

Deslauriers, Marguerite. 2007. *Aristotle on Definition*. Leiden: Brill.

Gagarin, Michael. 1981. *Drakon and Early Athenian Homicide Law*. New Haven, CT: Yale University Press.

———. 1986. *Early Greek Law*. Berkeley: University of California Press.

———. 2008. *Writing Greek Law*. Cambridge: Cambridge University Press.

Grethlein, Jonas. 2004. "Aeschylus's 'Eumenides' and Legal Anthropology." In *Nomos: Direito e sociedade na Antiguidade Clássica*, edited by Delfim Ferreira Leão, Livio Rossetti, and Maria do Céu Fialho, 113–125. Coimbra: Imprensa da Universidade de Coimbra; Madrid: Ediciones Clásicas.

Hansen, Mogens Herman. 1975. *Eisangelia: The Sovereignty of the People's Court in Athens in the Fourth Century B.C. and the Impeachment of Generals and Politicians*. Odense: Odense University Press.

Harrison, A. R. W. 1971. *The Law of Athens*. Vol. 2, *Procedure*. Oxford: Clarendon Press.

Herman, Gabriel. 1996. "Ancient Athens and the Values of Mediterranean Society." *Mediterranean Historical Review* 11: 5–36.

Jones, Horace Leonard, trans. 1924. *The Geography of Strabo*. Vol. 3. London: William Heinemann; New York: G. P. Putnam's Sons.

Jowett, Benjamin, trans. 1984. *"Politics."* In *The Complete Works of Aristotle: The Revised Oxford Translation*, edited by Jonathan Barnes, vol. 2, 1986-2129. Princeton: Princeton University Press.

Lanni, Adriaan. 2010. "Judicial Review and the Athenian 'Constitution.'" In *Démocratie athénienne—démocratie moderne: Tradition et influences*, edited by Alain-Christian Hernández, 235–276. Vandoeuvres-Geneva: Fondation Hardt.

Lipsius, Justus Hermann. 1908. *Das attische Recht und Rechtsverfahren: Mit Benutzung des Attischen Processes*. Vol. 2. Leipzig: Reisland.

MacDowell, Douglas M. 1978. *The Law in Classical Athens*. Ithaca, NY: Cornell University Press.

———. 1991. "The Athenian Procedure of *Phasis*." In *Symposion 1990: Vorträge zur griechischen und hellenistischen Rechtsgeschichte*, edited by Michael Gagarin, 187–198. Cologne: Böhlau.

Maine, Henry Sumner. 1861. *Ancient Law: Its Connection with the Early History of Society and Its Relation to Modern Ideas*. London: J. Murray.

———. 1883. *Dissertations on Early Law and Custom: Chiefly Selected from Lectures Delivered at Oxford*. London: J. Murray.

Millett, Paul. 1990. "Sale, Credit, and Exchange in Athenian Law and Society." In *Nomos: Essays in Athenian Law, Politics, and Society*, edited by Paul Cartledge, Paul Millett, and Stephen C. Todd, 167–194. Cambridge: Cambridge University Press.

Nehamas, Alexander. 1999. "Confusing Universals and Particulars in Plato's Early Dialogues." In *Virtues of Authenticity: Essays on Plato and Socrates*, 159–175. Princeton: Princeton University Press.

Osborne, Robin. 1985. "Law in Action in Classical Athens." *The Journal of Hellenic Studies* 105: 40–58.

————. 1996. *Greece in the Making, 1200–479 BC*. London: Routledge.

Rhodes, Peter J. 1979. "*ΕΙΣΑΓΓΕΛΙΑ* in Athens." *The Journal of Hellenic Studies* 99: 103–114.

Roberts, W. Rhys, trans. 1984. "*Rhetoric.*" In *The Complete Works of Aristotle: The Revised Oxford Translation*, edited by Jonathan Barnes, vol. 2, 2152-2269. Princeton: Princeton University Press.

Thür, Gerhard. 2004. "Law of Procedure in Attic Inscriptions." In *Law, Rhetoric, and Comedy in Classical Athens: Essays in Honour of Douglas M. MacDowell*, edited by Douglas L. Cairns and Ronald A. Knox, 33–49. Swansea: Classical Press of Wales.

Todd, Stephen C. 1993. *The Shape of Athenian Law*. Oxford: Clarendon Press.

————, trans. 2000. *Lysias*. Austin: University of Texas Press.

Wallace, Robert W. 1989. *The Areopagos Council, to 307 B.C.* Baltimore: Johns Hopkins University Press.

————. 1994. "The Athenian Laws against Slander." In *Symposion 1993: Vorträge zur griechischen und hellenistischen Rechtsgeschichte*, edited by Gerhard Thür, 109–124. Cologne: Böhlau.

————. 2000. "'Investigations and Reports' by the Areopagos Council and Demosthenes's Areopagos Decree." In *Polis and Politics: Studies in Ancient Greek History; Presented to Mogens Herman Hansen on his Sixtieth Birthday, August 20, 2000*, edited by Pernille Flensted-Jensen, Thomas Heine Nielsen, and Lene Rubinstein, 581–596. Copenhagen: Museum Tusculanum Press.

————. 2003. "*Phainein* in Athenian Laws and Legislation." In *Symposion 1999: Vorträge zur griechischen und hellenistischen Rechtsgeschichte*, edited by Gerhard Thür and Francisco Nieto, 167–181. Vienna: Verlag der Österreichischen Akademie der Wissenschaften.

————. 2006. "Withdrawing *Graphai* in Ancient Athens: A Case Study in 'Sycophancy' and Legal Idiosyncracies." In *Symposion 2003: Vorträge zur griechischen und hellenistischen Rechtsgeschichte*, edited by Hans-Albert Rupprecht, 57–66. Vienna: Verlag der Österreichischen Akademie der Wissenschaften.

————. 2009. "Charismatic Leaders." In *A Companion to Archaic Greece*, edited by Kurt A. Raaflaub and Hans van Wees, 411–426. Oxford: Blackwell.

2 / REVENGE AND PUNISHMENT

Eva Cantarella

THE RELATION BETWEEN REVENGE AND LAW HAS BEEN widely discussed in recent years. In the last decade several authors, starting with David Cohen, formulated new theories that are worth revisiting. Cohen, as is well known, highlights the tension between Athenian competitive values and the egalitarian spirit of the rule of law, yet he maintains and explicitly restates the conceptual distinction between revenge and civic punishment.[1] Other scholars, notably Danielle Allen and David Phillips, question this distinction at the conceptual level.[2] My objectives here are to challenge the objections of Allen and Phillips and to present new arguments in support of the conceptual distinction between revenge and civic punishment in ancient Athenian thought and practice.

One of Allen's points, not to say her main point, is the critique of the traditional understanding of the difference between revenge and punishment. The former is viewed as a reaction to a personal wrong involving the emotions of anger and resentment, and the latter as a consequence of wrongdoing based upon some general principles and administered with cool reason rather than emotion. In her opinion, anger together with personal interest "provided the *only* [italics mine] truly legitimate basis for an attempt to punish someone."[3] Prosecutors were culturally expected to show anger, as the cause of their court case needed a trial to restore their offended honor and reassess their social status: this was the function of punishment. There was, however, a proper way to display anger in court, which Allen positions within the Foucauldian idea that the Athenians (or Greeks, in her terms) attempted to control appetites denoted as "necessities" (like sexual desire, eating, and sleeping) by establishing an "economy of spending" for them. But anger, she argues, is also an emotionally necessary force, and like *erōs* ("sexual desire") produces a desire to change the social relationship (in the case of anger by destroying it, in

25

the case of *erōs* by creating it). Anger was regulated by an economy of spending parallel to the economy of spending of sexual desire. In respect to sexual desire, a man had to be temperate (*sōphrōn*) and limit his indulgence so as not to weaken himself. He had to avoid any desire for payment for overtly sexual purposes, or, in the case of same-sex relationships, for acting as the passive partner. The prosecutor was expected "to eschew prosecuting for payment, avoid indulging an excessive taste for provoking people and disrupting social relations, and reject serving as someone else's flunky."[4]

One weakness of this theory consists in applying to punishment the Foucauldian idea that Greek sexual morality, which Allen extends to the entire civic morality, proposed a model of self-control, continence, and measure freely chosen by the citizens, who would have developed these virtues internally because of the lack of external coercive rules. But this is not true. The Athenian sexual code did involve coercive rules, both social and legal. Pederastic courtship was governed by very strict social rules. It imposed a dissymmetry in age between the two lovers, and a very precise gift code.[5] A law attributed to Solon stipulated severe penalties for adults, except teachers, who entered a school for boys (Aeschin. 1.12); male prostitution was punished as *hetairēsis* ("unchastity") (Aeschin. 1.13); and a law punished the rape of a slave and, according to some scholars,[6] would have considered as statutory rape sexual relations with a boy under twelve (Aeschin. 1.14–16).

The fact that voluntary self-repression was not a general feature of Athenian society weakens one of the pillars of Allen's conception of punishment as an orchestrated exercise of anger. This, however, is not to deny that the prosecutor's anger could have a role as the emotion at the basis of enmity that, according to Phillips, induced the Athenians to address the courts.[7] In his opinion, trials were initiated in order to respect the rules governing *echthra*, in his definition "a socially recognized state of private active mutual hostility, with established norms governing its proper and expected conduct," an "institution," which included characteristics of the institution of the feud in paradigmatic feud cultures, such as medieval Iceland.[8] In his opinion, Draco's law (*IG* I³ 104) did not cancel this "institution." It simply transferred to the courts the satisfaction of the desire and social necessity to pursue the politics of *echthra*, with the courts serving as the *"primary locus"* (italics mine) for its pursuit. As a consequence, "we should not view the pursuit of *echthra* and the goal of law as opposing principles."[9] Rather, feud was transferred to the courts. As noted above, anger and enmity (*echthra*) could have a relevant role when the prosecutor was a private citizen. I will return to this later, after exploring Allen's and Phillips's arguments in favor of a different understanding of the concept of punishment in order to question their validity.

First, Allen denies that there was a basic difference between precivic and civic courts, basing her argument on a new reading of Aeschylus's *Oresteia* that, she writes, does not represent "a triumphalist advance from the system of revenge to the system of punishment."[10] In her opinion, precivic courts differed from civic courts only in the "forms of judicial proceedings."[11] The only detailed description of a precivic court, that of the trial represented on Achilles's shield (Hom. *Il.* 18.499–504), shows that the differences are not only procedural. I do not wish to discuss the many controversial aspects of this trial. Had the killer sought protection from the revenge of the relatives of the victim, as Wolff suggested?[12] Had the litigants voluntarily submitted their dispute to the *gerontes* ("elders") for settlement, as Gagarin proposes?[13] How was the dispute settled—with a *Beweisurteil*, as Thür argues?[14] The problems are many and they are significant. What matters here, however, is that the procedure (whatever it was) was not aimed at establishing the guilt of the defendant, which was taken for granted, whereas establishing guilt was exactly what the Areopagus was called upon to do. Demosthenes 23.29, on the one hand, insists on this role, saying that when someone is accused of homicide the polis punishes him only after a trial has established whether the accusation is true, and not before. The *gerontes* on the Shield of Achilles, on the other hand, in my opinion determined only whether the *poinē* ("blood-money") had or had not been paid. The trial before the Areopagus, therefore, did not differ from precivic justice only in the procedure used. It differed with regard to the substantive issue. The precivic courts acted in a world where the concept of crime did not yet exist. The same behavior was acceptable or unacceptable according to the persons involved. The necessity to react was uniquely a matter of balance between the "honor" of the interested persons; it was not a matter of justice. But the civic courts—as Draco's law shows—instead functioned in a world where general rules existed: homicide was a crime that was punished with predetermined and fixed penalties. And the courts' function was not to effect "honor reassessment" (albeit that was still an important motivation for initiating a trial), but rather to ensure that the rule of law was observed and that the penalty responded to the egalitarian principle that the life of citizens had the same value, regardless of their social standing. By transforming offenses into crimes, Draco's law gave to the courts an institutional function radically different from the function of the precivic ones.

Second, Allen asserts that "punishment in Athens was not coolly distant from anger." It was not "a dispassionate, disinterested, wholly legal affair, carried out by state agents removed from the private passions and anger of those who had been wronged by a fellow member of the city."[15] This view is shared by Phillips, whose hypothesis that courts served as the place where the politics of *echthra* were enacted leads to the inevitable consequence that the emotions which determined this personal relation between the litigants played a role in the decision of judges.[16] For Phillips as well as for Allen, then, emotions and law are not parts of incompatible spheres of experience. Their view is not entirely new. Paul Gewirtz, a key proponent of the "law and literature" movement, had already challenged the idea that the *Eumenides* represented the triumph of law as reason (masculine) over the emotions (feminine) that dominated the world of revenge.[17] Gewirtz questions whether law is in fact gendered in the *Oresteia*. Certainly, the forces of revenge (the Erinyes) are female and law is represented by Apollo and by the court that Athena—the woman-man, motherless, and husbandless goddess—establishes. But in the *Eumenides* the defeated Erinyes are not expelled by the polis but instead become part of the judicial system. Within law there is space also for the force of passions. Thus, law, to be just, must provide space for the emotions: a vision of law that finds expression in a current debate among philosophers, jurists, and politologists (see below).

Allen understands Athena's description of the Areopagus as "quick to anger" (*oxuthumon*, Aesch. *Eum.* 705) to imply that the Areopagus, "like the Erinyes, is expected to inspire fear in the citizenry and to ward off anarchy and tyranny, while being 'quick to anger.'"[18] But the LSJ lists many texts where *oxus* means "sharp/keen" (s.v. *oxus*), and translates *oxuthumon* in *Eumenides* 705 as "sharp to punish" (s.v. *oxuthumeō*). Thus, the semantic argument is not decisive; *oxuthumos* does not necessarily imply that the Areopagus is "allowed to persist in the use of anger" or that the Erinyes "never really became the 'well minded ones.'"[19] Allen asserts that the Erinyes abandoned their anger toward Athens only in the case of Orestes, but they otherwise retained it and could wield it against other wrongdoers. Athena seems to be asking that the Erinyes accede to her authority, particularly on this first occasion: "If you give holy reverence to Persuasion (*Peithō*)," she promises the Erinyes, "then you might remain" (*Eum.* 885, 887 [trans. Smyth 1926, here and below]). Nothing suggests that the Erinyes should respect Peithō on one occasion alone. And in fact, a couple of verses later the Erinyes, having abandoned hate (*methistamai kotou*; 900), explicitly disown vengeance completely and forever, vowing that the city's dust will "not drink the black blood of its people and through passion cause ruinous murder for vengeance" (δι' ὀργὰν ποινᾶς ἀντιφόνους; 981–982).

In my opinion both Allen and Phillips confuse social roles and civic institutions. The transformation of the Erinyes in *Eumenides* concerns their social role, not the moment of the civic response to homicide from which the institution of the Areopagus excludes them. In the trial they have the role of prosecutors, not that of judges. And the new civic judicial system does not require impartiality from its prosecutors. Athena requires impartiality (and therefore lack of emotional involvement) from the judges, who, as the goddess says, will judge according to truth (*etētumōs*; 488), without violating the dicasts' oaths (*dikastas horkious*; 483) with a vindictive sentiment (*ekdikon phrasein*; 489). The judges therefore could not be animated by the sentiment of revenge, even if the litigants were or could be.

Allen further asserts that judicial speeches fail to draw a sharp distinction between revenge and law. It is certainly true that the prosecutor's personal interest in condemning, often represented by his desire to seek redress, is clearly attested in some speeches. But in many cases the expression of his anger or enmity is accompanied by an attempt to show that he is acting in defense of the laws. Edward Harris investigates this point at length and discusses the most relevant texts.[20] Here I will note only two of the relevant passages, both from Demosthenes. First, in his speech against Meidias, Demosthenes compliments himself for his capacity to restrain his anger and not react violently to the public hubristic behavior of his enemy, deciding instead to seek redress before the court (Dem. 21.74–76). Demosthenes continues that for this reason he expects from the dicasts ("lay judges") the revenge that, to his credit, he chose not to exact privately, adding:

> I think that you should set up a precedent (*paradeigma*) for all to follow, that no one who wantonly assaults and outrages another should be punished by the victim himself in the moment of anger (*meta tēs orgēs*), but must be brought into your court, because it is you who confirm and uphold the protection granted by the laws to those who are injured. (Dem. 21.76 [trans. Murray 1939])

No less instructive is Demosthenes's explanation in his speech against Aristocrates of why the decree introduced by Aristocrates in favor of Charidemus was illegal. The decree that declared *agōgimos* ("liable to seizure") any person who killed Charidemus could be interpreted as an authorization to kill his killer without a trial. Demosthenes reasons that the decree thus allows an individual in certain cases to kill an *androphonos* ("one convicted of manslaughter"). However, only the Areopagus can convict an individual on the charge of *androphonia* ("manslaughter"), and only an individual who has been convicted on this charge can be seized if he attempts to flee and can be killed by his captor with impunity. But Aristocrates's decree violates this rule, for a person who brings someone before the *thesmothetai* (judicial officials) gives power over the wrongdoer to the laws, but the person who keeps him for himself (as Aristocrates's decree permits) retains the power for himself. In the first case, the offender is punished according to the law's will; in the second case, he is punished according to the will of the captor. And there is a great difference when it is law that decides the punishment (*timōria*) and when it is the enemy (*echthros*) (Dem. 23.32).

In my opinion these speeches express a very clear distinction between the personal motivation of the accusers and the institutional role of the dicasts. Personal motivation, being private, could include the desire for revenge. Prosecutors were not forbidden from expressing this desire as their own private feeling. However, this does not mean that the court would take the desire for revenge into account in reaching its decision. The court supports those who are wronged as the laws provide (Dem. 21.76). Or as Cohen observes in commenting on these passages in forensic speeches, "The rationale of punishment is expressed as advancing the public interest in deterring others from committing such wrongs."[21] Cohen, then, recognizes the existence of a sharp conceptual distinction between revenge and punishment. As he explicitly writes, it is not true that "litigation was no more than feud, or that Athenians were unaware of the values associated with the rule of law."[22] In his opinion, the rule of law existed and punishment was conceptually different from revenge. While I endorse this distinction, I disagree with Cohen's view that "the ideology of the rule of law was just that: an ideology of equality, impartiality, and justice that existed in tension with countervailing values . . . of conflict and judgment"; that is, the rule of the law existed in principle only.[23] I do not, however, intend to suggest that Athenian litigants based their cases strictly on the letter of the law and that the social status of the parties and their private lives, previous behavior, and emotions were irrelevant. But it is not possible to determine to what extent strategies based on agonistic values were successful in influencing the decisions of juries. The lack of evidence does not allow us to do more than speculate, and nothing authorizes us to exclude the possibility that jurors shared nonagonistic and nonviolent values.

Moreover, we must consider that to convince the dicasts of their good reasons, the logographers (speechwriters) often considered it necessary to misrepresent the laws, as Lysias does, for example, in his speech in defense of Euphiletus, who was accused of having murdered Eratosthenes, his wife's lover. To obtain his acquittal, Lysias focuses on the fact that Euphiletus killed his wife's lover to uphold a law that supposedly required a husband who caught his wife committing adultery to kill her lover on the spot (Lys. 1.29–34). This is a very interesting line of defense, since Lysias is blatantly lying. The law did not oblige the husband to kill his wife's lover; it simply stated that if he did, his homicide would be *dikaios* ("just"). Had the Athenian legal system been based on the economy of anger, or had it had as its goal the pursuit of the politics of *echthra* and not the rule of law, Lysias would not have needed to misrepresent the city's laws as he did. Lysias's effort to convince the jury that Euphiletus acted in obedience to a law that did not in fact exist clearly indicates that anger, enmity, and the desire for revenge were not sufficient reasons for the jury to decide a case in his client's favor. Cohen himself asserts that the logographers exploited arguments based on respect for the agonistic values and respect for the polis's good, and that the trial was intended to obtain this good.[24] Which was the victorious strategy? The fact that the logographers appealed to both leaves open both possibilities.

What emerges from the judicial speeches is that two different ethics coexisted in classical Athens: the old ethics of revenge and a more recent civic ethics inspired by cooperative values. Reading Cohen and those who follow his reconstruction, one has the impression that the civic ethics of the polis had practically no effect on the culture of the Athenians, which was still dominated by an archaic epic ethics of revenge. In my opinion, the fact that there was a change in ethical standards and a progressive diffusion of cooperative and egalitarian values providing the basis of the rule of law that accompanied the birth of the polis contradicts their view. To conclude, I believe that the unquestionable presence of agonistic values does not mean necessarily that these values were victorious in court. I will not address here the controversial topic of the relation between the dicasts and the demos, defined as the citizens who formed the *ekklēsia* ("assembly").[25] I will only recall that whatever the power relation between these two civic institutions, the dicasts, chosen by lottery that imposed on them special obligations, which they pledged to respect with the dicastic oath, were not ordinary citizens when they sentenced. They were citizens who had tasks and specific duties that obliged them not to be influenced by the agonistic arguments of the logographers.

Earlier we noted the distinction between the prosecutorial role of the Erinyes/Eumenides and the adjudicative role of the Areopagus. Here I would like to add that tragedy, like judicial oratory, attests to the presence and diffusion of an egalitarian culture in fifth-century Athens. As William Harris observes about the *Oresteia*:

> It is obvious that the Eumenides' prayer against violence is an attempt to display divine support for a basic code of political coexistence. The sentiment was unoriginal but its prominence in the *Oresteia* probably means that it had immediate relevance in the years after the reforms (462) and the murder of Ephialtes . . . The campaign against vengeful *kotos* ["grudge"] in the city in any case is reasonably discernible.[26]

Harris notes as well that the speech of Odysseus at the end of Sophocles's *Ajax* reveals very clearly the limits of enmity and the existence of a different standard of morality.[27] After Athena informs Odysseus of the intention of Ajax to seek revenge, Odysseus declares that even if Ajax is his enemy, considering the latter's state of madness, Odysseus himself will not take revenge in turn:

> Do not in any way let the violence of your hatred overcome you so much that you trample justice under foot. To me, too, this man was once the most hostile enemy in the army (*echthistos stratou*; 1336) from the day on which I beat him for possession of Achilles' arms. Yet for all that he was hostile towards me, I would not dishonor him in return or refuse to admit that in all our Greek force at Troy he was, in my view, the best and bravest. (Soph. *Aj.* 1334–1340 [trans. Jebb 1893])

A clear statement of the importance of the rule of law in the city's government is also found in Sophocles's *Antigone* when Creon declares that, in spite of the fact that Antigone is his niece and the fiancée of his son, nonetheless he will put her to death:

> If I am to foster my own kin to spurn order, surely I will do the same for outsiders. For whoever shows his excellence in the case of his own household will be found righteous in his city as well. But if anyone oversteps and does violence to the laws, or thinks to dictate to those in power, such a one will never win praise from me. (Soph. *Ant.* 659–65 [trans. Jebb 1891])

Egalitarian principles were shared by the Athenians. The polis had to come before the family. Sophocles wanted to remind his co-citizens of this; Antigone's behavior was a threat to the respect for civic ethics.

Even admitting that agonistic values dominated in the courts, this does not challenge the awareness emerging from classical oratory and tragedy of a conceptual difference between the response to a "tort" entrusted to the victims (or their relatives) and the response entrusted to third persons who were extraneous to the facts and impartial. As I said, in my opinion, to doubt the conceptual distinction between revenge and punishment means to confuse social ethics with institutional principles. It may well be true that for many Athenians, "going to law is not an alternative to personal vengeance, but a means of achieving it"; however, this does not mean that it was a function *assigned* to the courts, or that "written laws merely provide the Athenians with information about how to measure and apply anger," or that the Athenians "considered law as a wise advisor whose wisdom was ultimately of second rank to that of the judge."[28] Achieving personal revenge might be what induced prosecutors (or some prosecutors) to initiate a *dikē* ("private lawsuit") or a *graphē* ("public lawsuit"), but even those who initiated a trial for that reason knew that the courts inflicted punishment, and that punishment was conceptually different from revenge.

NOTES

1. See Cohen 1991, 1995, 2005.
2. See Allen 2000; Phillips 2008.
3. Allen 2000: 35.
4. Allen 2000: 163.
5. Koch-Harnack 1983.
6. E.g., Cohen 1991: 177–182.
7. Phillips 2008: 15.
8. Miller 1990.
9. Phillips 2008: 23.
10. Allen 2000: 20.
11. Allen 2000: 21.
12. Wolff 1946.
13. Gagarin 2008: 13–18.
14. Thür 1970.
15. Allen 2000: 20.
16. Phillips 2008: 20.
17. Gewirtz 1988. This interpretation had its roots in the nineteenth-century view (now discredited) that early cultures experienced a transition from matriarchy to patriarchy.
18. Allen 2000: 22.
19. Ibid.
20. Harris 2005: 129–138.
21. Cohen 2005: 221–222.
22. Cohen 1995: 88.
23. Ibid.
24. Cohen 1995: 95.
25. See, e.g., Hansen 2010.
26. Harris 2001: 162–163.
27. Harris 2001: 164.
28. Allen 2000: 174.

REFERENCES

Allen, Danielle S. 2000. *The World of Prometheus: The Politics of Punishing in Democratic Athens*. Princeton: Princeton University Press.
Cohen, David. 1991. *Law, Sexuality, and Society: The Enforcement of Morals in Classical Athens*. Cambridge: Cambridge University Press.

———. 1995. *Law, Violence, and Community in Classical Athens*. Cambridge: Cambridge University Press.

———. 2005. "Crime, Punishment, and the Rule of Law in Classical Athens." In *The Cambridge Companion to Ancient Greek Law*, edited by Michael Gagarin and David Cohen, 211–235. Cambridge: Cambridge University Press.

Gagarin, Michael. 2008. *Writing Greek Law*. Cambridge: Cambridge University Press.

Gewirtz, Paul. 1988. "Aeschylus's Law." *Harvard Law Review* 101.5: 1043–1055

Hansen, Mogens Herman. 2010. "The Concepts of *Demos, Ekklesia,* and *Dikastērion* in Classical Athens." *Greek, Roman, and Byzantine Studies* 50.4: 499–536.

Harris, Edward M. 2005. "Feuding or the Rule of Law? The Nature of Litigation in Classical Athens; An Essay in Legal Sociology." In *Symposion 2001: Vorträge zur griechischen und hellenistischen Rechtsgeschichte*, edited by Robert W. Wallace and Michael Gagarin, 125–141. Vienna: Verlag der Österreichischen Akademie der Wissenschaften.

Harris, William V. 2001. *Restraining Rage: The Ideology of Anger Control in Classical Antiquity*. Cambridge, MA: Harvard University Press.

Jebb, Richard C. 1891. *The Antigone of Sophocles*. Cambridge: Cambridge University Press.

———. 1893. *The Ajax of Sophocles*. Cambridge: Cambridge University Press.

Koch-Harnack, Gundel. 1983. *Knabenliebe und Tiergeschenke: Ihre Bedeutung im päderastischen Erziehungssystem Athens*. Berlin: Gebrüder Mann.

Miller, William Ian. 1990. *Bloodtaking and Peacemaking: Feud, Law, and Society in Saga Iceland*. Chicago: University of Chicago Press.

Murray, A. T., trans. 1939. *Demosthenes*: Orations. Vol. 5, Orations *41–49: Private Cases*. Cambridge, MA: Harvard University Press.

Phillips, David D. 2008. *Avengers of Blood: Homicide in Athenian Law and Custom from Draco to Demosthenes*. Stuttgart: Steiner.

Smyth, Herbert Weir. 1926. *Aeschylus*. Vol. 2, *Agamemnon, Libation-bearers, Eumenides, Fragments*. Cambridge, MA: Harvard University Press.

Thür, Gerhard. 1970. "Zum *dikazein* bei Homer." *Zeitschrift der Savigny Stiftung für Rechtsgeschichte, Romanistische Abteilung* 87: 426–444.

Wolff, Hans Julius. 1946. "The Origin of Judicial Litigation among the Greeks." *Traditio* 4: 31–87.

3 / HYPERIDES'S *AGAINST ATHENOGENES* AND THE ATHENIAN LAW ON AGREEMENTS

Michael Gagarin

SOMETIME IN THE EARLY 320S BCE, THE ATHENIAN POLI-
tician and *logographer* ("speechwriter") Hyperides wrote a speech for a certain Epicrates to deliver in his suit against Athenogenes, a metic of Egyptian origin (Hyp. 3, *Against Athenogenes*). The background to the case, according to Epicrates, is that he had been persuaded (or duped, as he claims)
by Athenogenes, when he agreed to buy Athenogenes's perfume business together with Midas and his two sons, the slaves who managed the business.
Epicrates had conceived a passionate desire for one of the sons and wanted to
buy his freedom, but Athenogenes, with the help of a brothel owner named
Antigona, persuaded him instead to buy the whole family together with their
perfume business, so that the slave boy would be under his complete control.
Epicrates was persuaded; he gathered together forty minas (4,000 drachmas),
the agreed-upon sale price, and brought it to Athenogenes, who read out to
him a written agreement he had prepared. The agreement referred to selling the business and the slaves together with any outstanding debt they might
have; Athenogenes assured him, he says, that these debts were not large. In
his eagerness to obtain the object of his desire, Epicrates reports, he paid little attention to the details, but quickly signed the agreement[1] and handed over
the money. Only later did he discover that Midas's debts amounted to almost
five talents (30,000 drachmas), far from the trivial amount Athenogenes had
claimed Midas owed. Epicrates, therefore, sued Athenogenes, probably for
damages (*blabē*).[2] It is not clear exactly what remedy he is seeking with the
suit; probably he either wants the sale canceled and his forty minas returned
or wants Athenogenes to assume Midas's debts.

In bringing the case, Epicrates faces an immediate and obvious difficulty:
as he tells the jury, "Athenogenes will soon be telling you that the law says,
whatever one person agrees with another is binding."[3] Since his agreement
with Athenogenes specified that Epicrates would assume Midas's debts, the

law in this form, if interpreted strictly, would seem to fatally weaken Epicrates's case. Therefore, he immediately adds a qualification: "Things that are just (*dikaia*), of course, (are binding) my friend; things that are not, it's the opposite: (the law) prohibits them from being binding."[4] He then adds that he will make things clearer from the laws themselves and proceeds to mention four other laws: one prohibiting lying in the agora (14), one requiring that a slave's defects be disclosed before a sale (15), one stating that children of women who were justly betrothed are legitimate (16), and one stating that a will is valid unless made under the influence of a woman or some other constraint (17). Epicrates then goes on to make several other arguments, in particular that an experienced businessman like Athenogenes must have known that Midas's debts were large, though he claimed that they were trivial; by contrast, he (Epicrates) could not be expected to know such things (19–20). Epicrates also adds the apparently unrelated accusation that Athenogenes had violated the law by leaving Athens rather than fighting at the battle of Chaeronea (29). But the heart of his case is that the agreement to purchase the slaves was unjust, at least with regard to Midas's debts, and thus it is not binding on him.

A number of other ancient sources, including other forensic speakers, also refer to this law (*nomos*) that whatever two people agree on is legally binding (*kurios*), and in recent years considerable attention has been given to what many scholars call the Athenian law on contracts, though I will call it the law on agreements. Scholars often discuss the law in the context of the Roman law of contracts and modern contract law; in particular, scholars debate whether Athenian contracts were real or consensual (both terms from Roman law) and what remedies may have been available to redress violations. Some of these scholars seem to lose sight of the fact that Athenian law is not Roman law, and that unlike Roman law, it does not usually define offenses in great detail or elaborate the precise conditions required for enforcement of a law. As others have also recently urged, however, in order to understand Athenian law it is essential to put aside preconceptions based on Roman law and begin with what the Athenians themselves tell us, especially in the forensic speeches.[5] Even Plato and Aristotle, though sometimes helpful on specific points, may be misleading if we try to apply their systematic reasoning to Athenian law, which more than most legal systems exemplifies Holmes's famous dictum, "The life of the law is not logic; it is experience."[6]

The aim of this chapter is to examine Epicrates's argument in Hyperides 3, which in my view has been widely misunderstood, and in so doing to shed light on the problem of understanding what an Athenian law really meant. But before we look at the argument, we must examine a number of issues pertaining to the law itself, including whether such a law really existed, how generally it was applied, and what its precise wording was.

Doubts about the existence of a law on agreements were first raised by Richard Maschke, who suggested that citations of the law by the orators are actually references to clauses taken out of context from various laws on other subjects, which included such a clause for reasons specific to each law.[7] Recently Maschke's view has been picked up by Domingo Aviles and Robert Wallace.[8] Reasons why scholars doubt the existence of a separate law include: first, the fact that authors refer to the law in different ways, suggesting that there may have been no fixed text and thus no written law; second, that the general form of the law and the absence of any sanction are uncharacteristic of Athenian or Greek law; and third, that there would have been no need for a general statute of this sort, since anyone who had been the victim when an agreement was violated could bring a suit for damages (a *dikē blabēs*) even without any such law.

Aviles presents the most extensive case against the existence of a general law. He cites a third-century BCE inscription from Ephesus (*Syll.*³ 364 = *IvEph* 4), which he calls a "statute" (though "decree" might be more appropriate), that gives rules for handling mortgage debt in the aftermath of a recent war, and he notes that it includes clauses allowing other sorts of arrangements besides that specified in the law, as long as the creditor and debtor agree (lines 75–77, 85–86). Although no such clause can be found in any surviving Athenian law, Aviles speculates that some Athenian laws similarly specified that any agreements between litigants that differed from the law, even those contrary to its provisions, were valid. Litigants and others (he argues) then quoted such clauses out of context, giving the impression that a provision which was written for a specific situation was a general law.

Aviles's speculation may seem attractive at first, but the problems he sees in accepting the existence of a general law on agreements are largely imaginary, and his solution is even more problematic. It may be true that a general law on agreements was not strictly necessary because the moral force of an agreement could have been considered by the court in any suit for damages (or any other suit); but by the same reasoning there was also no need for a special clause inserted into some other law allowing the parties involved to make an agreement that differed from the law. Parties to a dispute, whether or not it had reached the stage of litigation, could almost always make an agreement (i.e., reach an out-of-court settlement) that resolved the dispute in any way they wished, and the court would have no further involvement; such agreements are a common basis for *paragraphē* suits (counterindictments). And since there is a good bit of evidence in the orators for a general law and none for any provision in a specific Athenian law, there is no reason whatsoever to reject the former in favor of the latter.

As for why a general law on agreements was passed if it was not strictly necessary, we can only speculate, but one possibility is that the law was enacted at a time (perhaps the late fifth century) when written agreements were just beginning to be used, and its purpose would have been to emphasize that all agreements were to be binding, even if they were not put in writing. Or perhaps even earlier Solon decided to include such a law among his many laws even if it was not strictly necessary, because in his effort to resolve the conflict between the elite (*agathoi*) and the masses (*kakoi*), he thought it important to stress the need to abide by one's agreements. In any case, our ignorance of the reason for writing this law (and most other Athenian laws) is no obstacle to our accepting the existence of such a law.

Nor should the absence of a sanction disturb us. Although many Athenian laws include sanctions, others, such as provisions in Draco's homicide law (*IG* I³ 104) that specify who can prosecute or who can agree to reconciliation, have no sanction. It is also likely that laws regulating inheritance or allowing people to make a will also contained no sanction. In such cases, it would go without saying that anyone harmed by a violation of the provision could bring suit. Laws were written to address particular situations and were adapted to that situation; some laws may share common features, but in Athens no strict format or language was prescribed. The general law as stated by Epicrates is clear and to the point, and there is no reason why it could not have been an Athenian statute.

Furthermore, it should not surprise us that speakers refer to the law in different ways. Each litigant has his own case-specific reason for discussing the law, and thus each describes the law in ways that are relevant to his specific concerns. Forensic speakers naturally give versions of the law that favor their case, even if this means straying slightly from the exact wording of the law. But the essence of the rule—that whatever two people agree to is binding—is always mentioned, whether or not other qualifications are added. In short, there is no good reason why the law on agreements as cited by Epicrates could not be an Athenian law, and no reason to think that it might be only a clause taken out of context from some other law.

By contrast, there is clear positive evidence for the existence of a general law stating that all agreements are binding. To be sure, when forensic speakers refer to "the law" or "the laws," they may not have a specific statute in mind;[9] but in these cases, the speaker does not ask the clerk to read out to the court the text of the (written) law. When a speaker does ask that a law be read out, we can be confident that the law existed in the form it was read, since in

Athens, we are told (Dem. 26.24), death was the prescribed penalty for anyone who cited a nonexistent law.

The law on agreements was read out to the court in one surviving speech, Demosthenes 47. The speaker maintains that he and Theophemus agreed to delay the date on which a payment that the speaker owed to Theophemus was due. The speaker then asks the clerk to "read the law and the witness deposition that prescribes that whatever one person agrees with another is to be binding, so that (you will see that) I am no longer in default to him" (47.77). After the law and the deposition are read (no text of either is preserved), he then adds that "witnesses have testified to you that he agreed and postponed the day of payment for me" (47.78).[10] For this reason, the speaker claims, Theophemus violated the agreement by not waiting to collect the payment until the newly agreed-upon due date. We can be quite confident here that a written statute has been read by the clerk, that this statute in fact existed, and that it stated that agreements between two people are binding.[11] Indeed, the passage is as conclusive as any proof of a law's existence could be, except for those rare cases where a law happens to be preserved on an inscription.[12]

The law on agreements that was read out at Demosthenes 47.77 is thus a real Athenian (written) law; and Epicrates's reference to the same law in Hyperides 3.13 in almost identical language lends support to the view that these were the actual words of the law, or at least of this part of it.[13] The law may have contained no explicit sanction because it was taken for granted that if someone was harmed by a violation of an agreement, he could bring suit for damages, and the courts would have to hear his case because, according to the law, the agreement was legally binding (kurios) and thus enforceable in court.

The next issue we need to address is whether the law was binding generally for all agreements or, as some scholars have argued, only after there had been some concrete performance; in Roman terms, did the law apply to "consensual contracts" or only to "real contracts"?[14] Fritz Pringsheim's very influential conclusion was that the law applied only to "real contracts," where some specific performance had occurred, and that more generally, "the Greek law of sale" required that there be delivery of both goods and payment in order for there to be a valid sale.[15] Pringsheim, like Maschke before him, seems to have been motivated in part by an underlying evolutionary view of law that assumes a development from more formal to less formal arrangements.[16] Pringsheim's view was further developed by Hans Julius Wolff, and still has followers today.[17]

The view that only "real contracts" are binding is attractive, because if no part of the agreement has been fulfilled, then no one has suffered any harm and so neither party would have grounds for seeking damages. From this perspective, if, for example, I agree to buy your horse, the agreement becomes binding only after some specific performance—either I pay you or you deliver the horse; before this, either of us can break the agreement without consequences.[18] It is true that most disputes about agreements in the forensic speeches pertain to those where there has been some fulfillment (or some violation by nonfulfillment). Epicrates, for instance, has already paid forty minas for the perfume business, and Theophemus in Demosthenes 47 (see above) violated the agreement by not waiting until the newly agreed due date.

The agreement in Demosthenes 48, however, does appear to be a "consensual contract."[19] Callistratus tells us that he and Olympiodorus made an agreement that if either of them prevailed over other claimants to an estate, they would divide whatever part of the estate was awarded. When Olympiodorus is finally awarded the estate, however, he refuses to give Callistratus anything. Callistratus thus sues to obtain his share. He clearly thinks the agreement is binding and that Olympiodorus is obligated to give him half of the estate, even though he (Callistratus) has done nothing to create this obligation except make the agreement. True, the two parties had also agreed to work together, and one might perhaps argue that, at least for a while, this part of the agreement was fulfilled, and that as a consequence theirs was a "real contract" and thus binding for this reason; but Callistratus says almost nothing about this aspect of the agreement, and certainly does not base his claim on any previous assistance he might have given Olympiodorus. In fact, Olympiodorus will apparently base his defense on a claim that recently Callistratus has not fulfilled this part of the agreement, which indicates that he too thinks the agreement would be binding unless he can point to some specific reason why it is not. We can only conclude that this "consensual contract" is binding.[20]

A corollary of Wolff's theory is that Athenian courts could not compel "specific performance," the fulfillment of some part of the contract, but could only award damages. The agreement between Callistratus and Olympiodorus, however, is evidence that an Athenian court could render a verdict compelling specific performance, since this is clearly what Callistratus is seeking. The case is generally considered a suit for damages (a *dikē blabēs*), and it is hard to see any other procedure that might have been used, even though Callistratus has not in fact suffered any harm because of the award of the estate to Olympiodorus. Perhaps because of this, his language remains vague—he speaks only of Olympiodorus "wronging" (*adikein*) him—when he asks the court to decide in his favor. And the only ruling they could give in his favor would be that Olympiodorus must fulfill his part of the agreement—viz. specific performance.

Another kind of restriction on the application of the law of agreements was proposed by Gerhard Thür in his magisterial work on the legal procedure of challenging an opponent in connection with interrogating a slave under torture.[21] Thür takes his idea of agreement (*homologia*) from this procedure, where in rare cases the challenged party admits the point on which he was challenged; in Demosthenes 30.27, for instance, Onetor refused to allow a slave to be interrogated but instead agreed or admitted that Aphobus was farming a piece of land.[22] Thür speculates that similar admissions were made at pretrial hearings, where litigants could question one another and the other party had to answer (though not necessarily to agree),[23] and that the law stating agreements were binding meant that in the trial a litigant could not deny an admission he had made in the preliminary hearing. Thür also cites Demosthenes 56.2, which refers to a law that agreements made voluntarily (*hekōn*) are binding; he argues that the qualification is meant to distinguish agreements outside of litigation, where no compulsion is involved, from those in the pretrial hearing, where an answer (but not an agreement) was compulsory.

Thür concludes that ordinary agreements, such as the one Epicrates concluded with Athenogenes to buy the perfume shop, created no obligation but only documented the transaction. In this case, however, the transaction does not need documentation: Epicrates admits he made the agreement and it appears that Athenogenes will base his defense on it, arguing that Epicrates has an obligation to pay the debts he has incurred. In fact, as far as we can tell, the law on agreements is never cited with reference to anything admitted (or agreed to) at a pretrial hearing. When the context is clear, the law is always cited in reference to an agreement that was concluded before the litigation began.[24] Thür's theory is a clever bit of step-by-step deduction where each step may seem reasonable but the theory fails to account for most of the references to the law on agreements in the orators and elsewhere.

We are now ready to examine exactly what the law said, and in particular whether it contained any of several qualifications sometimes mentioned by orators and others. All mentions of or references to the law on agreements have been conveniently collected by Phillips, who groups them into four categories, beginning with the "unqualified" general law that whatever is agreed to is binding; this is the form cited by Epicrates in Hyperides 3.13 (see above), among others.[25] The other versions are that whatever is agreed to voluntarily is binding, whatever is agreed to in front of witnesses is binding, and whatever is agreed to is binding provided it is just or lawful.[26] After some discussion, Phillips concludes, correctly in my view, that the actual law most likely was unqualified and read simply: ὅσα ἂν ἕτερος ἑτέρῳ ὁμολογήσῃ, κύρια εἶναι ("whatever one person agrees on with another is to be binding"), without qualification.[27] In their discussions, litigants might add a qualification that was supportive of their case, probably thinking that the jury would accept the qualified version as essentially the same as the general law. In this they were probably correct, as we can see by briefly examining each of the qualifications in turn.

First, some speakers (e.g., Dem. 56.2) report the law as stating that all "voluntary" (*hekōn*) agreements are binding. Did an agreement have to be voluntary in order to be binding? Or to put it another way, would an Athenian court have enforced an agreement that was not voluntary—for instance, if one party had agreed only because the other party held a knife to his throat or had exerted some other form of compulsion? Even in a modern court, agreements made under such circumstances (a gun to the head) would normally not be enforced, and it is hard to imagine an Athenian court acting any differently. In fact, one can argue that even the simple, unqualified version of the law implies a voluntary agreement, because *homologein* (lit. "say the same thing"), like the English "agree," in itself implies a voluntary act; to sign a contract at gunpoint arguably does not qualify as agreeing. Thus, even if the text of the Athenian law on agreements did not specify "voluntarily," the law would be understood as including this qualification.[28]

The qualification that an agreement is binding only if it is made before witnesses is different, since an agreement without witnesses would still be considered an agreement. To be sure, in Athens most agreements, like most transactions of any sort, took place in front of witnesses, and the absence of witnesses could be grounds for doubting that the transaction had taken place or for questioning its details. But as far as we can tell, witnesses were not legally required; their role was to confirm the existence of the agreement, not to make the agreement valid. If one could convince a jury that the agreement had in fact been made (or if the two litigants agreed that it had been made), the absence of witnesses would not invalidate the agreement. In the case against Athenogenes (Hyp. 3), there is no mention of Epicrates having a witness when he made the agreement (though most commentators think he did), but if in fact he did not have one, he almost certainly could not use this as an argument against enforcement of the agreement. The presence of witnesses was part of virtually all Athenian agreements, but it was probably not required by law and it was not part of the meaning of the law.

What about an agreement that was unjust or unlawful? Would such an agreement have been binding? Athina Dimopoulou is almost certainly correct to maintain that, in view of the law prescribing death for anyone who shipped grain to any port besides Athens (Dem. 34.37, 35.50–51), no Athenian court would enforce an agreement to purchase grain abroad and ship it somewhere besides Athens.[29] Indeed, it is highly unlikely that anyone would seek enforcement of such a contract, since he would, in essence, be confessing to a capital crime. Similarly, if two persons agreed that they would both embezzle money from the state treasury and divide the proceeds equally, and one of them succeeded in embezzling, it is hard to imagine that the other person would sue for his share, arguing in court that the agreement to embezzle state funds should be enforced. If he did make such a claim, a jury would almost certainly not support him; more likely, he would himself be indicted for embezzlement. It seems clear, therefore, that in practical terms unjust agreements were not binding in Athenian law.

Many scholars, nevertheless, reject Epicrates's assumption that an agreement must be just or lawful in order to be binding, and argue that unjust agreements were in fact binding. This conclusion is primarily based on Demosthenes 48 (discussed above), where Callistratus and Olympiodorus agreed to join forces in seeking an inheritance and to divide equally whatever amount either one might receive. According to many scholars, this agreement was, as David Phillips puts it, "blatantly illegal (and hence, by definition, unjust)";[30] and yet Callistratus is openly seeking to enforce it. Was the agreement illegal? Claimants to an Athenian estate engage in all kinds of strategies, many of them quite devious, in order to advance their claim over the claims of others, but nothing in the orators suggests that joining forces with another potential claimant was either illegal or immoral.[31]

The agreement in Demosthenes 48 was made before reputable, named witnesses, and Callistratus reports it with no hint of embarrassment or excuse. In fact, he presents the agreement as a positive legal development—he and Olympiodorus had stopped arguing about which of them deserved the entire estate and had instead agreed to divide it equally.[32] Clearly neither he nor the witnesses see anything wrong with the agreement, nor does he expect the jurors to see anything wrong. And Olympiodorus almost certainly did not argue that the agreement should not be enforced because it was illegal or unjust. This case, then, provides no support for the view that an unjust or unlawful agreement was binding. Rather, it was generally understood that no one would ask an Athenian court to enforce an agreement that was clearly illegal or unjust. If someone did attempt to enforce such a contract, no court would support him; indeed, he would be more likely to be indicted himself. For all practical purposes, then, unjust or illegal agreements were not binding in Athens, and since this view was rooted in general assumptions about law and justice, it would not need to be stated explicitly in the law on agreements.

One other argument scholars sometimes advance in support of the view that an unjust or illegal agreement was nonetheless binding is that an agreement can put itself above the law. Stephen Todd notes, for example, that in Demosthenes 35.39 Androcles asserts that his agreement with Lacritus "allows nothing to be more authoritative (*ouden kuriōteron*) than its written terms, and no law or decree or anything else can be brought to bear against the agreement."[33] The agreement had also been mentioned earlier in the speech in similar terms: "concerning these matters, nothing is to be more authoritative (*kuriōteron mēden*) than the agreement" (13).[34] Both passages place the agreement above everything else.

At first sight these *ouden/mēden kuriōteron* clauses may seem puzzling: could Athenians add such a clause to an agreement to do something illegal, such as ship grain to some other port besides Athens, and then claim that their agreement was binding? It seems highly unlikely that the Athenians would allow their law to be ignored by the simple insertion of such a clause in an agreement; and indeed, they almost certainly did not.

As Edward Cohen explains, all private agreements with an *ouden kuriōteron* clause that we know of concern maritime trade, which by its nature was international and usually involved other cities and countries besides Athens.[35] A merchant might find himself involved in litigation in unpredictable circumstances at a foreign port where the laws were also unpredictable. Thus those who entered into a maritime agreement would understandably want to ensure that their agreement remained valid and binding even if it conflicted with some unpredictable legal situation elsewhere. Moreover, it is reasonable that these agreements included a clause putting their agreement above the law. However, such a clause would not allow the agreement to override an Athenian law in an Athenian court, and it has no relevance to Athenian agreements concerning matters that, unlike maritime trade, could not put themselves above the law and would not be enforced if they were illegal.

We may thus conclude that the Athenian law on agreements applied without qualification to all agreements (it being understood that "agreement" meant "voluntary agreement"), and that in practical terms, under Athenian law, agreements that were illegal or unjust would not be enforced in court and thus would not be considered binding. If this is correct, what then is Epicrates's argument in Hyperides 3? More specifically, why does he cite four other laws to support his case? A common view among scholars is that Epicrates cites these laws in order to support an argument from analogy to the effect that even though the qualification "just" is not explicitly stated in the law on agreements, it is legitimate to read this qualification into that law;[36] thus, the analogies provided by these other four laws allow us to interpret the law on agreements as applying only to agreements that are just. Phillips concludes that Epicrates is trying to convince the jury "to import an understood justice requirement into the general contract law."[37] He accomplishes this goal, Phillips argues, by positing "a unitary legislative intent to combat contractual fraud": if all Athenian laws form a unity because (as Athenians believed) they were all authored by Solon, and if several other laws contain a justice requirement, then the same requirement can be presumed for all laws, including the law on agreements, even if the law itself contains no such requirement.

If this is Epicrates's argument, I think scholars are right to question it, but I don't think it is. In my view, his argument begins from his understanding, shared by the jury and Athenians generally, that an agreement must be just in order to be enforceable. He indicates that this assumption would be widely accepted by inserting the particle *ge* ("of course") in his initial response to the idea that all agreements are binding: "those that are just, of course, my friend" (τά γε δίκαια ὦ βέλτιστε [Hyp. 3.13]). He assumes that not only will his audience agree, but his opponent, Athenogenes, will also agree; and indeed, it seems very unlikely that Athenogenes would attempt to argue that because the law on agreements does not specifically mention just agreements, it must apply to unjust as well as just agreements, and therefore his agreement with Epicrates is enforceable even if it is unjust.

The reason why Epicrates cites four additional laws is not, therefore, to show by analogy that the law applies only to just agreements, because this goes without saying. Rather, Epicrates's purpose in citing them is to prove that Athenogenes acted unjustly in persuading him to accept the terms of the agreement, and for this reason the agreement should not be enforced. The laws he cites serve this purpose by helping to define more precisely what kinds of conduct were considered unjust by Athenian legislators. Each of these four laws—prohibiting lying in the agora, concealing a slave's physical defects in a sale, misrepresenting the status of a woman being betrothed, and exerting improper influence (specifically, a woman's influence) on someone who is making a will—contains an example of conduct that the law treats as unjust and that is in some respect similar to Athenogenes's conduct in the present case.

First, consider the law about lying in the agora. Epicrates argues that Athenogenes lied, or at least concealed the truth, about the debts his slaves had incurred; it is unclear where the agreement was made, but even if it was not concluded in the agora, Athenogenes behaved in a way that one law explicitly prohibits: he lied in a business transaction. This law establishes a specific form of conduct as unlawful and thus unjust; and since Athenogenes engaged in similar conduct, his conduct was unjust and the agreement ought to be voided.

Similarly, the law prohibiting concealment of a slave's physical defects in a sale is relevant because Athenogenes engaged in similar conduct, concealing a slave's financial liabilities. This law does not apply directly to his own transaction, but it too shows that the type of deceptive conduct Athenogenes engaged in is similar to conduct which the law declares to be unjust. The same is true of the other two laws, which prohibit misrepresenting the facts in a betrothal agreement and improperly influencing someone drawing up a will: Athenogenes misrepresented the facts and the woman Antigona improperly influenced Epicrates to agree. As analogies, these four laws are imperfect, at best, but as examples of types of conduct that Athenian laws considered unlawful and thus unjust, they support Epicrates's position: in getting him to agree to buy the slaves, Athenogenes and Antigona engaged in unjust conduct, and therefore the agreement is unjust and should not be enforced.[38] Thus, Epicrates's argument does reflect the underlying assumption noted by Phillips that Athenian laws formed a unity, but not in the way he thinks.

As far as we can judge from the speech that we have, moreover, it seems highly unlikely that Athenogenes will argue that these four laws do not apply because the first only prohibits lying in the agora, not lying in one's own house (or wherever the agreement was made); the second only prohibits concealment of a slave's physical liabilities, not concealment of financial liabilities; the third speaks of a woman about to be betrothed and says nothing about a slave's condition; and the fourth applies to wills, not to sales. No, Athenogenes's defense will almost certainly be that he did not lie about anything, did not conceal or misrepresent anything, and did not exert improper influence. On the contrary, he read out the full text of the agreement to Epicrates, as Epicrates admits, and the agreement mentioned all the debts (though perhaps without details). Epicrates then willingly signed the agreement and paid the agreed price. Athenogenes can hardly be blamed if Epicrates did not listen closely when the agreement was read, or was so overcome with love that he acted foolishly in agreeing to the sale. The law is quite clear that agreements are binding, and he, Athenogenes, has made an open and honest agreement and has fulfilled all the obligations the agreement required of him. Now the court must enforce the law.

The dispute between Epicrates and Athenogenes is thus not a dispute about the meaning or interpretation of the law on agreements; it is a dispute about the facts of the case, specifically whether Athenogenes's and Antigona's conduct in persuading Epicrates to agree to buy the slaves, debts and all, accorded with Athenian standards of just conduct. The jury is being asked to judge not between differing interpretations of the law on agreements but between differing accounts or assessments of a series of events. The meaning of the law, as stated by Epicrates, is clear and would not have been disputed.

Finally, the above analysis of the meaning of the law on agreements, together with Epicrates's arguments about the law, have implications for the larger issue of interpreting Athenian laws, which may be worth elaborating. Without engaging in linguistic or philosophical discussion about "meaning," I propose that we think of four levels or stages of the meaning of a law that would make sense to a fifth-century Athenian: (1) the strictly literal meaning of the written text of the law, (2) the further implications of those words, (3) assumptions about the meaning stemming from common Athenian cultural values, and (4) interpretations urged by litigants as appropriate to the issues in their case.

This schema is only theoretical; in practice it is questionable whether one can isolate each stage from the others, and of course there will always be gray areas. The first two in particular are perhaps impossible to separate, since words arguably cannot be uttered without conveying both their denotation and their connotations. But in saying "whatever one person agrees with another is to be binding," one almost certainly does not intend to say that even an agreement made under severe duress, such as with a gun to one's head, is binding. Someone intending this meaning would probably rephrase the statement or add something to it indicating this. On the other hand, there are degrees of duress and there will always be a gray area around the precise amount of duress necessary to make an agreement invalid; but this does not invalidate our conclusion that the qualification "voluntary" would be taken for granted as an inherent connotation of the word "agree."

As for the third level of meaning of the law on agreements, I argued above that Athenians would assume the law applied only to agreements that were lawful and just, and that an unlawful or unjust agreement was not binding. But whereas "voluntarily" may be understood as implicit in the word "agreement," so that "involuntary agreement" can be considered a self-contradiction, the same cannot be said of "unlawful or unjust agreements," which are certainly conceivable. On the other hand, Athenians would generally not consider unlawful or unjust agreements binding—unlawful agreements because for practical reasons (discussed above) these would not be presented to any court for enforcement, and unjust agreements because Athenians, more than we do today, tended to equate law and justice, so that jurors would not wish to render a verdict that was considered unjust, even if it was legal in some technical sense. For this reason, Epicrates's claim that unjust agreements are not binding is also an accurate understanding of the meaning of the law. It is not his own interpretation that needs to be defended against a different interpretation, for it is highly unlikely that any Athenian would ever argue that unjust agreements are binding. Thus, although the text of the general law on agreements ("whatever one person agrees with another is binding") contained no explicit qualifications, it was implicit in the law that it applied only to agreements that were voluntary, lawful, and just. Accepting these qualifications as implicit, however, still leaves the fourth level, interpretation, where litigants could dispute the meaning of a law.

In elaborating his view, Phillips assumes a much simpler understanding of a law's meaning than I have proposed above, namely that "in fourth-century

Athens, what the law said was carved in stone; what the law meant was determined in each individual and independent case by the arguments of the litigants and the decision of the jury."[39] Underlying this analysis is the well known fact that Athenian laws were written with considerably less precision of detail than we today expect and generally require. The details included in a law today are intended to make the law's meaning and its applicability to specific cases clearer and more certain, and thus to prevent the sorts of disputes on these points that Phillips postulates for Athens. Take, for example, the law on perjury. The US civil code defines perjury as:

> When a person, having taken an oath before a competent tribunal, officer, or person, in any case in which a law of the United States authorizes an oath to be administered, that he will testify, declare, depose, or certify truly, or that any written testimony, declaration, deposition, or certificate by him subscribed, is true, willfully and contrary to such oath states or subscribes any material matter which he does not believe to be true; or in any declaration, certificate, verification, or statement under penalty of perjury, willfully subscribes as true any material matter which he does not believe to be true.[40]

Athenians would probably find this modern definition absurdly complex. For them, for example, the word "statement" alone would of course include declaration, certificate, and verification, and they would probably use a simple verb like "say" and assume it included "testify, declare, depose, or certify."

Conversely, because Athenians took for granted the evident meaning of words in their laws, even if this was not spelled out in the text, the less precise nature of their laws did not make them intolerably vague, just as the precise nature of our laws does not make them completely unambiguous. The law prohibiting lying in the agora, for example, almost certainly was meant to apply to lying in business dealings, and it presumably envisaged primarily misrepresentation of the quality or quantity of goods or of payment. It almost certainly did not apply to lying to a friend about your whereabouts the night before while you happened to be walking through the agora. For the Athenians, these implications of the law could be assumed; there was no need to add more precise language to clarify the simple text. They were not uncomfortable with legal language that relied on a common understanding of the use of words, resulting in laws whose meaning (as I defined it earlier) included the implicit understandings conveyed by the ordinary language of that text.

This would still leave room for disputes about the full meaning of a law or about its application to a specific case, but such disputes may have been less common than Phillips seems to think. In their annual oath, all jurors swore "to judge according to the laws (*kata tous nomous*)," and because of the severe penalty for citing a nonexistent law (see above), they could have confidence that the texts of laws that were read out in court were accurate. But in cases where the meaning of a law or its applicability to the case at hand was disputed, the jury would need some guidance, which could come only from the arguments of the two litigants.[41] Like many others, Phillips maintains (wrongly, as I have argued above) that Hyperides 3 is such a case. He sees here an example of "the democratic principle that permitted any Athenian to assert his interpretation of the law and rewarded the litigant whose interpretation proved most persuasive to a citizen jury."[42] This view appears to suggest that litigants had a free hand to interpret Athenian laws as they wished. I would argue, however, that common Athenian values and beliefs significantly constrained the range of possible interpretations of the bare text of the law.

Phillips's view seems attractive in part because Athenian litigants did not face the sort of restraints imposed by judges on modern litigants. Thus, they often seek to interpret the law, and sometimes do it in ways that appear clearly misleading, such as when Euphiletus in Lysias 1 argues that the law establishes death as the punishment for adultery and therefore the law required him to kill Eratosthenes, or that the law set a more severe penalty for adultery than for rape. These arguments are, at best, misleading interpretations of Athenian laws. But such cases are less common than often thought, and there frequently seems to be no dispute at all about the meaning of a law, even though Athenian laws are generally written with far less precision and fewer details than most modern laws.

In other words, because Athenian laws made less effort to specify precise details, they cannot be understood as literally and precisely as modern laws; but they also should not be seen as open to a nearly unlimited range of interpretation. Athenian laws may leave more room for disputes about interpretation than laws do today, but they still pose significant restraints on the arguments of litigants.

NOTES

1. Epicrates's words are: "he immediately sealed the agreement . . . adding Nikon of Kephisia's name to mine" (σημαίνεται τὰς συνθήκας εὐθὺς . . . προσεγγράψας μετ᾽ ἐμοῦ Νίκωνα τὸν Κηφισιέα [Hyp. 3.8]). All translations in this chapter are the author's. It is possible that Athenogenes wrote Epicrates's name on the agreement, but I think it more likely that Epicrates did.

2. Whitehead 2000: 268.

3. Hyp. 3.13: ὁ νόμος λέγει, ὅσα ἂν ἕτερος ἑτέρῳ ὁμολογήσῃ, κύρια εἶναι. "Binding" is my translation of *kurios*, whose basic meaning is "authoritative."

4. Hyp. 3.13: τά γε δίκαια, ὦ βέλτιστε· τὰ δὲ μὴ τοὐναντίον ἀπαγορεύει μὴ κύρια εἶναι.

5. E.g., Wallace 2014.

6. Holmes 1963: 5.

7. Maschke 1926: 159–171.

8. Aviles 2012 [2015]; Wallace 2014.

9. Cf., e.g., Aeschines's assertion that "all the laws" forbid anyone to write false statements in public decrees (Aeschin. 3.50).

10. Dem. 47.77–78: ἀνάγνωθί μοι τὸν νόμον καὶ τὴν μαρτυρίαν, ὃς κελεύει κύρια εἶναι ὅ τι ἂν ἕτερος ἑτέρῳ ὁμολογήσῃ, ὥστε οὐκέτι ἦν αὐτῷ δήπου ὑπερήμερος. ΝΟΜΟΣ. ΜΑΡΤΥΡΙΑ. ὡς μὲν τοίνυν ὡμολόγησε καὶ ἀνεβάλετό μοι τὴν ὑπερημερίαν, μεμαρτύρηται ὑμῖν.

11. Wallace (2014: 216) resists this conclusion, maintaining (among other things) that in 47.77 it "remains unclear . . . why the speaker juxtaposes the following *homologia* clause with 'the deposition.'" But this "juxtaposition" is only an impression created by the English translation, where a literal translation, "the law and the witness deposition that prescribes," may seem to suggest that the deposition is prescribing something (which would make no sense). To avoid this, some editors (e.g., Murray 1939) reverse the order in Greek and read τὴν μαρτυρίαν καὶ τὸν νόμον. But in Greek, the relative pronoun ὅς is masculine, and thus the antecedent of ὅς is clearly the masculine τὸν νόμον ("law"), not the feminine τὴν μαρτυρίαν ("testimony"), no matter what the order of the nouns. Thus, in Greek, it is clearly the law that prescribes, not the testimony.

12. The same law was probably also read out at Dem. 48.11, but the speaker's words at this point—"the law according to which we wrote our contract with one another" (τόν τε νόμον . . . καθ' ὃν τὰς συνθήκας ἐγράψαμεν πρὸς ἡμᾶς αὐτούς)— are not specific enough for one to be certain exactly what law is being requested.

13. The two speakers use identical words, but their word order is slightly different.

14. There is no evidence that the Greeks themselves ever distinguished between these two types of agreement.

15. Pringsheim 1950: 26–43.

16. On which see Cohen 2006.

17. Wolff 1968.

18. There might, of course, be consequences if the buyer needed the horse or the seller needed the money for some other reason.

19. Gagliardi 2014: 192–194.

20. Wolff's theory (1968: 530–531)—that the basis of Callistratus's claim is that as soon as Olympiodorus was awarded the estate, half of it automatically belonged to Callistratus, so he can sue because he is being deprived of property that is already his own—has no support in the text. Carawan (2006, and more briefly in 2007) develops the theory that most Athenian agreements were "real contracts," and those that were not real were binding not because "consensual contracts" were binding, but be-

cause they provided for the settlement of previous differences between the two parties (confirmed by oaths). In these cases, it was the settlement that the agreement confirmed that made it binding; the agreement by itself was not binding. But the law says nothing about a past settlement, nor does the agreement in Dem. 47 (see n. 32).

21. Thür 1977: 152–158; see also 2013: 8–9.

22. Onetor made the admission well before the pretrial hearing, but he may have repeated it at the hearing.

23. Thür (2013: 8) cites a law from Dem. 46.10, that opposing litigants had to answer one another, a law usually cited in connection with the *erōtēsis*, or questioning of an opponent during the trial. He then cites a law mentioned in Dem. 42.12, which is there applied to an agreement made between the two parties (not an admission by one party) well before the trial.

24. In, e.g., Dem. 48.11 the agreement that is cited was made before any litigation at all over the inheritance in question began, and long before Callistratus decided to sue; see Aviles 2012 [2015]. In Dem. 42.12 the speaker says that in order to avoid rushing into court, he agreed to meet with his opponent, presumably to try to settle their dispute without litigation. And in Dem. 56.2 it is clear that the law is cited with reference to a maritime contract made long before any litigation on the matter began. Conversely, when a person is said to have agreed or admitted something during the pretrial hearing, there is no mention of this admission being binding (e.g., Dem. 29.31–32).

25. Phillips 2009: 93–94.

26. Given the close connection between law and justice in Athens, "illegal" and "unjust" amounted to almost the same thing. Phillips (loc. cit.) sees lawful as a "subset" of just.

27. Phillips 2009: 105.

28. One of the referees asks whether a person who agrees to pay a ransom in order to obtain his release would be thought to act voluntarily. Consider the case of Eratosthenes, caught in bed with Euphiletus's wife in Lysias 1. He offers Euphiletus money to release him (apparently a common outcome in adultery cases). Euphiletus does not agree, but if he did agree, both would be obliged to honor the agreement. However, Euphiletus would probably not release Eratosthenes until the money had been paid, so that there would be no question of Eratosthenes not fulfilling the agreement. On the other hand, if the money was paid and Euphiletus did not release him, Eratosthenes or his relatives on his behalf could surely sue for his release and perhaps for additional damages too.

29. Dimopoulou 2014.

30. Phillips 2009: 96.

31. Cf. Isoc. 11.20–21, where Theopompus denies that he could have made an agreement to join forces with Stratocles in contesting the estate because their two claims competed directly with one another; he suggests, however, that two other claimants might have made such an agreement because their claims did not compete directly. There is no hint in his argument that either agreement would have been unjust or unlawful.

32. Carawan (2007: 77; cf. n. 20) argues that the agreement between the two men was binding because it settled a previous dispute between the two. But Callistratus nowhere attributes any significance to the fact that the agreement was also a settlement. He cites the settlement to reinforce the idea that the two agreed to an equal division of property, but, as he repeatedly emphasizes, his case rests on the agreement to divide the estate equally in the future, not the fact that they divided proceeds equally during a settlement of their past differences.

33. Todd 1993: 59. Dem. 35.39: ἡ μὲν γὰρ συγγραφὴ οὐδὲν κυριώτερον ἐᾷ εἶναι τῶν ἐγγεγραμμένων, οὐδὲ προσφέρειν οὔτε νόμον οὔτε ψήφισμα οὔτ' ἄλλ' οὐδ' ὁτιοῦν πρὸς τὴν συγγραφήν.

34. Dem.35.13: κυριώτερον δὲ περὶ τούτων ἄλλο μηδὲν εἶναι τῆς συγγραφῆς.

35. Cohen 2014.

36. E.g., Phillips 2009: 106–114.

37. Phillips 2009: 115.

38. Harris (2007: 364) takes a position close to mine: "Since the law does not define the term unjust in this context, Epicrates examines other laws for guidance about how to interpret the term." But his analysis rests on the false assumption that the law on agreements explicitly stated that unjust agreements are not binding. It is unclear why he makes this assumption, but in an earlier article (2000: 49) he similarly assumes, without explanation, that the law includes the qualification "willing."

39. Phillips 2009: 119.

40. 18 USC §1621.

41. Gagarin 2014.

42. Phillips 2009: 117.

REFERENCES

Aviles, Domingo. 2012 [2015]. "The Athenian Law(s) on *Homologia*." *Mouseion* 12.1, 56—ser. 3: 51–71.

Carawan, Edwin. 2006. "The Athenian Law of Agreement." *Greek, Roman, and Byzantine Studies* 46.4: 339–374.

———. 2007. "Oath and Contract." In *Horkos: The Oath in Greek Society*, edited by Alan H. Sommerstein and Judith Fletcher, 73–80, with notes 236–238. Exeter: Bristol Phoenix Press.

Cohen, Edward E. 2006. "Consensual Contracts at Athens." In *Symposion 2003: Vorträge zur griechischen und hellenistischen Rechtsgeschichte*, edited by Hans-Albert Rupprecht, 73–84. Vienna: Verlag der Österreichischen Akademie der Wissenschaften.

———. 2014. "Private Agreements Purporting to Override Polis Law: A Response to Athina Dimopoulou." In Gagarin and Lanni, *Symposion 2013*, 277–286.

Dimopoulou, Athina. 2014. "Ἄκυρον ἔστω: Legal Invalidity in Greek Inscriptions." In Gagarin and Lanni, *Symposion 2013*, 249–275.

Gagarin, Michael. 2014. "Rhetoric as a Source of Law in Athens." In Gagarin and Lanni, *Symposion 2013*, 131–151.

Gagarin, Michael, and Adriaan Lanni, eds. 2014. *Symposion 2013: Vorträge zur griechischen und hellenistischen Rechtsgeschichte.* Vienna: Verlag der Österreichischen Akademie der Wissenschaften.

Gagliardi, Lorenzo. 2014. "La legge sulla ὁμολογία e i vizi della volontà nei contratti in diritto ateniese." In Gagarin and Lanni, *Symposion 2013*, 177–214.

Harris, Edward M. 2000. "Open Texture in Athenian Law." *Dike* 3: 27–79.

———. 2007. "Did the Athenian Courts Attempt to Achieve Consistency? Oral Tradition and Written Records in the Athenian Administration of Justice." In *The Politics of Orality*, edited by Craig Richard Cooper, 343–370. Leiden: Brill.

Holmes, Oliver Wendell. 1963. *The Common Law.* Edited by Mark DeWolfe Howe. Boston: Little, Brown.

Maschke, Richard. 1926. *Die Willenslehre im griechischen Recht.* Berlin: Georg Stilke.

Murray, A. T., trans. 1939. *Demosthenes: Orations.* Vol. 5, Orations *41–49: Private Cases.* Cambridge, MA: Harvard University Press.

Phillips, David D. 2009. "Hyperides 3 and the Athenian Law of Contracts." *Transactions of the American Philological Association* 139: 89–122.

Pringsheim, Fritz. 1950. *The Greek Law of Sale.* Weimar: Böhlaus.

Thür, Gerhard. 1977. *Beweisführung vor den Schwurgerichtshöfen Athens: Die Proklesis zur Basanos.* Vienna: Verlag der Östereicheischen Akademie der Wissenschaften.

———. 2013. "The Statute on *Homologein* in Hyperides' Speech *Against Athenogenes.*" *Dike* 16: 1–10.

Todd, Stephen C. 1993. *The Shape of Athenian Law.* Oxford: Clarendon Press.

Wallace, Robert W. 2014. "Did Athens have Consensual Contracts? A Response to Lorenzo Gagliardi." In Gagarin and Lanni, *Symposion 2013*, 215–221.

Whitehead, David. 2000. *Hypereides: The Forensic Speeches; Introduction, Translation, and Commentary.* Oxford: Oxford University Press.

Wolff, Hans Julius. 1968. "Die Grundlagen des griechischen Vertragsrechts." In *Zur griechischen Rechtsgeschichte*, edited by Erich Berneker, 483–533. Darmstadt: Wissenschaftliche Buchgesellschaft.

4 / SLAVES OPERATING BUSINESSES: LEGAL RAMIFICATIONS FOR ANCIENT ATHENS— AND FOR MODERN SCHOLARSHIP

Edward E. Cohen

SCHOLARS HAVE LONG RECOGNIZED (IN ALBERTO MAFFI'S words) the "leading role" of slaves in Athenian commercial activity.[1] Because traditional Athenian concepts of manliness (*andreia*) valorized only cultural, military, and political pursuits; condemned all commerce as inherently servile; and insisted that farming alone provided a proper economic arena for the "free man" (*anēr eleutheros*), Athenian society was highly receptive to slave enterprise.[2] The Athenian institution of "slaves living independently" (*douloi chōris oikountes*) permitted unfree persons to conduct their own businesses, to establish their own households, and sometimes even to own their own slaves—with little contact, and most importantly, virtually without supervision from their owners.[3] But only minimal academic attention has been directed to the paradox of an Athenian economy dependent on slave entrepreneurs operating within a legal system that supposedly treated slaves as nullities, a system absolutely closed to slave participation (except perhaps as witnesses through torture [see n. 27 following]).

Extensive evidence and multiple studies, however, have demonstrated that legal systems invariably develop mechanisms to close significant gaps that may arise between changed societal reality and traditional juridical principles.[4] Athens was no exception.

Some years ago, in my book on Athenian banking, I set forth certain legal "adaptations" seemingly developed to accommodate commercial needs arising from the reality of fourth-century Athenian businesses (*ergasiai*) operated by slaves with little if any involvement by their masters.[5] These adaptations included recognition of slaves' responsibility for their own business debts, court acceptance of slaves and free noncitizens as parties and witnesses in commercial litigation (in contravention of the general rules allowing access to polis courts only to citizens of the polis), and acceptance of mercantile "agency" as a mechanism to overcome remaining legal disabilities.[6] Although Michael Gagarin—himself always receptive to new ideas and new approaches—has called attention to Greek legal historians' tendency simply to ignore paradigm-challenging arguments,[7] in recent years there has in fact been a boomlet in scholarly consideration of the juridical response to slave enterprise at Athens.[8]

Accordingly, at this conference on "Greek Law in the 21st Century," it seemed appropriate first to consider modern historians' recent efforts to reject (and even to athetize) evidence confirming slave entrepreneurs' liability for their own debts, and historians' similar attempts to nullify testimonia supporting slaves' participation in commercial litigation. Then I will consider in economic context the factors that virtually mandated a system of credit at Athens in which slaves bore legal responsibility for their own business obligations—a system consonant with the Roman juridical principles that in a different time and in a different society likewise effectively limited owners' liability for the financial obligations of slaves independently operating businesses.

I. STRUGGLING AGAINST THE EVIDENCE

In 2008, Maffi and the late Mario Talamanca published conflicting valuable papers concerning masters' legal liability for debts incurred in businesses operated by slaves. Maffi argued from Roman law principles[9] that Athenian slaves operating businesses were not personally liable for obligations arising from such commerce (as I had contended); rather, their masters were solely and invariably so obligated. When a slave was sold, the new master became liable for these obligations.[10] In response to Maffi, Talamanca insisted that evidence from Greek sources—and not Roman conceptions—must govern our interpretation of the legal and economic aspects of Athenian business practices, and that "*le fonti parlano con molta nettezza contro, non a favore della ricostruzione [di Maffi]*."[11]

Central to this conflict is the dispute chronicled in Hyperides 3 (*Against Athenogenes*, delivered between 330 and 324) involving the only domestic Athenian business "deal" known in detail—the purchase and sale of a retail perfume business operated by a slave, Midas, with his two sons.[12] Athenogenes, an Egyptian resident at Athens, sold Midas and his sons to Epicrates, an Athenian citizen, who assumed, by written agreement, liability for the shop's debts. The buyer claims to have undertaken these liabilities only because he was misled by the seller, who had claimed that the business's obligations were minimal. In the course of narrating Epicrates's version of the facts, the Greek text repeatedly and explicitly reports the slave-businessman Midas as personally owing the debts, remarkable evidence that the *douloi*, and in particular the father, Midas, were at least primarily liable for these commercial obligations. At Hyperides 3.10 the purported language of the actual purchase agreement provides that the buyer will be liable for whatever obligations the slave "Midas owes to anyone." Section 6 describes how the seller persuaded the buyer to be responsible for "whatever money" Midas and his sons "owe," and section 9 refers to "the creditors to whom Midas was indebted" (literally, "to whom it was owed by Midas"). In section 20, the buyer complains that the seller actually knew of "Midas owing (this money)."[13]

Against the clarity of this Athenian evidence (set forth by Hyperides, in Talamanca's phrase, "con molta nettezza") stand silence and Roman legal theory. The "silence" is not only the absence of any effort by Maffi to explain (away) Hyperides's characterization of the slaves' debts, but also the absence of an Athenian law governing responsibility for debts incurred by *douloi* operating businesses. Under a statute attributed to Solon, a slave's master was clearly liable for noncontractual wrongs ("torts") committed by a *doulos*. When a slave was acquired by a new owner only after occurrence of a delict, the law (cited in Hyp. 3) appears even to have specifically placed liability for such damage on the person owning the slave at the time that a tortious wrong was committed.[14] But this law is entirely silent about a master's liability for contractual obligations incurred by slaves. Since the debts at issue in the case of Athenogenes arose entirely from business commitments, Louis Gernet has pointed out that an owner's liability for such debts was not addressed by this or any other statutory law: otherwise the litigant would have appealed to such legislation instead of utilizing the early law dealing with slaves' wrongful "actions," which was at most applicable only by analogy to "contractual obligations."[15] The absence of provisions relating to slaves' contractual debt is not surprising: the independent operation of businesses by *douloi* represented a commercial reality of the fourth century that could not have been anticipated by an earlier law enacted in a period prior to the monetization of the Athenian economy.[16]

But in many instances, on a number of theoretical bases (e.g., characterization of the *doulos* as agent for his owner, joint liability for joint undertakings), a master could have been held liable for contractual obligations incurred by his slaves, even in the absence of an owner's general liability for the contractual commitments of a *doulos*. A master's liability, for example, would easily and clearly have arisen from conventional banking operations by a free proprietor and his staff of slaves. In other cases, a master's responsibility for, or lack of liability for, a slave's contractual commitments would have been (in barristers' parlance) an evidentiary issue. Despite his insistence that his only involvement with Midas's business was the receipt of monthly accountings, Athenogenes—as an alleged owner of three perfumeries, an habitué of the fragrance area of the agora, and a successor to his parent(s) and grandparent(s) as a seller of scents—would have found it difficult to persuade arbitrators or jurors of his noninvolvement in Midas's fragrance *ergasia*.[17] The uncertainty of a court's ultimate decision on his involvement explains Athenogenes's insistence on Epicrates's explicit assumption of the loans pertaining to the bankrupt business operated by the slaves whom Epicrates was acquiring—a nugatory and unnecessary effort if Maffi were correct in his contention that when a slave was sold, the new master became liable for the obligations of the business, and the old master was freed from liability.[18]

Masters' potential liability also explains bankers' entry into leases (*misthōseis*) with their own slaves. Thus the *douloi* Xenon, Euphraeus, Euphron, and Callistratus—while still enslaved—as principals operated the largest bank in Athens, that of Pasion. Only upon completion of the lease term did their owners "set them free" (*eleutherous apheisan*), "being quite satisfied" with how they (the owners) had been treated (Dem. 36.13–14).[19] During the ten years in which the leasing arrangement had been in force (Dem. 36.37), the slaves' only involvement with their owners appears to have been annual payment of a sizeable fixed rental (an entire talent per year) in return for the slaves' retention of the net income resulting from operation of the bank. Although all assets under the slaves' control, including all of the assets of the *trapeza* ("bank"), would have remained exposed to creditors, the bank owner's other assets would have been protected from banking obligations incurred after commencement of the lease.[20] Furthermore, a formal lease would have eliminated any inference that a slave was acting as agent for his master in entering into a banking commitment, or that they were co-venturing—possible bases for finding a master legally responsible for a slave's contractual debts, even in the absence of general legislation mandating this obligation. In contrast, such a rental arrangement between a bank owner and slave would have lacked economic justification if the master had remained potentially liable for bank obligations incurred after the lease had become effective: the owner would then have limited his right to receive income while retaining unlimited liability for losses. But the slaves of Apollodoros and Pasicles, the bank owners, paid their masters exactly the same rent as the free person who had previously leased the *trapeza* (Dem. 36.12), not an increased sum, as might be expected if their status as slaves had in fact increased their masters' liability for contractual obligations incurred by the bank during the period of their lease.

Like the testimony of Hyperides *Against Athenogenes* regarding an unfree businessman's personal liability for debts, the evidence offered by Demosthenes 36 and 45 for lease arrangements between master and slave contradicts prevailing academic dogma, and here too scholars have sought to athetize the ancient sources rather than to abandon modern doctrine. Hans Klees, for example, argues that the bank lease (*misthōsis*) between owners and slaves reported at Demosthenes 36.13–14 does not offer a "reliable basis" ("*gesicherte Grundlage*") for concluding that unfree bankers could actually enter into trapezitic leases with their masters. He finds Demosthenes's explanation for the manumission suspect, viz., the owners were "quite satisfied" with how they had been treated (36.14). Klees reasons that since a slave has a duty to serve his master, an owner need not feel appreciative of slaves' service— presumably even when slave tenants, according to Demosthenes, had paid their masters a total of ten talents (perhaps six million dollars on a purchasing power parity basis). According to Klees, the passage is clearly idiosyncratic ("*ohne Parallele*") and should therefore be disregarded.[21] Stephen Todd, in contrast, does not urge outright disregard of the text, suggesting rather that the phrase *eleutherous apheisan* does not really mean "set them free." He offers an alternative translation: the owners "bindingly declared that they (the slaves) were free of legal claims," a release rather than a manumission, thus eliminating the need to attribute slave status to the lessees who, on Todd's reading, were not being freed after termination of the lease and therefore need not have been unfree during the term of the lease.[22] But Todd's translation is impossible: the phrase *eleutherous apheisan* is formulaic Greek for manumission of slaves,[23] and is routinely translated as "set them free" or "enfranchised them." A. R. W. Harrison explicitly taught almost fifty years ago that the phrase does *not* mean "released them from their obligations," a lesson that has also been proffered by Gernet and Douglas MacDowell.[24] Yet efforts to nullify this evidence persist. Maffi does not challenge the manumission but does claim that the *misthōsis* is not really a lease: it should be treated rather as an *apophora* ("sharing arrangement").[25] Characterization of this lease as an *apophora*, however, is precluded by the text of Demosthenes 36, which explicitly characterizes the arrangement with the slaves not as a "sharing arrangement" (*apophora*) but as the lease of the deposits (*parakatathēkai*) and the operation (*ergasia*) arising from these deposits.[26]

Yet contractual arrangements with slaves, including extensions of credit directly to unfree persons operating businesses and banks on their own, would have been juridically meaningful (because legally enforceable) only if such unfree persons could be parties to commercial litigation. Although slaves were in general totally devoid of legal capacity—deprived of the right even to be witnesses in legal proceedings[27]—it has long been generally accepted that slaves did have full access to Athenian courts as parties and as witnesses in at least one category of cases, the important "commercial maritime" suits (*dikai emporikai*), where "standing" was accorded without regard to the personal status of litigants.[28] Analogously, I have further suggested that unfree persons independently operating their own businesses could also be parties in commercial cases involving banking (*dikai trapezitikai*)—a "sphere," in Harrison's words, "allied" to maritime commerce—and mining (*dikai metallikai*).[29] Maffi, however, insists that Demosthenes 37, a mining case, "confirms" that slaves could not participate for their own account in such cases.[30] Here again the actual evidence speaks, in Talamanca's words, "con molta nettezza contro, non a favore della ricostruzione [di Maffi]."[31]

Demosthenes 37 deals with loans involving a mining business—a mine and a workshop (*ergastērion*) employing thirty slaves who processed the silver obtained underground—operated by Pantaenetus.[32] During Nicobulus's absence from Athens—according to Pantaenetus because of an alleged default on a loan advanced in part by Nicobulus—Antigenes, Nicobulus's slave, had seized the *ergastērion*, taking control over Pantaenetus's property and improperly seizing silver.[33] Pantaenetus has sued Nicobulus, but Nicobulus insists that on these facts, Pantaenetus instead—in MacDowell's translation—"should have initiated the case against the slave" (Dem. 37.51).[34] Once again, the clear language of the text asserts the possibility (the speaker actually insists on the juridical necessity) of suit against a slave operating a business on his own—in this case the *ergastērion* that has been seized by the slave Antigenes. Gernet sees the passage as demonstrating that "when the slave has acted at the master's direction, it is the master who should be sued; when he has acted on his own, the slave himself should be sued."[35]

Other texts confirming the availability of Athenian courts to slaves in commercial disputes similarly have evoked determined resistance from modern scholarship defending modern theses threatened by the ancient evidence. In Demosthenes 55, a case set in the context of rights to real property, a plaintiff (according to the defendant) has concocted false contracts and has sued the defendant's slave: the litigant argues that the suit should not have been brought against the slave since the *doulos* was not acting independently of his master's direction.[36] Todd, however, insisting on the modern dogma that a slave "could be neither plaintiff nor defendant," dismisses the evidence as "obscure."[37] And Pancleon, engaged in commercial pursuits in a fuller's shop, seeks in Lysias 23 to avoid a court action on the grounds that he is a Plataean, only to be met by the plaintiff's introduction of evidence that he is in fact a slave. Of course, the plaintiff's presentation of proofs of servitude would justify pendency of the case only if slaves actually could be parties to business-oriented lawsuits. Todd, however, objects to "the assumption that the speaker's aim in convincing the court of Pancleon's slave status is to continue with the case."[38] Todd's counterassumption—that the plaintiff is really trying to lose the case which he has initiated—seems methodologically less desirable than an effort to understand the text as transmitted.

2. UNDERSTANDING THE EVIDENCE

"L'acquisto di uno schiavo che esercita un'attività commerciale
comporta anche l'acquisto dell'azienda da lui gestita, in particolare
del passivo inerente allo svolgimento di quell'attività."[39]

No Athenian evidence confirms Maffi's belief that on the sale of an Athenian slave operating a business, legal liability for that business's obligations is automatically transferred from the slave's former owner to the slave's new owner. Against the Athenian evidence that argues "with considerable clarity" (in Talamanca's words) against his hypothesis, Maffi turns to Roman commercial law. Although, in my opinion, Roman theory and/or practice should not be employed to refute Athenian sources, I do not agree with Talamanca that Maffi's resort to Roman parallels is inherently deleterious ("inutile"),[40] for the Roman economy, like the Athenian, was heavily dependent on the operation of businesses by unfree persons.[41] In fact, the treatment of a slave's *peculium* (the commercial assets used by a slave [*servus*] in commercial transactions) in Roman law provides a useful example of how a slave's legal nullity can be reconciled with legal recognition of a slave's direct responsibility for business obligations in a system, whether Roman or Greek, in which economic activity gave prominence to slaves operating businesses autonomously.[42] But Romanists' treatment of the *peculium* also illustrates the inadvisability, if not the impossibility, of seeking to mechanically impose analogies from Roman law on Athenian business procedure in defiance of the actual Athenian evidence, for—beyond the very different circumstances of a very different civilization—these Roman law principles are themselves often based on highly disputed and fragmentary source material. Not surprisingly, then, of those Roman slave-businessmen referenced by Maffi as most analogous to the Athenian *douloi chōris oikountes*, the Roman *gestores* and *institores*, "direct evidence is scarce."[43] Yet it is generally accepted that the *institor* was a mere agent of the Roman master, while the *gestor* functioned as an independent businessman.[44] Analogously to Athenian owners of slaves autonomously operating businesses, Roman masters (*domini*) were not responsible for the debts of slave *gestores*; creditors could collect only from the *gestor's* own *peculium*[45]— the assets devoted to the business—as Maffi himself recognizes.[46] Although the *peculium* is sometimes described as a "legal fiction,"[47] it was a legal fiction on which creditors could rely: in the entire vast surviving juridical corpus of Roman legal material, there is not a single example of a master ever attempting to withdraw a *peculium* as to which an action at law was pending.[48] Maffi, however, arbitrarily chooses to analogize the Athenian slave-businessman not to the independent Roman slave-businessman, the *gestor*, but to the Roman agent, the *institor*, whose master, he believes, was fully liable for debts incurred by his slave "manager."[49] This is a false analogy, because, as Gernet pointed out almost seventy years ago, there is absolutely no evidence for the existence at Athens of anything like the *actio institoria* which imputed to masters liability for the debts of Roman *institores*.[50] Fortunately, however, students of ancient Athens need not dispute Roman law, debating which category of Roman slave is precisely analogous to the Athenian *doulos chōris oikōn*. The actual Athenian structure of credit, as presented by Hyperides, offers far greater insight into Athenian commercial law than suggestions based on the functioning of another economy at another time.

Under Maffi's formulation, the original master could avoid all liability for his business-related debts merely by selling the unfree business operator to a third party, even to a person entirely lacking assets. As Talamanca asks,[51] how could credit ever be reasonably extended under the Maffi hypothesis—since the borrower/slave owner can free himself of obligation without the lender's consent or even knowledge? In contrast, the actual content of the Greek text—loans made directly to a businessman/*doulos* for the repayment of which the slave is responsible (*opheilei*)—accords well with the known structure of Athenian credit. Even if an unfree person had no other assets, a loan to a slave independently operating a business could be, and was, fashioned as a loan made against, and secured by, the assets of that business— a conventional form of credit extension at Athens.

In fact, at Athens, credit was seldom extended *without* underlying security. Large numbers of surviving *horoi* throughout Attica attest to financing secured by real estate. Numerous court cases deal with conflicts over the assets of a business (especially wholesale and retail merchandise) pledged in whole or in part as security for a loan. Even so-called "friendly loans" (*eranoi*) were generally collateralized by valuable property.[52] And given the opacity of personal assets at Athens, which seem largely to have been held in the so-called *aphanēs ousia*, the "invisible economy,"[53] how could a would-be creditor ever obtain reliable knowledge of an individual's creditworthiness? How could a lender ever collect against assets held in obfuscated forms intended to frustrate creditors (and tax collectors)? But the assets of a business *were* ascertainable, and lenders in the fourth century had developed sophisticated and effective techniques to control such property once encumbered.[54]

In the Athenogenes case, of course, the purchaser, Epicrates, had no difficulty in evaluating the assets and liabilities of the business—once he found other persons to help him.[55] To explain his sloth, Epicrates insists that he is a mere Athenian citizen, a farmer with no business experience, ignorant of the laws, entering into an agreement and assuming liabilities only because he lusted after the slave-businessman's son and had ignored all other aspects of the transaction.[56] In short, he manifests the Athenian concept of manliness (*andreia*) which held commercial pursuits in contempt, a value system apparently not shared by his slave-businessman, Midas, or by the Egyptian seller, Athenogenes (who is characterized by Epicrates as "commercially savvy" (*agoraios*) (Hyp. 3.3). Such citizen ignorance of the law apparently caused no widespread difficulty at Athens: slaves and foreigners conducted a large part of business activity, and the law accommodated itself to this reality. Modern scholars should do the same.

NOTES

1. Maffi 2008: 207: ". . . in Grecia il ruolo degli schiavi è indubbiamente primario nel mondo degli scambi commerciali." Cf. Bitros and Karayiannis 2006; Garlan 1988: 60–69; Gernet [1960] 1964: 164.

2. See Bitros and Karayiannis 2008; Cohen 2003; Hanson 1995: 214–219.

3. The overwhelming majority of scholars identify the *chōris oikountes* as slaves (Kamen 2011: 44; Valente 2012; Tordoff 2013: 8), but a few (most recently Zelnick-Abramovitz 2005; Fisher 2006, 2008) believe that the term, depending on context, can refer to both present slaves (*douloi*) and freed slaves (*apeleutheroi*). Canevaro and Lewis (2014: 95) opine that "although some slaves in Athens did fall in this position" (i.e., were *douloi chôris oikountes*), "their number and significance has been somewhat exaggerated." Cf. Klees 2000: 15–17; Cohen 2000: 145–154; Hervagault and Mactoux 1974; Perotti 1974; Partsch 1909: 135–140.

4. See most recently the introduction and various essays in Black and Bell 2011; Smith 2007. Cf. Grillo et al. 2009; Nelken and Feest 2001.

5. Cohen 1992.

6. Cohen 1992: 90–101.

7. Gagarin 2001: opening paragraphs (cf. McGinn 2014: 84).

8. On "agency" as a possible mechanism to overcome slaves' legal disabilities, for example, see Harris 2013; Acton 2014: 32; Cohen forthcoming.

9. Maffi (2008: 206) insists, correctly in my opinion, on "diritto commerciale romano" as "util[e] anche per lo studio del diritto ateniese dell'economia."

10. Maffi 2008: 212. According to Maffi, however, a buyer and seller might by contract exclude the transfer of liability for the debts by excluding the transfer of the assets of the business ("in termini romani, un acquisto degli schiavi senza peculio," 213).

11. Talamanca 2008: 224.

12. See Lanni 2006: 163–164; Zelnick-Abramovitz 2005: 217–218, 220; Scafuro 1997: 61–64. The absence from our corpus of other cases involving sales should not be interpreted as establishing that legal disputes relating to property were in fact rare at Athens. Harrison (1968: 200 n. 1) has identified no fewer than fifteen additional forensic presentations whose contents have not been preserved but whose titles suggest a focus on issues involving property.

13. Hyp. 3.6: ὅσον μέντοι ὀφείλουσιν ἀργύριον; 9: οἱ χρῆσται, οἷς ὠφείλετο παρὰ τῷ Μίδᾳ; 10: καὶ εἴ τῳ ἄλλῳ ὀφείλει τι Μίδας; 20: ὀφείλοντα Μίδαν τὰ χρήματα ταῦτα.

14. Hyp. 3.22: [Σόλων] εἰδὼς ὅτι πολλαὶ ὠναὶ γίγνονται ἐν τῇ πόλει, ἔθηκε νόμον δίκαιον . . . τὰς ζημίας ἃς [ἂν ἐργάσ]ωνται οἱ οἰκέται καὶ τὰ ἀ[- - -]ατα διαλύειν τὸν δεσπότην παρ' ᾧ [ἂν ἐργάσ]ωνται οἱ οἰκέται. ("Knowing that many sales are made in the city, [Solon] passed a law . . . [stating that], 'Damages and [- - -] caused by slaves are to be paid by the master who owned the slaves at the time they caused them.'" [trans. Cooper 2001, here and below]) For *ʒēmias ergaʒesthai* ("damages caused") as descriptive of a slave's noncontractual wrongdoing, see Wyse 1967: 506.

15. Gernet [1960] 1964: 161–162.

16. For the extraordinary impact of the dissemination of coined money and the resultant fourth-century monetization of the Athenian economy, see Schaps 2004, 2008; Shipton 2001; Picard et al. 2008: 147–151.

17. Hyp. 3.19: οὗτ[ος] δέ, ὁ ἐκ τριγονίας [ὢν] μυροπώλης, καθ[ήμε]νος δ' ἐν τῇ ἀγο[ρᾷ] ὅσαι ἡμέραι, τρία [δὲ μυ]ροπώλια κεκτη[μένος], λόγους δὲ κατὰ μῆνα λαμβάνω[ν, οὐκ] ᾔδει τὰ χρέα. ἀλλ' ἐν μὲν τοῖς ἄλλοις οὐκ ἰδιώτης ἐστίν, πρὸς δὲ τὸν οἰκέτην οὕτ[ως ε]ὐήθης ἐγένετο. ("[But] this fellow, who is a third-generation perfume seller, who sits in the Agora every day, who owns three perfume stalls, and who receives accounts every month, he did not know about his debts? In other regards he is no amateur, but with regard to his own slave he was a complete simpleton?") See also Hyp. 3.11: καταλαβόντες αὐτὸν πρὸς τοῖς μυροπωλίοις . . . ("We found him [Midas] near the perfume shops . . .").

18. Maffi 2008: 212: "l'acquisto di uno schiavo che esercita un'attività commerciale comporta anche l'acquisto dell'azienda da lui gestita, in particolare del passivo inerente allo svolgimento di quell'attività."

19. Dem. 36.13–14: ἐμίσθωσεν ὕστερον Ξένωνι καὶ Εὐφραίῳ καὶ Εὔφρονι καὶ Καλλιστράτῳ . . . τὰς παρακαταθήκας καὶ τὴν ἀπὸ τούτων ἐργασίαν αὐτὴν ἐμισθώσαντο . . . καὶ ἐλευθέρους ἀφεῖσαν ὡς μεγάλα εὖ πεπονθότες. . . . ("[that he (Apollodorus, the son of Pasion) later] leased [the bank] to Xenon, Euphraeus, Euphron, and Callistratus . . . they took a lease on the deposits and the investment of the deposits only . . . and being very satisfied with the way they (the owners of the slaves) had been treated, they set them (the slaves) free . . ." [trans. MacDowell 2004, here and below]).

20. Of course, the owner would still have been liable for repayment of deposits left with him prior to effectiveness of the lease: Athenian law's nonrecognition of businesses as juridical persons ensured that liability.

21. Klees 1998: 153–154.

22. Todd 1994: 137 n. 31.

23. See, e.g., Hyp. 3.6: εἶθ' ὕστερον, ὅτε ἄν σοι δοκῇ, ἀφῇς αὐτοὺς ἐλευθέρους . . . ("and later, at your own convenience, set them free . . ."); Dem. 57.34: . . . ἢ ὡς ἐδούλευσεν ἢ ὡς ἀφείθη ἐλευθέρα. (". . . or that she had lived as a slave or had been set free." [trans. Bers 2003])

24. Harrison 1968: 176 n. 2. See also, Gernet 1954–1960, vol. 1: 209 n. 2; [1960] 1964: 163; MacDowell 2004: 157–158 n. 27.

25. Maffi 2008: 213: "la *misthosis* . . . deve essere interpretato, se si tratta davvero di schiavi, come una *apophora*."

26. Dem. 36.13: τὰς παρακαταθήκας καὶ τὴν ἀπὸ τούτων ἐργασίαν αὐτὴν ἐμισθώσαντο ("they leased the deposits and the business related to the deposits").

27. For slaves' general inability to bring lawsuits, see Pl. *Grg.* 483b; Dem. 53.20. Their testimony could be utilized only to the extent that it was extracted under formalized torture, a form of proof that emphasized the normal evidentiary incapacity of the *doulos*. See Thür 2005: 150–151; Kamen 2013: 13–14. See p. 54.

28. Maffi 2008: 214; Garlan 1988: 55; Paoli [1930] 1974: 107; Cohen 1973: 121; Gernet [1960] 1964: 162–164.

29. Harrison 1968: 176. On the *dikai trapezitikai*, see Gernet [1938] 1964: 176–177; *dikai metallikai*, MacDowell 2006.

30. Maffi 2008: 215.

31. Talamanca 2008: 224.

32. On Dem. 37, see Harris 2006: 190–199; Carey and Reid 1985: 105–159.

33. Dem. 37.25: καταστήσας Ἀντιγένην τὸν ἑαυτοῦ οἰκέτην εἰς τὸ ἐργαστήριον τὸ ἐμὸν τὸ ἐπὶ Θρασύμῳ κύριον τῶν ἐμῶν . . . ("[Nicobulus] posted his slave Antigenes at my workshop at Thrasymus to take charge of my property . . ." [trans. MacDowell 2004, here and below]); 22: ἀφελέσθαι κελεύσας Ἀντιγένην τὸν ἑαυτοῦ οἰκέτην τὸ ἀργύριον τοῦ ἐμοῦ οἰκέτου. . . ("[Nicobulus] ordered his slave Antigenes to take away from my slave the cash . . .").

34. Dem. 37.51: ἔδει . . . λαχόντ' ἐκείνῳ τὴν δίκην.

35. Gernet 1954–1960, vol. 1: 228: "Lorsque l'esclave a agi sur l'ordre du maître, c'est le maître qui est actionné: lorsqui'il a agi de son chef, c'est lui-même."

36. Dem. 55.31–32: συνθήκας οὐ γενομένας ἀπήνεγκεν . . . Καλλάρῳ τὴν αὐτὴν δίκην δικάζονται. καίτοι τίς ἂν οἰκέτης τὸ τοῦ δεσπότου χωρίον περιοικοδομήσειεν μὴ προστάξαντος τοῦ δεσπότου; ("he [the plaintiff] produced an agreement which had never been made . . . [the plaintiffs] bring this same suit against Callarus [the defendant's slave]. And yet what slave would wall in his master's land without orders from his master?" [trans. Bers 2003]).

37. Todd 1993: 187 with n. 35.

38. Todd 1994: 131 n. 18.

39. Maffi 2008: 212.

40. Talamanca 2008: 228.

41. Maffi 2008: 206–207. Cf. Chiusi 1991; Di Porto 1984. On slaves' autonomous operation of financial businesses at Rome, see Petrucci 2002: 105–114, 118–127.

42. On the *peculium*, see Cerami et al. 2002, passim; Andreau 1987: 613–615, 631–632.

43. Aubert 1994: 5.

44. Berger 1953: s.vv. *institor, negotiorum gestio*.

45. Aubert 1994: 414; Andreau 1999: 68.

46. Maffi (2008: 214 n. 36) chronicles the "schiavo gestore di un'impresa 'peculiare,' in cui . . . il *dominus* risponde dei debiti solo entro la capienza del *peculium*."

47. Andreau 1999: 68.

48. Watson 1987: 43.

49. Maffi (2008: 214 n. 36) peremptorily rejects analogy to the Roman law treatment of the *gestor*: ". . . ad Atene, contrariamente a quel che pensa Cohen, l'attivo del 'peculio' non costituisce un limite alla responsabilità del padrone."

50. Gernet [1960] 1964: 162: ". . . il n'y a pas, à Athènes, l'équivalent de l'*actio institoria* du droit romain."

51. Talamanca 2008: 226–227.

52. Finley 1985: 85, 100–106.

53. Gabrielsen 1994: 54–56; Cohen 1992: 191–215.

54. See Cohen 1992: 61–189.

55. Hyp. 3.9–11.

56. Hyp. 3.26: [οὔτε μυροπώλη]ς εἰμὶ οὔτ' ἄλλην τέχνην ἐργάζο[μαι, ἀλ]λ' ἅπερ ὁ πατήρ μοι ἔδωκεν χωρία ταῦτα γεωργῶ, . . . ("I am [not a perfume seller] and do not practice any other trade, but I farm this small piece of land that my father gave me, . . ."); 8: ἦσαν δὲ αὗται συνθῆκαι πρὸς ἐμέ· ὧν ἐγὼ ἀναγιγνωσκομένων μὲν ἤκουον, ἔσπευδον μέντοι ἐφ' ὃ ἧκον τοῦτο διοικήσασθαι. ("This [the agreement just read out] was the agreement with me. Although I listened to what was being read, I was more anxious to complete the business I had come for.") Epicrates claims to have tried to cure his ignorance of legal matters in Hyp. 3.13: οὕτω με διατέθηκας καὶ περίφοβον πεποίηκας μὴ ἀπόλωμαι . . . ὥστε τούς τε νόμους ἐξετάζειν καὶ μελετᾶν νύκτα καὶ ἡμέραν, πάρεργα τἄλ[λα π]άντα ποιησάμενον. ("You have made me so fearful of being brought to ruin . . . that I have been forced to study and examine the laws night and day to the neglect of all else.").

REFERENCES

Acton, Peter. 2014. *Poiesis: Manufacturing in Classical Athens*. Oxford: Oxford University Press.

Andreau, Jean. 1987. *La vie financière dans le monde romain: Les métiers de manieurs d'argent; IVe siècle av. J.-C.-IIIe siècle ap. J.-C.* Rome: École française de Rome.

———. 1999. *Banking and Business in the Roman World*. Translated by Janet Lloyd. Cambridge: Cambridge University Press.

Aubert, Jean-Jacques. 1994. *Business Managers in Ancient Rome: A Social and Economic Study of Institores, 200 BC–AD 250*. Leiden: Brill.

Berger, Adolf. 1953. *Encyclopedic Dictionary of Roman Law*. Philadelphia: American Philosophical Society.

Bers, Victor, trans. 2003. *Demosthenes, Speeches 50-59*. Austin: University of Texas Press.

Bitros, George, and Anastasios Karayiannis. 2006. "Morality, Institutions, and Economic Growth: Lessons from Ancient Greece." *Munich Personal RePEc Archive Paper* 994. https://mpra.ub.uni-muenchen.de/994/1/MPRA_paper_994.pdf.

————. 2008. "Values and Institutions as Determinants of Entrepreneurship in Ancient Athens." *Journal of Institutional Economics* 4: 205–230.

Black, E. Ann, and Gary F. Bell, eds. 2011. *Law and Legal Institutions of Asia: Traditions, Adaptations, and Innovations.* Cambridge: Cambridge University Press.

Canevaro, Mirko, and David Lewis. 2014. *"Khōris oikountes* and the Obligations of Freedmen in Late Classical and Early Hellenistic Athens." *Incidenza dell'Antico: Dialoghi di storia greca* 11: 91–121.

Carey, Chris, and R. A. Reid, eds. 1985. *Demosthenes: Selected Private Speeches.* Cambridge: Cambridge University Press.

Cerami, Pietro, Andrea Di Porto, and Aldo Petrucci. 2002. *Diritto commerciale romano: Profilo storico.* Turin: Giappichelli.

Chiusi, Tiziana J. 1991. "Landwirtschaftliche Tätigkeit und *actio institoria.*" *Zeitschrift der Savigny-Stiftung für Rechtsgeschichte, Romanistische Abteilung* 108: 155–186.

Cohen, Edward E. 1973. *Ancient Athenian Maritime Courts.* Princeton: Princeton University Press.

————. 1992. *Athenian Economy and Society: A Banking Perspective.* Princeton: Princeton University Press.

————. 2000. *The Athenian Nation.* Princeton: Princeton University Press.

————. 2003. "The High Cost of *Andreia* at Athens." In *Andreia: Studies in Manliness and Courage in Classical Antiquity,* edited by Ralph M. Rosen and Ineke Sluiter, 145–165. Leiden: Brill.

————. Forthcoming. "Overcoming Legal Incapacity at Athens: Juridical Adaptations Facilitating the Business Activity of Slaves." In *Legal Documents in Ancient Societies* VI: *Ancient Guardianship; Legal Incapacities in the Ancient World,* edited by Michele Faraguna and Uri Yiftach-Firanko. Trieste: University of Trieste Press.

Cooper, Craig, trans. 2001. "Hyperides." In *Dinarchus, Hyperides, and Lycurgus,* translated by Ian Worthington, Craig Cooper, and Edward M. Harris, 88–181. Austin: University of Texas Press.

Di Porto, Andrea. 1984. *Impresa collettiva e schiavo 'manager' in Roma antica (II sec. a.C.–II sec. d.C.).* Milan: Giuffrè.

Finley, Moses I. 1985. *Studies in Land and Credit in Ancient Athens, 500–200 BC: The Horos Inscriptions.* Reprint with new introduction by Paul Millett. New Brunswick, NJ: Transaction Publishers. First published in 1952 by Rutgers University Press.

Fisher, Nick. 2006. "Citizens, Foreigners, and Slaves in Greek Society." In *Companion to the Classical Greek World,* edited by Konrad Kinzl, 327–349. Malden, MA: Blackwell.

————. 2008. "'Independent' Slaves in Classical Athens and the Ideology of Slavery." In *From Captivity to Freedom: Themes in Ancient and Modern Slavery,* edited by Constantina Katsari and Enrico Dal Lago, 121–146. Leicester: University of Leicester.

Gabrielsen, Vincent. 1994. *Financing the Athenian Fleet: Public Taxation and Social Relations*. Baltimore: Johns Hopkins University Press.

Gagarin, Michael. 2001. Review of *Law and Social Status in Classical Athens*, edited by Virginia J. Hunter and Jonathan Edmondson. *Bryn Mawr Classical Review* 2001.10.03. http://bmcr.brynmawr.edu/2001/2001-10-03.html.

Garlan, Yvon. 1988. *Slavery in Ancient Greece*. Ithaca, NY: Cornell University Press.

Gernet, Louis. [1938] 1964. "Sur les actions commerciales en droit athénien." In *Droit et société dans la Grèce ancienne*, 2nd ed. rev., Paris: Sirey, 173–200. First published in 1938 in *Revue des études grecques* 51: 1–44.

———. [1950] 1964. "Aspects du droit athénien de l'esclavage." In *Droit et société dans la Grèce ancienne*, 2nd ed. rev., Paris: Sirey, 151–172. First published in *Archives d'histoire du droit oriental* 1950: 159–187.

———, ed. 1954–1960. *Démosthène, Plaidoyers civils*. 4 vols. Paris: Les Belles Lettres.

Grillo, Ralph, Roger Ballard, Alessandro Ferrari, André J. Hoekema, Marcel Maussen, and Prakash Shah, eds. 2009. *Legal Practice and Cultural Diversity*. Farnham, UK: Ashgate.

Hanson, Victor Davis. 1995. *The Other Greeks: The Family Farm and the Agrarian Roots of Western Civilization*. New York: The Free Press.

Harris, Edward M. 2006. "When is a Sale not a Sale? The Riddle of Athenian Terminology for Real Security Revisited." In *Democracy and the Rule of Law in Classical Athens: Essays on Law, Society, and Politics*, by Edward M. Harris, 163–206. Cambridge: Cambridge University Press. First printed in 1988 in *Classical Quarterly* 38: 351–381.

———. 2013. "Were there Business Agents in Classical Greece? The Evidence of Some Lead Letters." In *The Letter: Law, State, Society, and the Epistolary Format in the Ancient World*, edited by Uri Yiftach-Firanko, 105–124. Wiesbaden: Harrassowitz.

Harrison, A. R. W. 1968. *The Law of Athens*. Vol. 1, *The Family and Property*. Oxford: Clarendon Press.

Hervagault, Marie-Paul, and Marie-Madeleine Mactoux. 1974. "Esclaves et société d'après Démosthène." In *Actes du colloque 1972 sur l'esclavage*, 57–102. Paris: Les Belles Lettres.

Humphreys, Sally C. 1985. "Social Relations on Stage: Witnesses in Classical Athens." *History and Anthropology* 1: 313–373.

Kamen, Deborah. 2011. "Reconsidering the Status of χωρὶς οἰκοῦντες." *Dike* 14: 43–53.

———. 2013. *Status in Classical Athens*. Princeton: Princeton University Press.

Klees, Hans. 1998. *Sklavenleben im klassischen Griechenland*. Stuttgart: Steiner.

———. 2000. "Die rechtliche und gesellschaftliche Stellung der Freigelassenen im klassischen Griechenland." *Laverna* 11: 1–43.

Lanni, Adriaan. 2006. *Law and Justice in the Courts of Classical Athens*. Cambridge: Cambridge University Press.

MacDowell, Douglas M., trans. 2004. *Demosthenes, Speeches 27–38*. Austin: University of Texas Press.

————. 2006. "Mining Cases in Athenian Law." In *Symposion 2003: Vorträge zur griechischen und hellenistischen Rechtsgeschichte*, edited by Hans-Albert Rupprecht, 121–131. Vienna: Verlag der Österreichischen Akademie der Wissenschaften.

Maffi, Alberto. 2008. "Economia e diritto nell'Atene del IV secolo." In *Symposion 2007: Vorträge zur griechischen und hellenistischen Rechtsgeschichte*, edited by Edward M. Harris and Gerhard Thür, 203–222. Vienna: Verlag der Österreichischen Akademie der Wissenschaften.

McGinn, Thomas A. J. 2014. "Prostitution: Controversies and New Approaches." In *A Companion to Greek and Roman Sexualities*, edited by Thomas K. Hubbard, 83–101. Malden, MA: Wiley-Blackwell.

Nelken, David, and Johannes Feest, eds. 2001. *Adapting Legal Cultures*. Portland, OR: Hart Publishing.

Paoli, Ugo Enrico. [1930] 1974. *Studi di diritto attico*. Milan: Cisalpino-Goliardica. First published by R. Bemporad e Figlio.

Partsch, Joseph. 1909. *Griechisches Bürgschaftsrecht: Das Recht des altgriechischen Gemeindestaats*. Leipzig: Teubner.

Perotti, Elena. 1974. "Esclaves ΧΩΡΙΣ ΟΙΚΟΥΝΤΕΣ." In *Actes du colloque 1972 sur l'esclavage*, 47–56. Paris: Les Belles Lettres.

Petrucci, Aldo. 2002. *Profili giuridici delle attività e dell'organizzazione delle banche romane*. Turin: Giappichelli.

Picard, Olivier, Michèle Brunet, Jean-Christophe Couvenhes, Amélie Perrier, Franck Prèteux, and François Rebuffat. 2008. *Économies et sociétés en Grèce ancienne, 478–88 av. J.-C.: Oikonomia et économie*. Paris: SEDES.

Scafuro, Adele C. 1997. *The Forensic Stage: Settling Disputes in Graeco-Roman New Comedy*. Cambridge: Cambridge University Press.

Schaps, David M. 2004. *The Invention of Coinage and the Monetization of Ancient Greece*. Ann Arbor: University of Michigan Press.

————. 2008. "What was Money in Ancient Greece?" In *The Monetary Systems of the Greeks and Romans*, edited by William V. Harris, 38–48. Oxford: Oxford University Press.

Shipton, Kirsty M. W. 2001. "Money and the Élite in Classical Athens." In *Money and Its Uses in the Ancient Greek World*, edited by Andrew Meadows and Kirsty M. W. Shipton, 129–144. Oxford: Oxford University Press.

Smith, Peter J. 2007. "New Legal Fictions." *Georgetown Law Journal* 95: 1435–1495.

Talamanca, Mario. 2008. "Risposta a Alberto Maffi, 'Economia e diritto nell'Atene del IV secolo.'" In *Symposion 2007: Vorträge zur griechischen und hellenistischen Rechtsgeschichte*, edited by Edward M. Harris and Gerhard Thür, 223–228. Vienna: Verlag der Österreichischen Akademie der Wissenschaften.

Thür, Gerhard. 1977. *Beweisführung vor den Schwurgerichtshöfen Athens: Die Proklesis zur Basanon*. Vienna: Verlag der Österreichischen Akademie der Wissenschaften.

————. 2005. "The Role of the Witness in Athenian Law." In *The Cambridge Companion to Ancient Greek Law*, edited by Michael Gagarin and David Cohen, 146–169. Cambridge: Cambridge University Press.

Todd, Stephen C. 1993. *The Shape of Athenian Law*. Oxford: Clarendon Press.

———. 1994. "Status and Contract in Fourth-Century Athens." In *Symposion 1993: Vorträge zur griechischen und hellenistischen Rechtsgeschichte*, edited by Gerhard Thür, 125–140. Cologne: Böhlau.

Tordorff, Rob. 2013. "Introduction: Slaves and Slavery in Ancient Greek comedy." In *Slaves and Slavery in Ancient Greek Comic Drama*, edited by Ben Akrigg and Rob Tordoff, 1–62. Cambridge: Cambridge University Press.

Valente, Marcello. 2012. "Demostene e Arpocrazione a proposito dei '*choris oikountes*.'" *Rivista storica dell'Antichità* 42: 95–115.

Watson, Alan. 1987. *Roman Slave Law*. Baltimore: Johns Hopkins University Press.

Wyse, William. 1967. *The Speeches of Isaeus*. Cambridge: Cambridge University Press. First published in 1904 by Cambridge University Press.

Zelnick-Abramovitz, Rachel. 2005. *Not Wholly Free: The Concept of Manumission and the Status of Manumitted Slaves in the Ancient Greek World*. Leiden: Brill.

5 / TOWARD A NEW SHAPE OF THE RELATIONSHIP BETWEEN PUBLIC AND PRIVATE LAW IN ANCIENT GREECE

Alberto Maffi

IN PREPARING FOR THIS CONFERENCE, I WAS THINKING that we need to reevaluate the corpus of principles or doctrines which represent the scholarly heritage of the last century, being aware that we do not have a shared theoretical framework or an "overall structure of the system,"[1] like the pandectistic system for Roman law. It is quite amazing that, after *The Greek Law of Sale* by Fritz Pringsheim of 1950, no monographs on contracts have been written, and after *Eigentum und Besitz* by Arnold Kränzlein of 1963, no monographs on ownership. We only have articles on the interpretation of single sources or groups of sources: this is also true even for the Symposia, where the papers about private law number no more than thirty out of four hundred. One could say that the awareness of the absence of ancient juridical conceptualization has discouraged theoretical research on the "juristische Denkformen," as Hans Julius Wolff proposed.[2] After Wolff, not only have his theories not been seriously reexamined, but no new attempt has been made to explore this field. So it was my intention to discuss some of the traditional topics concerning private law, like "ownership" and "obligations."

But, while working on my paper, I realized that I had to start from more general premises: it is impossible to speak of private law without first addressing the problem of the relationship between public law and private law in the Greek world, because such a distinction is certainly present from remote times, not only in the legal sphere, but more generally in political and cultural matters.

My chapter is therefore divided into three parts. In the first part I will briefly summarize the current state of studies in Greek law. In the second part I shall discuss the relationship between public law and private law in relation to the nature and functioning of the Greek polis as a state. In the third part I shall discuss some cases concerning the interaction between public and private governance.

There is no doubt that today the study of Greek law in Europe begins with the work of the founders of the Symposia: Wolff, Arnaldo Biscardi, and Joseph Mélèze Modrzejewski. We can say that it was Wolff who traced the main lines for the renewal of the discipline: he was so influential that the Symposia have maintained, in essence, the structure that Wolff had given them. All of us who developed the study of Greek law under the auspices of the Symposion (and related "Schattengesellschaft") looked at the work of Wolff as a new start.

Wolff was a legal historian "à part entière" (as we used to say not long ago), who knew and taught Roman as well modern German and common law. This quality allowed him to put the finest tools of legal investigation to the service of a fundamentally new goal: to identify the specific nature of Greek law, that is, the system of concepts that underlies legislation and the everyday practice of law. Certainly we can find scholars before Wolff (such as Ugo Enrico Paoli, Louis Gernet, Pringsheim with his still fundamental *The Greek Law of Sale*, and, in the previous generation, Josef Partsch, Ernst Rabel, and others) who had sought to define the specific character of Greek legal thought and practice. The work of these scholars is still very valuable, but it is piecemeal, whereas Wolff felt the need for a global reconstruction. Although his research was conducted with a high degree of legal technicality, Wolff was aware that there were no lawyers in ancient Greece, and thus no reflection on the legal dimension; therefore, he substantially devalued Greek philosophical thought on law and State. Instead, he thought it necessary to extract the legal "Denk-formen" that were only implicit in the historical and literary sources. For this reason he invited historians and philologists to the first Symposion, in 1971. Wolff clearly had such personal qualities that he could provide a link between lawyers and nonlawyers, and thus could take advantage on the legal side of the data that came from the contributions of historians and philologists.

Since Symposion 1985 a new component has begun to exert influence on the relations between lawyers and nonlawyers in our field. Three scholars who were destined to play a leading role in the Gesellschaft attended that Symposion: Douglas MacDowell, David Cohen, and Michael Gagarin (who were followed after 1990 by Robert Wallace, Stephen Todd, Edward Cohen, and Edward Harris). All these scholars helped to give the study of Greek law new direction, which is well summarized by Todd and Paul Millett: "Law and legal process in Athens were embedded in society, so that questions about Athenian law are in the last resort anthropological questions about the Athenians."[3] The absence of a purely legal discussion in ancient Greece (compared with Roman law) led these scholars to believe that the law in Greece was conceived as pure empirical practice constantly adapting to the demands posed by socioeconomic factors. Starting from this point of view, in recent decades the most important field of inquiry became the Athenian law courts and Athenian procedure. Procedure was and is, of course, a main topic for European historians of law as well, and so it was for Wolff himself, as it still is today for his most important pupil, Gerhard Thür. But the strict legal method, applied by Wolff in his studies on the origins of procedure and particularly on the *paragraphē* (counterindictment for illegal procedure), as well as in his commentaries on forensic speeches, was gradually replaced by a perspective that saw the peculiar organization of legal procedure in classical Athens as a manifestation of political and social confrontation and not as a complex mechanism carefully regulated by law. Wolff had stressed that legal issues (the "Komplex juristischer Denkweise, Organisationsformen und Methoden") had to be investigated "from a legal point of view," a position with which I agree.[4] To some extent my criticism of Wolff's detractors is also directed at Gagarin's understanding of Greek procedure. In his important recent works concerning this topic he has reiterated that procedure was characterized by "open forensic debate and free judicial decisions";[5] moreover, Gagarin, who does not share the radical point of view of many American and British scholars who see Athenian litigation as a competition for status in a feuding society,[6] speaks of a tendency to avoid using writing in the legal process.[7] In my opinion Athenian procedure, like Gortynian, does not always imply free decisions by the judges, as Gagarin believes, and oral procedure does not necessarily imply informal procedure.

II. DEMOCRACY AND THE RULE OF LAW

The extraordinary growth of studies on Athenian democracy over the past thirty years, which has developed mainly in the Anglophone world, has led to a confrontation between those who emphasize the prevalence of the popular will expressed by the Assembly and those who believe that the government organs were subordinate to the constitutional law, or "democracy versus rule of law." In my opinion both positions are legitimate, in the sense that the first focuses on how politics used institutions to achieve its purposes, while the second focuses primarily on the way in which institutional mechanisms were built through legal rules (metaphorically we could say "physiology versus anatomy"). In fact it is a debate that has a long history: I refer to the synthesis of a famous Italian political philosopher, Norberto Bobbio, who juxtaposed the idea of legal positivism (*non sapientia sed auctoritas facit legem*) from Plato to Hobbes and Max Weber with the concept of rule of law (*lex facit regem*) from Aristotle to Hans Kelsen.

Without denying the legitimacy of the first approach, as a legal historian I side with the advocates of the rule of law. The Greeks invented the legal dimension of life, which is represented by its own laws. One may debate the nature of the code of Hammurabi, but I think its differences from the Greek legal universe are clear.[8] The laws that the city approved freely, not the justice of the sovereign, were the benchmark for the conduct of the members of the community, not only as individuals but also as political actors. Thus, I would partly—but not totally—agree with Mogens Hansen's understanding of the relations between the institutions of formal government.[9] Hansen restricts the public sphere to what we would call constitutional law. But the public sphere goes beyond the strictly constitutional field, which comprises the competences of constitutional bodies and the relations between them. *Ta koina* or *ta dēmosia* covers the whole sphere of public interest from the perspective of the modern jurist, and would encompass not only constitutional law but also administrative law.[10]

This raises the problem of the legal classification of persons acting in the public interest and of the acts performed by them, or more generally, the problem of the structure of the Greek State. I will not discuss the controversy triggered more than a decade ago by Moshe Berent, except to say that Berent's thesis of a stateless polis was not well received.[11] In particular, Greg Anderson concluded that state and society would be neither wholly differentiated nor entirely "fused." They would be forever entwined in a kind of mutually dependent, mutually constitutive embrace, which should be defined not as interaction, but as intra-action.[12] In my opinion, Anderson's solution does not untie the knot of the dualism between state and society. I am more inclined to accept the view expressed by Hansen that "it is also true that the Greek polis is usually identified with its citizens, but we must not forget that it is also often seen as an impersonal abstract power above both rulers and ruled."[13] Thus the notion of state remains a valid heuristic tool for studying the Greek polis. In my opinion, to understand how the polis works as a state, the legal approach can be very useful. In particular, I would like to ask whether people acting in the public interest are subject to rules, and if so, what are those rules?

Hansen devotes a very interesting paragraph to this topic in his discussion of "Government and Administration":

> In a modern state decisions are made by governments and parliaments and carried into effect by a hierarchically organized network of professional civil servants, usually chosen by their superiors. In a democratically organized Greek polis decisions were made in assemblies and popular courts, and carried into effect by magistrates (*archai*) elected or selected by lot for

a term of, usually, one year [so that the polis] possessed, if not a hierar-chical bureaucracy of professional civil servants, then a very sophisticated network of magistrates empowered to implement the decisions made in assemblies.[14]

I have three comments to make. First, Hansen's observations hold for most poleis, not just the ones with an inclusive (i.e., "democratic") system of gov-ernment. Second, is it only the magistrates who implement public policy, or do others also act on behalf of the polis? Third, are there general rules con-cerning the performance of acts in the public interest, what I would call "ad-ministrative law," that are specific to the Greek polis?

Noteworthy is the fact that the study of "administrative law" has not en-tered into the Anglophone debate, despite some attempts to study the issue, such as a chapter by the late A. H. M. Jones titled "How Did the Athenian Democracy Work"?[15] One possible explanation for this lack of interest is found in Todd's observation that administrative law "is a term which until the twentieth century has effectively been restricted to Continental European Systems," where it would be "a special body of rules applied to contracts or other obligations in which the state is involved as one of the parties."[16] Only in the twentieth century did a branch of administrative law develop in En-gland, which employed "judicial review to examine the behavior of a wide va-riety of public bodies and statutory corporations," with particular attention to the prevention of abuses of power. In Continental doctrine, after Georg Busolt and Heinrich Swoboda concluded in their brief chapter on "Form der Verwaltung" that the Athenian government conformed to the criteria of le-gality,[17] the scholar who probably made the greatest contribution to this field was Ulrich Kahrstedt, with his *Studien zum öffentlichen Recht Athens*.[18] But, ac-cording to Todd, "there is in Athens very little which corresponds with mod-ern administrative law." In particular, "in the absence of an Athenian doc-trine of contract, it is hard to see how Athenians would have made sense of the special contractual position enjoyed by the state in Continental jurisdic-tions." Otherwise, Athenian law knows only actions for offenses committed by "public officials"([Dem.] 25.71; Lys. 9, 24, 17). Todd hesitantly concludes that "the primary purpose of Athenian 'administrative' law was not so much to right public wrongs as to execute failed political leaders."[19]

These observations by Todd are very sketchy, but perhaps sufficient to ex-plain the apparent lack of interest in this topic on the part of Anglo-American scholars. Peter Rhodes, whose research has made an important contribution to our understanding of Athenian democratic institutions, rightly places the work of Kahrstedt in the track of the traditional "Staatskunde" (or "Staatsaltertümer"), which (in his words) seeks to answer the question: "What was the machinery and how did it work?"[20] Yet Rhodes, in observing that Kahrstedt liked legality, manifests a vaguely contemptuous attitude toward the juridical approach. The same attitude devaluing a strictly juridical approach can probably be seen in the colossal scholarly output of Hansen.

In more recent times, scholars have paid attention to some areas of public administration in Athens, such as the power of magistrates like *agoranomoi* ("overseers of the marketplace") and *astunomoi* ("overseers of the city"), administration of the mines of Laurion, financial administration, and public contracts. What is lacking, however, with the exception of the pioneering article by Lene Rubinstein,[21] is a broader approach that examines the functioning of the polis in terms of public-private relations, focused on the dialectic between *archon* ("magistrate") and *idiotēs* ("private citizen"), which is already evident in Homer.[22] In this regard, we must remark that insofar as the relationship between public and private concerns the definition of the Greek state, the issue goes far beyond the debate about the definition of Athenian democracy. Starting from a definition of the Greek state and focusing on the dichotomy between public and private, let us ask the two fundamental questions we have anticipated: Who acted in the public interest, and according to what rules? In modern theory and practice the state acts both as a sovereign entity distinct from its own citizens, applying specific rules that are qualified as public law, and as a body which places itself at the same level as individuals, building relationships governed by rules of private law (for example, when the state sells or leases public property). But in both cases, public bodies are acting on behalf of the state. Thus, in considering the polis, I think we should, on the one hand, identify the actors who operate in the public interest, and on the other, define the rules under which they operate.

The actors certainly include the magistrates, who acted in the public interest, thus embodying what today would be called the executive or "agents of the polis and its laws."[23] But citizens were also directly involved in the management of public interests,[24] both in local bodies and at the central level, so that not only were they directly affected by the positive and negative relationships they had with the state (polis and/or demos), but they themselves were called upon to manage public interests together with or instead of the magistrates. From this perspective, the characterization of the polis I have outlined finds an unexpected correspondence with various transformations of public functions that are being implemented in some European countries. The modern state has built itself on a clear separation between the actions of the state-person, exclusively pursuing public interests through its organs, and the actions of private bodies pursuing private interests. I believe this achievement has been one of the most important distinctions between the conception of the polis and the modern state.

I use the past tense, because in recent years Europe has undergone a change of mentality through acknowledgment of the principle of "subsidiarity" in both a vertical and a horizontal sense. On the one hand, the state's exclusive competence to manage the main spheres of public interest is now shared with local bodies or organs; on the other hand, a collaboration between public authorities and citizens or private associations is not only allowed but recommended, so that the identification of the public sphere with the state and the private sphere with its citizens is now not as clear-cut as it was in the last two centuries. In Italy this recently led to an important change in article 118 of the Constitution, amended by the following new paragraphs:

> 1. Administrative functions are attributed to the municipalities except that, to ensure their uniformity, they are conferred to provinces, metropolitan cities, regions, and state, on the basis of the principles of subsidiarity, differentiation, and adequacy.
> 2. State, regions, metropolitan cities, provinces, and municipalities shall promote the autonomous initiatives of citizens, individually and in groups, to carry out activities of general interest, based on the principle of subsidiarity.

The first is what is called "vertical subsidiarity," that is, collaboration between public organs on different levels. The second is what is called "horizontal subsidiarity." It may be possible and profitable to apply the principle of subsidiarity in studying the interaction between the different local bodies (such as tribes and demes) and the polis on the one hand (vertical subsidiarity), and between the polis with its magistrates and the citizens on the other hand (horizontal subsidiarity).[25]

As for the applicable rules, it is not easy to identify principles generally recognized and shared. We cannot say that the magistrates apply public law and citizens acting in the public interest apply private law because they are private persons. The law that has to be applied to acts affecting the public interest does not automatically depend on the qualification of the agent. Surely the magistrates must be obeyed (a point on which Wallace insisted),[26] and it is true that, at least in some cases, individuals who carry out public functions are also subject to the magistrates, like the *trierarchs* ("outfitters of triremes") facing the *strategoi* ("commanders").[27] But even though they have no power to command, individuals are not excluded from responsibility for the management of public interests, as would be the case if they only had to obey the orders of the magistrates. A puzzling Athenian decree of 325/4 (*IG* II² 1629, lines 233–242) prescribes accountability before the *euthunos* ("public examiner") for both the magistrate (*archon*) and the private citizen (*idiotēs*).[28]

In my opinion, it is very difficult to find a reliable criterion for assessing whether individuals acting in the public interest or being personally liable for the consequences of acts of the polis as abstract power are subject to rules of public law. Wallace explained that "the evidence for Athenian legal regulations and procedures is complex in part because different laws sometimes contained their own, idiosyncratic provisions."[29] In his response to Wallace, Harris objected to the characterization of Athenian law as idiosyncratic, preferring instead to say that "Athenian law contained some actions with distinctive procedural features suited to the nature of the substantive offense."[30] In my opinion, Harris's view is too narrow; the aim of the laws was not merely to adapt the procedure to the nature of the offense. But Wallace's view is too pessimistic, for it makes it impossible to identify Wolff's famous "Denkformen."

As mentioned above, the usefulness of studying the Greek state from the two points of view, whose importance I have emphasized (public authorities vs. individuals),[31] must be verified through concrete contexts of action in the public interest. In the third part of my paper I suggest some examples illustrating this.

III. STATE SOVEREIGNTY AND CITIZEN PARTICIPATION

The first area where the interaction between the exercise of state sovereignty and the direct participation of citizens is particularly important is financial organization. In an influential article, Kurt Latte supposed that, originally, the income and expenditures, and credits and debts, of the community were allocated directly to the members of the community.[32] As regards income, Latte saw a turning point in the decision made by Themistocles to allocate the revenues of the mines of Laurion to the construction of the fleet instead of dividing them among the citizens. That act, which initiated the fifth-century Athenian state, would not have been conceivable in some areas of Greece that were based on a "collectivist" economy, such as the Peloponnese and Crete (at least until the third century BCE). These areas had a system of redistribution among the citizens not only of agricultural products but also of fines and of spoils of war.[33]

As regards expenditures and debts, Latte stressed the persistence of collective responsibility in the classical period, especially in international relations. He was referring specifically to *androlepsia* ("seizure of foreigners") and more generally to the phenomenon of *sulē* ("right of seizure"), as, for example, in Demosthenes 51.13, which refers to collective responsibility for the misdeeds of *trierarchs*, or Demosthenes 35.13, in which a contract clause prohibited an Athenian merchant ship to layover where there were *sulai* against Athenians. Benedetto Bravo, author of the most important recent study of *sulān* ("seizure"), has denied that there was a collective responsibility, arguing instead that executive acts were only allowed against a foreign debtor.[34] But this thesis, despite the keenness of Bravo's arguments, was not widely accepted.[35] This issue should also be reconsidered with regard to relations regulated by international treaties. Some important texts are quoted by Rubinstein: the Athens-Selymbria treaty (*ML* 87, lines 22–25), where the debts of *idiotai* to *idiotai* were distinguished from debts of an *idiotēs* to the *koinon* ("public treasury"), or of the *koinon* to an *idiotēs*, and the Athenian decree for Neapolis (*ML* 89, lines 52–53), where Athenian *strategoi* were required to ensure that the citizens of Neapolis were not offended by an *idiotēs* or by the *koinon poleōs* (here, "an official acting on behalf of the polis").[36] I would add, in a different frame of international relationships, the so-called foundation decree of the Second Athenian League (*IG* II² 43, lines 35–46), in which an Athenian was not allowed to buy a house in allied territory through sale or mortgage. One wonders how the Athenian state (or the Athenian magistrates) could have prevented this act.

Lastly, the loan agreements between a city and a foreign private citizen are very important. Of particular interest are, for example, the well-known contracts concluded by Arkesine, a small town on the island of Amorgos, in the late fourth or early third century BCE (*IG* XII.7 67B; *IG* XII.7 69).[37] Both of them contain the clause that the creditor is entitled to guarantee his loan "on the common goods of the city and on private property of citizens and foreign residents, asking from each the total amount of credit . . ." One may wonder whether this clause may be considered a response to the problem posed by Aristotle (*Pol.* 1276a8–16) and discussed by Hansen: "When an oligarchy or a tyranny changes into a democracy . . . some people are reluctant to fulfill public contracts on the grounds that the recipient was not the polis but the tyrant, and they are unwilling to meet other obligations of a similar nature."[38] Whatever the political regime of Arkesine, no citizen could have disclaimed the debt in the future. In other cases, however, such as those involving Chalcedon ([Arist.] *Oec.* 1347b20–30) and Teos-Lebedos (*Syll.*³ 344, lines 18–20), it is expressly stated that the city will pay the public debts with the *koinoi prosodoi* ("public revenue").

Another area of great importance from the legal point of view concerns the way in which the polis made a public claim on the property of a citizen (e.g., the state's confiscation of private property). In an influential article,[39] Thür argued that the polis made use of a peculiar procedural tool, the *diadikasia* ("suit to decide between claimants"), in two cases of public interest: in an *apographē*,[40] "if you had a prior claim on an about-to-be-confiscated estate, you could assert that you had a better right to it than the state did,"[41] and the procedure took the form of a *diadikasia*; and in an action brought by a *trierarch* against his predecessor, claiming that the latter had not returned the equipment of the ship. According to Thür, in these cases *diadikasia* was used because the parties were not on the same level (in the sense, if I understand correctly, that the creditor cannot exercise a "Zugriffsrecht" against the city that confiscates the goods of a public debtor, as would be usual between private persons). The same principle explains the use of the *diadikasia* by exiles readmitted into the polis who claim the refund of all or part of their former estates. Thür concludes that the aim of the *diadikasia* was to ensure "den Freiheitsraum des Bürgers vor staatlichen Eingriffen in sein Vermögen."[42] I observe that there is a difference between confiscation where the claimant is the state and situations where the trial is between individuals. It is true that the *trierarch* is an *idiotēs* in the exercise of a public duty, but the exiles are suing as private citizens. So I am not convinced that the *diadikasia* characterizes only public claims.

Last but not least is the issue of the role of the citizen as volunteer prosecutor (*ho boulomenos*). The role of the citizen as prosecutor in a *graphē* ("public lawsuit") has been widely studied in relation to its degeneration represented by the figure of sycophant. What interests me here is again the legal treatment of such a figure, a theme that in the last ten years has been the subject of several significant studies.[43] As Wallace states, "The prosecutor who failed to receive one-fifth of the dicasts' votes or a plaintiff who did not 'follow through' (*epexelthein*) his case to trial were both subject to two punishments: a 1000 drachma fine, and some permanent restriction of their ability to prosecute future cases."[44] The main areas where the intervention of citizens was expected were the prosecution of public debtors and the control of the magistrates. Concerning public debtors, in a recent article, which remains the most important contribution in the field, Virginia Hunter has highlighted the paradox arising from the fact that "the polis had no state structures or officials dedicated to identifying and bringing to justice the majority of public debtors," so that "the identification of such debtors was a civic duty on the part of *ho boulomenos*, who brought the case on his own initiative whatever his motive."[45] Rubinstein has shown that in classical and Hellenistic Greece the control of magistrates took several forms: the involvement of other magistrates; the control exercised by the successors in the same magistracy; a college of prosecutors appointed by a deliberative body; and a public action brought by a volunteer prosecutor.[46]

The figure of the volunteer prosecutor thus presents a double paradox. On the one hand, his primary role was to respond to a need for implementing the law, as confirmed by Lycurgus's famous statement that the most important things that preserve the city are the law, the accuser (*katēgoros*), and the juryman (1.3–1.4). On the other hand, the volunteer prosecutor exposed himself to heavy risk. In a widely cited article, Robin Osborne has argued that in Athens "the prosecution was faced with a choice of procedure," and he has suggested that "the capacity to fit actions to men was a primary quality of Athenian legal procedure." Consequently, "the choice of action is likely to be determined by factors more closely linked to the nature and relative status of victim and offender than to the nature of the breach of the law," since "the Athenian law courts were a public stage upon which private enmities were played out."[47] Although Osborne's view has the backing of a well-known passage of Demosthenes (22.25–22.29), I am not convinced by his thesis. In my opinion, the nature and relative status of victim and offender had a secondary role and only served to provide persuasive arguments of a conventional character. The wide choice of actions is better explained by the fact that the volunteer prosecutor was not paid, and neither were the magistrates, unlike the citizens who attended the *ekklēsia* (assembly) or the courts. Thus there was a need to encourage the participation of citizens in the service of the public interest through judiciary prosecution; the rewards attached to certain types of procedures certainly served this purpose, as did the availability of a wide range of public and private actions. At the same time, since penalties were established to avoid spurious charges, it is no wonder that under these conditions only professional politicians (*hoi politeuomenoi*) assumed the role of volunteer prosecutor.

The aim of this chapter was to show that to understand the functioning of the polis as a state, we must call into question the traditional boundaries between public law and private law. Developing categories of analysis and classification of public and private persons and of the acts performed by them in the public interest may open a new path in the study of a very important aspect of the Greek legal mentality. Such a research perspective may also help us understand more completely and adequately the nature and the discipline of legal transactions that we are accustomed to placing in an exclusively private or public field. This remark applies also to the judicial process. The distinction between public and private trial, so important to Roman law and the modern world, has yet to be investigated in a systematic way for the Greek world. Given the importance that this distinction, invented by the Greeks, continues to have in today's world, research into the relationship between the public and private spheres seems to me to be a very important task for twenty-first century studies in the field of ancient Greek law.

NOTES

1. Todd 1993: 15.
2. Wolff 1975.
3. Todd and Millett 1990: 15.
4. Wolff 1975.
5. Gagarin 2005: 34–35.
6. See particularly Cohen 1995: 87: "In examining the social context of Athenian litigation, this chapter suggests that much litigation should be viewed as a form of feuding behavior, and that it was acknowledged as such by Athenian judges and litigants." See also Osborne 1985: 48 (cited below n. 47).
7. Gagarin 2008a: 110–121, 176–205. For a different evaluation of the role of writing in Greek procedure, see Faraguna 2008 with the response of Gagarin 2008b.
8. Gagarin 2006 is an important contribution illustrating these differences.
9. Hansen 2002.
10. This issue was dealt with recently by Macé 2012, but he does not address the legal aspects of these concepts.
11. Berent 2000.
12. Anderson 2009.
13. Hansen 2002: 22.
14. Hansen 2002: 16–17.
15. Jones 1958: Chapter 5.
16. Todd 1993: 300.
17. Busolt and Swoboda 1920: 630.
18. Kahrstedt 1934–1936.
19. Todd 1993: 300–302.
20. Rhodes 2003: 35.
21. Rubinstein 1998.
22. Cantarella 1979; Polignac and Schmitt Pantel 1998.
23. Rubinstein 1998: 133.
24. Another individual who, especially in the fourth century BCE, carries out a very important public function is the *rhētor*. See the debate generated by Ober 1989.
25. There are of course other modern approaches that are useful in discussing our topic. See, e.g., Rosenberg 2007.
26. Wallace 2005.
27. As stressed by Rubinstein 1998.
28. For a detailed discussion of the law, see Piérart 1971; cf. Rubinstein 1998: 129.
29. Wallace 2006: 58.

30. Harris 2006: 70–71.

31. See Azoulay 2014 and the other important contributions in *Annales: Histoire, sciences sociales; Politique en Grèce ancienne* 69.3.

32. Latte 1946–1947.

33. See the oath of Dreros for the distribution of fines among the *hetaireiai* ("association of citizen men") (*IC* I.ix 1, lines 124–125, 134–135); see also the agreement between Gortyn and Rhitten (*IC* IV 80, lines 6–7).

34. Bravo 1980.

35. See, e.g., Gauthier 1982.

36. Rubinstein 1998.

37. For discussion of these texts, see Migeotte 1984: 168-183, nos. 49 and 50.

38. Hansen 2002: 23.

39. Thür 1982.

40. The term *"apographē"* refers to a written catalogue of the property of a man in debt to the state, the process of denunciation of the debtor, and the judicial hearing arising out of the case.

41. Todd 1993: 121.

42. Thür 1982: 68.

43. Harris 1999; Rubinstein 2000, 2003; Wallace 2006.

44. Wallace 2006: 57.

45. Hunter 2000: 36.

46. Rubinstein 2012.

47. Osborne 1985: 48.

REFERENCES

Anderson, Greg. 2009. "The Personality of the Greek State." *The Journal of Hellenic Studies* 129: 1–22.

Azoulay, Vincent. 2014. "Repolitiser la cité grecque, trente ans après." *Annales: Histoire, sciences sociales; Politique en Grèce ancienne* 69.3: 689–719.

Berent, Moshe. 2000. "Anthropology and the Classics: War, Violence, and the Stateless Polis." *Classical Quarterly* n.s. 50: 257–289.

Bravo, Benedetto. 1980. "*Sulān*: Représailles et justice privée contre des étrangers dans les cités grecques; Étude du vocabulaire et des institutions." *Annali della Scuola Normale Superiore di Pisa: Classe di Lettere e Filosofia*, ser. 3, 10.3: 675–987.

Busolt, Georg, and Heinrich Swoboda. 1920. *Griechische Staatskunde*. Vol. 1. Munich: C. H. Beck.

Cantarella, Eva. 1979. *Norma e sanzione in Omero: Contributo alla protostoria del diritto greco*. Milan: Giuffrè.

Cohen, David. 1995. *Law, Violence, and Community in Classical Athens*. Cambridge: Cambridge University Press.

Faraguna, Michele. 2008. "Oralità e scrittura nella prassi giudiziaria ateniese tra V e IV sec. a.C." In *Symposion 2007: Vorträge zur griechischen und hellenistischen*

Rechtsgeschichte, edited by Edward M. Harris and Gerhard Thür, 63–82. Vienna: Verlag der Österreichischen Akademie der Wissenschaften.

Gagarin, Michael. 2005. "The Unity of Greek Law." In *The Cambridge Companion to Ancient Greek Law*, edited by Michael Gagarin and David Cohen, 29–40. Cambridge: Cambridge University Press.

———. 2006. "Inscribing Laws in Greece and the Near East." In Rupprecht, *Symposion 2003*, 9–20.

———. 2008a. *Writing Greek Law*. Cambridge: Cambridge University Press.

———. 2008b. "Response to Michele Faraguna." In *Symposion 2007: Vorträge zur griechischen und hellenistischen Rechtsgeschichte*, edited by Edward M. Harris and Gerhard Thür, 83–86. Vienna: Verlag der Österreichischen Akademie der Wissenschaften.

Gauthier, Philippe. 1982. "Les saisies licites aux dépens des étrangers dans les cités grecques." *Revue historique de droit français et étranger*, ser. 4, 60.4: 553–576.

Hansen, Mogens Herman. 2002. "Was the Polis a State or a Stateless Society?" In *Even More Studies in the Ancient Greek Polis*, edited by Thomas Heine Nielsen, 17–48. Stuttgart: Steiner.

Harris, Edward M. 1999. "The Penalty for Frivolous Prosecutions in Athenian Law." *Dike* 2: 123–142.

———. 2006. "A Response to Robert Wallace." In Rupprecht, *Symposion 2003*, 67–72.

Hunter, Virginia J. 2000. "Policing Public Debtors in Classical Athens." *Phoenix* 54.1–2: 21–38.

Jones, A. H. M. 1958. *Athenian Democracy*. New York: Frederick A. Praeger.

Kahrstedt, Ulrich. 1934–1936. *Studien zum öffentlichen Recht Athens*. 2 vols. Stuttgart: Kohlhammer.

Kränzlein, Arnold. 1963. *Eigentum und Besitz im griechischen Recht des fünften und vierten Jahrhunderts v. Chr.* Berlin: Duncker und Humblot.

Latte, Kurt. 1946–1947. "Kollektivbesitz und Staatsschatz in Griechenland." *Nachrichten von der Akademie der Wissenschaften in Göttingen, Philologisch-Historische Klasse* 6: 64–75. Reprinted in *Kleine Schriften zu Religion, Recht, Literatur und Sprache der Griechen und Römer*, edited by Olof Gigon, Wolfgang Buchwald, and Wolfgang Kunkel, 294–312. Munich: C. H. Beck, 1968.

Macé, Arnaud, ed. 2012. *Choses privées et chose publique en Grèce ancienne: Genèse et structure d'un système de classification*. Grenoble: Jérôme Millon.

Migeotte, Leopold. 1984. *L'emprunt public dans les cités grecques: Recueil des documents et analyze critique*. Québec: Édition du Sphinx; Paris: Les Belles Lettres.

Ober, Josiah. 1989. *Mass and Elite in Democratic Athens: Rhetoric, Ideology, and the Power of the People*. Princeton: Princeton University Press.

Osborne, Robin. 1985. "Law in Action in Classical Athens." *The Journal of Hellenic Studies* 105: 40–58.

Piérart, Marcel. 1971. "Les *euthynoi* athéniens." *L'Antiquité classique* 40: 526–573.

Polignac, François de, and Pauline Schmitt Pantel, eds. 1998. "Public et privé en Grèce ancienne: Lieux, conduites, pratiques." Special issue, *Ktèma* 23.

Pringsheim, Fritz. 1950. *The Greek Law of Sale*. Weimar: Böhlaus.

Rhodes, Peter J. 2003. *Ancient Democracy and Modern Ideology*. London: Duckworth.

Rosenberg, Shawn W., ed. 2007. *Deliberation, Participation, and Democracy: Can the People Govern?* New York: Palgrave Macmillan.

Rubinstein, Lene. 1998. "The Athenian Political Perception of the *Idiotes*." In *Kosmos: Essays in Order, Conflict, and Community in Classical Athens*, edited by Paul Cartledge, Paul Millett, and Sitta von Reden, 125–143. Cambridge: Cambridge University Press.

———. 2000. *Litigation and Cooperation: Supporting Speakers in the Courts of Classical Athens*. Stuttgart: Steiner.

———. 2003. "Volunteer Prosecutors in the Greek World." *Dike* 6: 87–113.

———. 2012. "Individual and Collective Liabilities of Boards of Officials in the Late Classical and Early Hellenistic Period." In *Symposion 2011: Vorträge ʒur griechischen und hellenistischen Rechtsgeschichte*, edited by Bernard Legras and Gerhard Thür, 329–354. Vienna: Verlag der Österreichischen Akademie der Wissenschaften.

Rupprecht, Hans-Albert, ed. 2006. *Symposion 2003: Vorträge ʒur griechischen und hellenistischen Rechtsgeschichte*. Vienna: Verlag der Österreichischen Akademie der Wissenschaften.

Thür, Gerhard. 1982. "Kannte das altgriechische Recht die Eigentumsdiadikasie?" In *Symposion 1977: Vorträge ʒur griechischen und hellenistischen Rechtsgeschichte*, edited by Josef Mélèze Modrzejewski and Detlef Liebs, 55–69. Cologne: Böhlau.

Todd, Stephen C. 1993. *The Shape of Athenian Law*. Oxford: Clarendon Press.

Todd, Stephen C., and Paul Millett. 1990. "Law, Society, and Athens." In *Nomos: Essays in Athenian Law, Politics, and Society*, edited by Paul Cartledge, Paul Millett, and Stephen C. Todd, 1–18. Cambridge: Cambridge University Press.

Wallace, Robert W. 2005. "'Listening to' the *Archai* in Democratic Athens." In *Symposion 2001: Vorträge ʒur griechischen und hellenistischen Rechtsgeschichte*, edited by Robert W. Wallace and Michael Gagarin, 147–158. Vienna: Verlag der Österreichischen Akademie der Wissenschaften.

———. 2006. "Withdrawing *Graphai* in Ancient Athens: A Case Study in 'Sycophancy' and Legal Idiosyncrasies." In Rupprecht, *Symposion 2003*, 57–66.

Wolff, Hans Julius. 1975. "Juristische Gräzistik—Aufgaben, Probleme, Möglichkeiten." In *Symposion 1971: Vorträge ʒur griechischen und hellenistischen Rechtsgeschichte*, edited by Hans Julius Wolff, Joseph Mélèze Modrzejewski, and Dieter Nörr, 1–22. Cologne: Böhlau Verlag.

6 / *"HEILIGES RECHT"* AND *"HEILIGE GESETZE"*: LAW, RELIGION, AND MAGIC IN ANCIENT GREECE

Martin Dreher

GREEK SACRED LAW IS OFTEN NEGLECTED IN THE STUDY of Greek law. One reason is certainly that sacred law has many features in common with nonsacred law; in many respects it is not distinctive. Therefore my chapter starts with problems of definition. What is sacred law (*heiliges Recht*), and what are sacred laws (*heilige Gesetze*)?

In what follows I will concentrate on the more juridical aspects of the subject, that is, on the regulation of religious matters, especially cult practice. Up to now the categorization of sacred law has been influenced, almost exclusively so, by the practices of authors compiling corpora of the *leges sacrae*. But for the study of Greek sacred law, these collections, limited to inscriptions, are not sufficient. For example, they explicitly exclude laws on cults honoring individuals, both living and dead, nor do they include laws on sacred wars, or sacred truces, or documents on *asulia* ("inviolability"). Of specific interest should also be curse tablets, a class of documents oscillating between religion (or official cult practice) and extralegal magic.

The opinions of modern scholarship on the forms of sacred laws, on their issuing authority, and on the sanctions these laws impose on transgressors are not always convincing. Furthermore, little attention has been given to questions such as: How and when did changes to sacred law occur in the course of Greek history? What kind of juridical competence and jurisdiction did the priests of the sanctuaries have? Which cases concerning sacred delicts did the regular courts or the regular institutions adjudicate and for which cases did the Greeks establish special tribunals?

On the basis of these considerations I will conclude that it would be useful to have some form of handbook of Greek Sacred Law.

1. HEILIGES RECHT (SACRED LAW) AND
HEILIGE GESETZE (SACRED LAWS)

The topic of ancient Greek law and religion has not been studied, on the whole, very intensively. It seems to me that scholars of the history of ancient religion, on the one hand, are not so much interested in legal questions, but search instead for points of contact with historical, philosophical, anthropological, sociological, or psychological approaches. Scholars of ancient law, on the other hand, often seem to consider religion as a kind of spiritual subject far from the concrete field of juridic facts and strict juridic thinking. Furthermore, religion is not a subject adapted to the traditional questions and to the traditional divisions of law decisively shaped by Roman law, such as the classical division by the jurist Gaius into the law of persons, the law of things, and the law of actions. As is the case for Roman law, scholars are mainly interested in Greek civil law, especially in problems of social status, kinship, marriage, inheritance, and purchase and contract, most of which are elements of private law (*Privatrecht*).[1] In contrast, religion and cult practice in ancient Greece were predominantly a public affair, and therefore one would put it into the sphere of public law. In addition, sacred law does not contribute very much to our knowledge of procedural law, the other field in which juridical scholars have a deep interest.

Perhaps for all these reasons, we do not find a treatment of sacred law in some of the fundamental works on Greek law; in some cases there is not even a reference to it or to the cultic sphere of Greek society.[2] But perhaps that too is not due to a lack of interest on the part of these scholars, but rather is due to the belief that a separate study is not required, since the cultic sphere, having no specific legal substance and procedure, was integrated into the same legal system that embraced both the sacred and the profane spheres of society.[3]

At this point we must clarify what we mean by "the sacred," beginning with a discussion of the terms that are relevant to our subject. There is no Greek term designating the entire area of law and religion. *Hieros nomos* ("sacred law") is sometimes used, but only for single, specific regulations of very different practices. It was, as Robert Parker says, "not so much a fixed category of thought for the Greeks as a form of expression that they sometimes fell into."[4]

The Latin *ius sacrum* ("sacred law"), often identified with *ius divinum* ("divine law") or *ius pontificium* ("law of the priests"),[5] had a wider significance. Up to the time of Ulpian (c. 200 CE) it was largely considered to be part of the *ius publicum*, or public law (D.1.1.1.2). At the same time, there appears to have been a conceptual separation of the sphere of private law from that of sacred law; we can observe a differentiation between *ius sacrum* and *ius publicum* already in the well-known tripartition expressed by Quintilian in the first century CE: *genera sunt tria: sacri, publici, privati iuris* ("There are three types: sacred, public, and private law"; Quint. *Inst.* 2.4.33). The content of *ius sacrum*, however, is obscure. It has been defined as

> a collection of public prayer formulas with short instructions for how to use them. These central elements were progressively mixed with some precepts and instructions about how to celebrate cult, which were given to the magistrates in the form of the official priestly advice.[6]

Yet even if Roman authors used the term *ius sacrum*, it was never a fixed corpus in written form. We have to imagine a kind of virtual code kept in mind by the priests and based upon oral tradition and the written *commentarii*.[7] The concrete application of the *ius sacrum* acquired some importance only in the formal debate of the priests with the senate or the magistrates about an actual and precise problem.[8] Nevertheless, modern authors use the term *ius sacrum* in a much broader sense, parallel to its modern equivalents.

In modern languages the situation is more complicated. German scholars of the nineteenth century spoke of *heiliges Recht* (sacred law), *geistliches Recht* (spiritual law), *göttliches Recht* (divine law), and *Priesterrecht* (law of the priest). They also often used *Sakralrecht*, but in a wide sense not confined to sacrifices as in other combinations with the word "*sakral.*" Scholars included here the doctrine of the gods, cultic and sacrificial laws, constitutions of priesthoods, sacred criminal law, and so on.[9] Usually these scholars were experts on Roman law, and therefore their terminology referred to Roman law.

The publication in 1920 of Kurt Latte's influential book *Heiliges Recht* provided a very sharp turning point. Latte dedicated his book to Greek sacred law with the subtitle *Untersuchungen zur Geschichte der sakralen Rechtsformen in Griechenland*.[10] His main interest was in elements of the transition from sacred to profane law. From this limited perspective, the scope of the term "*heiliges Recht*" underwent a similar restriction. For Latte it is confined to religious elements within the nonsacred, profane law,[11] and it is an important part of the formula he uses in the subtitle, *sakrale Rechtsformen*. Latte's interest is confined, however, to criminal law and private law (*Straf- und Privatrecht*); he excludes from his analysis the *eigentliche Tempelrecht* (law of the temples). I have noted this focus already in my earlier remarks on Roman law and consider it problematic, as I will explain below.

Even before the publication of Latte, other scholars had established another category within the area of law and religion, but they did not put it under the general heading *heiliges Recht*. Johannes von Prott and Ludwig Ziehen published in two volumes a collection of legal regulations on religious matters that they called *heilige Gesetze*; or in Latin, *leges sacrae*; in English, "sacred laws"; in French, *lois sacrées*; and in Italian, *leggi sacre*.[12] But neither von Prott and Ziehen nor their successor, Franciszek Sokolowski, in his three volumes on *lois sacrées* provide a sound definition of this kind of law.[13] Philippe Gauthier refuted the categorization completely on the grounds that there was not a real unity in these collections and it was difficult to understand why many laws were not included.[14] But the majority of scholars accepted it,[15] and Sokolowski's collection was often considered so sufficient that editors of other corpora of inscriptions decided to exclude the sacred laws from their own collections.

In the most recent corpus of Eran Lupu, *Greek Sacred Law: A Collection of New Documents*, the editor puts more weight on definition than did his predecessors.[16] He admits that the term "sacred laws," as he uses it, "hardly constitutes a well-defined genre." But he offers two minimal criteria for his category: first, the document must be prescriptive, either in grammatical form (e.g., using the imperative) or implicitly. Second, "their subject matter . . . must be or pertain to religion and particularly to cult practice." He adds that rather than serving only a marginal role in an otherwise noncultic context, the cultic subject must provide the focus of the provisions.

This limitation may be justified for a corpus of inscriptions, where complete texts, rather than only those passages thought to be relevant, are presented.[17] A similar consideration is valid for a further criterion of Lupu, namely that the sacred rules must refer to the *regular* cult practice of the polis. His exclusion of non-recurring festivals or of cults for persons living or dead can, however, stand only as a pragmatic criterion for a corpus.

Lupu's book (its first edition from 2005) had not been published when Parker wrote his two important articles on our subject (published in 2004 and 2005).[18] The later one on "Law and Religion" in *The Cambridge Companion to Ancient Greek Law* does not introduce the subject as systematically as one might expect in a companion. Rather, Parker begins his essay with the decidedly unsystematic pronouncement that in the present contribution, "a bundle of issues" would be united, before he proceeds abruptly to the first of its three sections, the headings of which indicate the organization of the relevant material. I cite the third heading first, "Religious Forms of Legal Action: *Heiliges Recht*."[19] In the discussion that follows this heading, Parker accepts the most important items treated by Latte, namely the oath and the curse (*ara*), but he criticizes, rightly in my opinion, the evolutionary concept of the German scholar. We will return to this below.

Under his first heading ("The Regulation of Cult: 'Sacred Laws'"), Parker summarizes his previous article, "What Are Sacred Laws?"[20] I discuss Parker's response to this question in greater detail in the next section, but it is necessary to make one specific point here. To underline his thesis that it was mainly the secular institutions of the polis that enacted sacred laws, a view that is by no means wrong, Parker asserts that these same institutions also initiated the consultation of oracles.[21] This assertion confuses the categories. It is not the polis that enacts a sacred law concerning the procedure of the oracle. On the contrary, the oracle is, in this case, a religious element playing a particular role in the legislation of the polis. It can determine or influence the decision of the polis and therefore we are in the sphere of *heiliges Recht* in the sense of Latte. For this procedure it does not matter if the law or decree of the polis concerns a predominantly profane matter, for example, the foundation of a colony, or a religious matter such as the question, "To which god shall we sacrifice to save our country from the plague?" The latter case, however, is not only part of *heiliges Recht*, but also, insofar as the decision concerns a religious matter, a *heiliges Gesetz* of its own, and we understand that our division is, like all definitions, an abstraction which in reality does not always appear in its pure form.

In the second section, titled "'Impiety': Laws against Religious Offenses," Parker treats sanctions against religious offenders. He mentions five concrete *sacrilegia* ("religious offenses") known from Athens, namely, "wrongdoing concerning a festival, theft of sacred money, impiety, temple robbing," and lastly, "offenses concerning sacred olive trees."[22] Parker never mentions in this context the term *asebeia* ("impiety"), which the Greeks used for these offenses.[23] Even more confusing is his exclusion of this category of laws from sacred laws. Evidently in this section he defines sacred laws as those that regulate cult practice, but he does not offer another term on the same scale for his laws against religious offenses.[24]

More explicitly than Parker, Alberto Maffi adheres to the distinctions of Latte.[25] He says even more explicitly than Latte himself that *Tempelrecht* (he does not use *heilige Gesetze*) was a specific application of *sakrale Rechtsformen*, but that he himself, like Latte, concentrates on criminal and private law. In his words it is "opportuno distinguere fra 1. elementi sacrali nell'ordinamento giuridico della polis," which would be *heiliges Recht* according to Latte, "e 2. l'elemento giuridico nel funzionamento della sfera sacrale," which would be Latte's *Tempelrecht*. Maffi assigns to the first category not only, like Latte, the oath, the curse, and murder, but also *hierosulia* and *asebeia*, which I would assign to the second one, as I will argue later.[26]

My conclusions concerning these terminological issues are as follows. Greek religion was not regulated by a specific category of law comparable to, for example, canon law of the Catholic Church. Neither was religion the source for all Greek law as Sharia law is for some Islamic states. When religion needed regulation, this regulation was provided by the polis, as the polis also regulated other fields of political and social life. Religion was, therefore, in a legal sense only one specific subject of the law of the polis,[27] albeit a very important one.

The relations between law and religion traditionally have been divided into two categories. This division makes sense and has often been adopted, although not consistently enough. The first category encompasses sacred elements integrated into the law of the polis. It should be called, following Latte in part, *sakrale Rechtsformen*, that is, sacred or sacral legal forms. The second category comprises juridical regulations of the religious sphere; it is and should be referred to with the generally accepted term *heilige Gesetze* (*leges sacrae*, or "sacred laws"), that is, with "law" understood in a wide sense that encompasses decrees by different authorities. We must also presume that not the laws themselves but only their objects can be considered sacred in the sense of belonging to the cultic sphere. Latte's *Tempelrecht* has the same meaning, but the term should be dismissed: on the one hand, for the pragmatic reason that it is not used by other scholars, and on the other, because it could be misunderstood as referring in the stricter sense only to temples instead of to all cultic fields. Finally, we also need a term that embraces both categories, and this term can only be *heiliges Recht*, or better *Sakralrecht*, that is, sacred law.

2. THE LAW AND THE GODS

Religion, mostly in the form of cult practice, was a very important part of polis life. In Greek belief, the polis was substantially connected with the world of the gods, and the fate of the polis depended to a large extent on the benevolence of the gods. Without the will of the gods, nothing could be achieved.

From the beginning, the law, like all other parts and institutions of the polis, stood under the protection of the gods, especially under the protection of Zeus, the holder of the highest power. Human justice as an abstract concept was personalized, transferred to the divine sphere, and imagined as Dikē, daughter of Zeus (e.g., Hes. *Theog.* 901–903; *Op.* 255–285). The *basileis* ("chieftains") in epic poetry dispense justice on instruction by Zeus; and they hold the same symbol of judicial power as he does, the scepter (e.g., Hom. *Il.* 9.96–99; *Od.* 11.568–571; cf. Hes. *Theog.* 84–92).

Latte held that in the beginning, religion was the only source of justice and that the polis later took over the charge to set and administer the law. He has been clearly and correctly criticized insofar as there was no sharp chronological or systematic break after which the law of the polis replaced religious law.[28] In reality, religious legal forms did not, as Latte held, die away. On the contrary, their importance continued into historical times. Latte rightly hinted at one way (though his critics have not paid much attention to it) that the character of law and justice—if we are allowed to use these terms for such early times—differed before the existence of the polis (and, in my opinion, the existence of the polis as a state) and after the foundation of institutional power. The appointment of magistrates responsible for justice and the associated requirement that all members of the polis bring their claims before a court are two of the most important markers of the establishment of the early Greek state.[29] Before and after this fundamental step, the administrators of justice deferred to the gods to legitimate their position and their decisions.[30] Lawgivers like Zaleucus and Charondas appear only some time later in the archaic period, when the polis-state was already in existence. We know very little about their actual rhetoric; certainly they insisted that their laws would be blessed by the gods, but with the exceptions of the Spartan Lycurgus, who is believed to have acted with the support of the Delphic oracle, and some of the Cretan poleis, the ancient traditions do not stress that the early lawgivers needed an intense and strong divine legitimation for their legislation. Hence it seems that the Greeks accepted wise men as creators of their laws, and they were convinced that these men acted in accordance with the will of the gods. Greek religion was not a religion of illumination, and neither the law itself nor the judges were believed to depend in some way on a god or on a holy text given by a god.[31]

How, then, are the gods involved in the judicial sphere of the polis? They are thought of as the proprietors of sacred places, of the territory of the sanctuary, or *temenos* (including its natural resources like trees or water), of the altars, temples, and other buildings on the site, and of all the more or less precious things that formed the property of a sanctuary. Therefore the gods are treated, at least in some aspects, as juridical persons with certain rights (even if they could not be physically present).[32] We have already mentioned that the law stood under the protection of the gods, especially of Zeus. But it must be asked more specifically: How far did the gods themselves interfere in human affairs by acting as judges?[33] The clearest example of such divine interference is the "trial by ordeal," which is known from several early European cultures.[34] Scholars vary in their opinions about the use of this procedure by early Greek communities, but the famous trial by ordeal at Mantineia shows that at least one polis employed it in historical times.[35]

3. FORMS OF SACRED LAW

Latte treats the following as sacred elements in Greek law: in legal procedure, oaths sworn by litigants, witnesses, and the judges; in penalties, sacred fines to a named deity, curses, and fines for the desecration of graves; and in legal transactions, contracts and manumissions. In the section titled "Religious Forms of Legal Action: *Heiliges Recht*," Parker does little more than summarize these items.[36]

In his much more comprehensive overview of *heiliges Recht*, Maffi too begins with the oath in public life. Before discussing the oaths of litigants and of judges in lawsuits, he treats curses, distinguishing public curses (*arai*) from private ones.[37] In my opinion there is no reason to consider *maledizioni private* (private curses), that is, curse tablets or curses on funerary monuments, as sacred elements in Greek law. These curses perhaps may be accepted as sacred insofar as they invoke a deity that is included in the official cults of the polis. But one may doubt whether the Greeks also attributed a sacred character to those curses that invoked dangerous spirits or dubious demons of the underworld, entities they would not have called *hieroi*, to bind or seriously injure the cursed person. In any case, because the author of the curse seeks justice for himself, resorting only to the immediate help of a supernatural force without the intercession of any legal institution, these curses stand outside the law. Furthermore, curses in a lawsuit, generally called judicial curses (*defixiones iudiciariae*), are not, contra Maffi, elements of law; on the contrary, this category of curse more than any other seeks to undermine the normal legal procedure by preventing the cursed person—for instance, the opposing litigant, his witness, or his advocate—from taking part in the lawsuit, and the judges from determining the sentence. Finally, many of these curses were probably forbidden and so were contrary to the law. As Maffi recognizes, we do not have as clear evidence for the illegality of these curses in Greek law as we have in Roman law, but there is a famous passage in Plato's *Laws* where the use of magic to harm another is sanctioned with severe punishment.[38] I do not mean to suggest that we exclude the curse tablets completely from our general subject of law, religion, and magic. But I would like to argue that these curses do not belong in either of the two categories discussed up to now, namely *sakrale Rechtsformen* and *heilige Gesetze*. Such curses require a distinct category, described as, for example, "religion, magic, and justice outside the polis institutions."

Maffi treats illegal acts with religious relevance in the second part of his first section.[39] He begins with the religious implications of murder, which Latte analyzed only in part, and then examines *hierosulia* and *asebeia*. Once again I do not see why these items should be, in Maffi's heading, "Elementi sacrali nell'ordinamento giuridico della polis." *Hierosulia*—the damage to or theft of sacred things or the violation of cultic rules—seems to belong clearly to the second of our basic categories, that is, sacred laws as regulations of the cultic sphere.[40] "Protection of sanctuaries" is one of the headings in Lupu's collection of sacred laws, and the delicts falling under *hierosulia* surely belong to this category.⁴¹ The same is true for *asebeia*. Even if this is, admittedly, a broader term that does not refer to specific laws, *asebeia* is, as Maffi recognizes, the failure to respect the gods. Therefore, the aim of its prosecution is, like that of *hierosulia*, to protect the sacred sphere of the polis. It is established in an ordinary law and does not include a specific religious element.

Parker sees *asebeia* as the main substance of the entire category of sacred laws. Under the heading "'Impiety': Laws against Religious Offenses," he summarizes the five specific delicts known from Athens cited above.⁴² In contrast to Maffi, Parker does not distinguish between *asebeia* and *hierosulia*. With the assignment of *asebeia* to the category of sacred laws, we have already begun the consideration of this second form of *Sakralrecht* (see above). To conclude this discussion of *asebeia*, I would suggest that we not treat it as a separate category; rather, insofar as *asebeia* has many different aspects, we should distribute the attested lawsuits where *asebeia* is alleged to the different kinds of sacred laws as categorized, for example, by Lupu.⁴³

Because the early editors of the corpora did not develop a clear system for identifying and organizing sacred laws, it has been the task of later scholars to do so. Parker's essay "What Are Sacred Laws?" seems to promise a clear systematization.⁴⁴ But since he is primarily interested in whether sacred laws are really laws in a technical sense (we will come back to this problem), his list of sacred laws is a rather loose compilation of examples and remains in any case incomplete. As subject matter of the laws he mentions: the protection of sanctuaries; the correct organization of festivals, especially the panhellenic ones; calendars, which do not seem to be, but in fact are, laws; priestly emoluments (especially the portions of the sacrifices that were given to priests); the terms of tenure for priesthoods; funerary laws (with a question mark); and finally, rules concerning purity.

In his 2009 collection of new documents, Lupu provides the most complete summary of the category that we have. In his table of contents he organizes the entire corpus of sacred laws into four chapters: "Sanctuaries and Sacred Space" (where we find the abovementioned "protection of sanctuaries" as a subcategory), "Cult Officials," "Cult Performance," and "Festivals and Ceremonies."⁴⁵ Maffi, in the section titled "L'elemento giuridico nel funzionamento della sfera sacrale" of his entry in the *Thesaurus Cultus et Rituum Antiquorum*, concentrates mainly on the competences assigned to priests in sacred laws.⁴⁶ He maintains that the administration of the sacred by priests also includes a juridical element. He focuses his presentation on this element, analyzing the exclusive competence of priests in controlling persons who seek asylum in sanctuaries as the most prominent expression of this authority. I do not agree with Maffi's interpretation of *hikesia* ("supplication") and *asulia*, and remain convinced that priests had a much more informal role and that they only exceptionally made formal juridical decisions on *hiketai* ("suppliants").[47] Their general competence to pronounce sentences was, in my opinion, limited to the imposition of relatively small fines on persons who caused disturbances in sanctuaries or during festivals.[48] The complex relationship between the judicial competence of priests and of the juridical institutions of citizens and other specially created juridical bodies forms the last part of Maffi's article.[49]

It is worth commenting briefly on the institution of asylum (*asulia*), insofar as no editor of sacred laws has considered this topic. Its juridical importance lies not so much, as Maffi maintains, in the role of the priests, but much more in the regulations themselves. *Asulia* does not become a subject of political regulation before the Hellenistic period. Only then do we find decrees from Hellenistic kings, from other Greek poleis, and from the Roman Senate recognizing the inviolability of particular sanctuaries.[50] This recognition is a legal act in itself, and it has some legal consequence, though on an international scale.

This interstate perspective in reference to the relation between law and religion has been rather neglected by modern scholars. Future research on law and religion should consider the decisions of, for example, amphictyonies (administrative bodies of sanctuaries, especially the Delphic one) and symmachies (alliances, such as the Peloponnesian League or the Athenian naval leagues)—for instance Athens's decisions concerning the sanctuary of Apollo at Delos.[51] Other topics that should be considered in a study of sacred law encompassing the international sphere are decisions to wage a sacred war aimed at protecting the sanctuary at Delphi and regulations concerning the sacred truce for the panhellenic festivals at Olympia and elsewhere. Attention should also be paid to violations of these regulations, especially the sanctions against violators.

4. ENFORCEMENT OF SACRED LAW

Inscriptions provide the lion's share of evidence for sacred law. The authors of corpora of sacred laws deal with this fact by including inscriptions to the exclusion of all other types of evidence, such as literary, numismatic, and papyrological sources. They tend, furthermore, to include only the more complete inscriptions in their corpora and to present the individual inscriptions intact rather than distributing the various provisions of one and the same inscription to different parts of their corpora according to topic. Finally, they include only those inscriptions whose main purpose is to regulate sacred affairs; texts in which sacred matters have only a secondary importance are largely excluded. All of these decisions are acceptable for a corpus of sacred laws, but they exclude precious material concerning the relation between law and religion.[52] A systematic presentation of the subject must not be constrained by these limitations, but should consider all of these kinds of information in its analysis.

One much-discussed question is whether sacred laws were laws *sensu stricto*, that is, obligatory rules that could be enforced and, when transgressed, envisaged the imposition of sanctions on the transgressor. All editors of corpora of *leges sacrae* imply that these laws were either enforceable by some official institution of the polis or merely recommendations based on sacred conventions and traditions that were issued by various types of authorities. This position has recently been endorsed by Parker:

> Sacred laws correspond more or less to one of two ideal types. The first, what one might call from its commonest instantiation "don't cut sacred wood," is a true law, issuing from the assembly like any other. The second, "how to deal with a haunting" as it may be, is more a recorded convention than a law; it derives from exegetical tradition, its aim is to advise, and it lacks sanctions and procedures for enforcement.[53]

I agree in principle with Parker, but I want to stress one point that he does not consider. When Parker reflects on the authors or initiators of his second category, the exegetic convention, he relies on inscriptions that make it clear that private individuals could set up these rules. But Parker does not consider that these laws would not have been written for publication in a sanctuary without the approval of the local administration of the sanctuary or even of the larger political body. We must assume this especially for the panhellenic sanctuaries at Delphi and Olympia, where space was limited and the competition for display in the best locations must have been intense. But it will have been the same in most sanctuaries. To display an inscription, a quite heavy piece of stone or metal, must have required the approval of the respective authorities.

Fred Naiden agrees with Parker's opinion that religious regulations, as he prefers to call them rather than laws, seldom include sanctions.[54] According to Naiden, who follows an earlier definition of the term "law" that requires inter alia inclusion of a sanction, these regulations are not laws. I have responded at length to Naiden's unconvincing views in an earlier article.[55] It is useful to include here two of my earlier arguments against his position because they are relevant in the present context. First, it is not in fact the case that sacred laws are rarely sanctioned. Fines in particular, both big and small, are not all that uncommon in sacred laws.[56] And second, if it is indeed the case that there are on the whole fewer sanctions in sacred laws than there are in others (i.e., profane laws), it is important to note that the Greeks feared divine punishment, which could be even harsher than sanctions imposed by man. As Lene Rubinstein observes (pers. comm.), mechanisms to enforce a sacred law may have been known to all people, making their recording in writing unnecessary.

To conclude this discussion of the enforcement of sacred laws, we consider what procedures could be used to compel obedience to them. No procedures were necessary in cases in which the Greeks expected divine punishment should someone disobey a law. It was also left up to the gods to punish a person who had committed perjury under oath or who had sworn an oath that included a self-curse should he or she commit perjury. Parker insists that some phrases threatening *asebeia* must be understood as making a transgressor not legally "liable to a charge of impiety," but morally, in the sense "let him be accounted impious."[57] Punishment is left to the gods. Yet *asebeia* was the charge most often brought against somebody for a religious offense, both in Athens and in some other places. *Asebeia* is a very broad accusation; the ancient sources attest many different behaviors that served as the grounds for a charge of *asebeia*. It is important to note that this charge evidently did not necessarily require the transgression of a specific law; it was sufficient to allege that someone had disobeyed religious tradition and the accepted religious standards of the community.[58]

Beyond the charge for *asebeia* we have little evidence for other religious procedures and for the eventual consequences in case of conviction. If somebody did not pay a sacred fine, we may assume the person could be treated like a public debtor. And a sanction is sometimes stated for a priest or a magistrate who fails to exact a fine that was due (e.g., *LSCG* 89, lines 14–16); in other cases he may have been accused of neglecting to perform his official duties.

As in the case of other lawsuits, the presumption was that a private person was interested in prosecuting someone. Perhaps the Greeks considered that in most cases it was left to the individual to respect all of the regulations concerning sacrifices and behavior in sanctuaries in general. Often an admonition may have been sufficient. Only in serious cases that put at risk the fortune of the entire community or ones that were politically motivated—both of which apply, for instance, to the violation of the herms in 415 BCE and to the famous trial of Socrates[59]—do we hear of a lawsuit, often against politicians like Alcibiades in the case of the herms.

I conclude with a brief discussion of questions and problems for future research. Maffi identifies several important features that deserve more attention from scholars.[60] They concern the office of priests—in particular, their functions, duties, and rights in the legal sphere. In my view, specific questions, *exempli gratia*, could be: What kind of cultic staff is mentioned in the sacred laws? Up to what amount in fines could cultic personnel impose on wrongdoers in sanctuaries and during festivals? In which cases are the civic magistrates competent? Which legal decisions were left up to the priests? Which cases do the regular institutions of the polis, such as the assembly or the *dikastēria* ("law courts"), decide? In which situations and for which offenses did the polis constitute extraordinary juridical bodies (*Sondergerichte*) such as the *hieroi* ("priests") at Andania? To what extent did foreign judges decide on religious matters?

All of these issues, together with those already considered in earlier studies, should be treated in the future with greater attention to chronological development and regional differences. These deficiencies are characteristic of most of the works cited in this essay. Parker, for example, does not distinguish adequately between laws from the archaic period and others from the Hellenistic or Roman periods. But during these centuries the position of priests, for instance, changed in fundamental ways: the sale of cultic offices is a relatively late practice, and the legal recognition of *asulia* for sanctuaries begins only in the Hellenistic period. Severe sentences for the cutting of sacred olive trees, which are attested early on at Athens, were later abolished.[61]

Furthermore, greater attention should be paid to the differences between oligarchies and democracies and to the contexts of peace and war. It seems, for instance, that in the period of the devastating Peloponnesian War (431–404 BCE), the Athenians were more sensitive to religious matters and paid more attention to their obligations to the gods than they did before the war.[62] If under these conditions someone committed an offense against a deity, it seemed to the community much more serious and worthy of indictment than was the case in peacetime.[63]

If we take into account these observations, it will be worthwhile to initiate further investigations in the areas of law, religion, and magic. We need, of course, collections of the material, especially analyses of specific inscriptions and a usable collection of the curse tablets, along the lines of the *Thesaurus Defixionum Magdeburgensis*, for the study of ancient magic. But, as noted above, all this must be combined with the literary tradition. In this way, one supersedes the limitations of the corpora of sacred laws. Such basic research tools will also make it possible to move beyond the study of specific aspects and compose an overview, and perhaps also a handbook, of the relations among law, religion, and magic in ancient Greece.

NOTES

1. See Sealey 1994: 60–63.

2. E.g., Biscardi 1982; 1999; Cohen 1989; Sealey 1994. Cf. Gernet [1938] 1968: 30; Paoli [1933] 1968: 54–55.

3. For this view, see Maffi (1982: 36), who argues convincingly against "la separazione fra diritto sacrale e diritto della polis."

4. Parker 2004: 67.

5. E.g., Berger 1919; Simon 1975; Schiemann 1999. For the terms *sacer—sanctus—religiosus*, see Schumacher 2006: 1–3.

6. Scheid 2006: 19, referring to similar formulations of Magdelain 1995: 73–74.

7. Scheid 2006: 19.

8. Ibid.

9. Berger 1919: cols. 1292, 1296.

10. Parker (2005: 68–70) recognizes the importance of Latte's book (but see n. 36 below) and translates its subtitle: *Investigation on the History of Sacral Legal Forms in Greece.*

11. Maffi 1982 has shown that there is a difference, but not a strict contradiction, between the sacred (*hieros*) and the profane (*hosios*).

12. Prott and Ziehen 1896–1906.

13. Sokolowski 1955, 1962, 1969.

14. Gauthier 1996: 572, cited by Parker 2004: 57.

15. E.g., Robertson (2010: 3): "Greek inscriptions regulating sacred matters, sacred laws so called, are a large and varied class. . . . They are seldom laws in the sense of enactments by an official body but rather customs of self-evident authority"; Gagarin (2011: 101): "Despite being a modern creation, the term 'sacred laws' has proven useful." For other formulations, e.g., religious regulations, *réglements religieux*, cult regulations, "which are not significantly more transparent than 'sacred law,'" see the discussion of Carbon and Pirenne-Delforge 2012: 163–170 (quotation, 170). They themselves suggest the expression "ritual norms," which "helps to dispel the notion of strict 'law,' decree, or regulation . . . while at the same time acknowledging the degree to which Greek inscriptions record both ancestral and innovative ritual practice" (quotation, 171–172). Instead of *sacred* norms, they prefer to collect *sacrificial and purificatory* ones.

16. Lupu 2009: 5–9 (quotations, 9, 5). The criticism of Carbon and Pirenne-Delforge (2012: 166 and passim) that Lupu's criteria are vague is not justified.

17. We should be aware nevertheless that the Greeks themselves defined a law as *hieros* ("sacred") even if its sacred character was only marginal. See Velissaropoulos-Karakostas 2011: 69–70.

18. Parker 2004, 2005.

19. Parker 2005: 61.

20. Parker 2005: 61–63, summarizing Parker 2004.

21. Parker 2005: 62.

22. Parker 2005: 64.

23. Todd (1993: 307–315), to the contrary, considers under the heading "Religion and the Law" almost exclusively cases of *asebeia*.

24. Parker 2004: 65, however, seems to include regulations on *asebeia* in the category of sacred laws.

25. Maffi 2012: 143.

26. See p. 92. Maffi 2012: 147–148. Maffi (personal correspondence) dissociates himself from the distinction imposed by the editors of the section. Maffi would not now assign *hierosulia* and *asebeia* either to the first or to the second of his categories.

27. See, e.g., Parker 2004: 58; Lupu 2009: 5–6; Gagarin 2011: 101.

28. See Maffi 1982: 38–39 with further references.

29. Dreher 1983: 46–52.

30. Schiemann 2001: 808.

31. See also Maffi 1983: 249 contra Wolff. The assertion is valid despite the fact that, e.g., Athenian judges had to swear an oath at the beginning of their period of service. In this case the gods were simply guarantors that the judges kept to the laws of the polis. The god-given *agraphoi nomoi* (unwritten laws) are not relevant in this context. For the latter, see Gagarin 2008: 33–34. Cf. Hansen in this volume.

32. The many legal consequences of this fiction lie beyond the scope of the present study. For further discussion, see Dreher 2014: 5–15.

33. Versnel (2002: 52–66) identifies in certain curse tablets, whose texts he refers to as judicial prayers or prayers for justice, the role of the gods as judges in a trial corresponding to the procedure in a law court. He argues that the authors of these tablets invoked divine justice; the god or the goddess was asked to act as judge and even as prosecutor in a kind of lawsuit between the author as plaintiff and the cursed person as defendant. See my arguments contra with references (Dreher 2010: 323–325).

34. Bartlett 1986.

35. *IPArk* 8. See also Maffi 2007: 222–232. Doubts that early Greek communities employed this procedure may be based in part on the fact that there is no hint of its use at Athens, the community for which we have the most evidence. For the gods as judges, see Dreher 2014: 16–17.

36. Parker 2005: 68–79. His detailed examination of the different forms of slave emancipation (77–79) refutes Latte's evolutionary interpretation of sacred law.

37. Maffi 2012: 144–146.

38. Plat. *Leg.* 933a–e; cf. Plat. *Rep.* 364b. See also Collins 2008: 139–141.

39. Maffi 2012: 146–148.

40. Cf. p. 90.

41. Lupu 2009: 21.

42. Parker 2005: 64.

43. See the Table of Contents in Lupu 2009: vii–ix.

44. Parker 2004.

45. Lupu 2009: vii–viii. I do not enumerate here the three to eleven subheadings of each chapter. The third chapter ("Cult Performance") has the greatest number (eleven) of subcategories of the four chapters. Carbon and Pirenne-Delforge (2012) do not mention this detailed summary when they criticize Lupu for not giving adequate definitions of sacred laws.

46. Maffi 2012: 148–150.

47. Maffi 2012: 148–149. Cf. Dreher 1996: 86–89.

48. For such summary fines, see Rubinstein in this volume.

49. Maffi 2012: 149–150.

50. See Dreher 1996: 89–91; Rigsby 1996: passim.

51. Dreher 1995: 198–272.

52. Carbon and Pirenne-Delforge (2012: 173–180) note that they intend to address my second and third points in their forthcoming project, "Collection of Greek Ritual Norms" (CGRN), but they say nothing about the first. A broader collection of the evidence is the aim of Georgoudi 2010.

53. Parker 2004: 65.

54. Naiden 2008.

55. Dreher 2008. Carbon and Pirenne-Delforge (2012: 167) comment that Naiden offers "a valuable perspective" without taking into account my critique.

56. See, e.g., the discussion of Harter-Uibopuu 2002 on the law of Andania.

57. Parker 2004: 65.

58. See, e.g., *ID* 98.B, lines 24–30, the case of the Athenian *Amphiktuones* (representatives of the Amphictyony) at Delos, with Dreher 1995: 203–215. The complete epigraphic evidence is treated by Delli Pizzi 2011.

59. For both cases, see, e.g., Todd 1993: 310–315.

60. Maffi 2012: 148–150.

61. For sale of priesthoods, see Buraselis 2008; for *asulia*, cf. above n. 50; for sacred olives, see Horster 2006.

62. Thucydides (3.82–85) notes that the overwhelming cruelty of the civil war in Corcyra destroyed the traditional respect for the gods.

63. As Rubel (2000) convincingly argues.

REFERENCES

Bartlett, Robert. 1986. *Trial by Fire and Water: The Medieval Judicial Ordeal*. Oxford: Clarendon Press.

Berger, Adolf. 1919. "*Ius sacrum*." In *Paulys Real-Encyclopädie der classischen Altertumswissenschaft*, edited by Wilhelm Kroll, vol. 10.2, cols. 1292–1300. Stuttgart: J. B. Metzler.

Biscardi, Arnaldo. 1982. *Diritto greco antico*. Milan: Giuffrè.

———. 1999. *Scritti di diritto greco.* Edited by Eva Cantarella and Alberto Maffi. Milan: Giuffrè.

Buraselis, Kostas. 2008. "Priesthoods for Sale: Comments on Ideological and Financial Aspects of the Sale of Priesthoods in the Greek Cities of the Hellenistic and Roman Periods." In *Religion and Society: Rituals, Resources, and Identity in the Ancient Graeco-Roman World*, edited by Anders Holm Rasmussen and Susanne William Rasmussen, 125–131. Rome: Quasar.

Carbon, Jan-Mathieu, and Vinciane Pirenne-Delforge. 2012. "Beyond Greek 'Sacred Laws.'" *Kernos* 25: 163–182.

Cohen, David. 1989. "Problems, Methods, and Models in the Study of Greek Law." *Zeitschrift der Savigny-Stiftung für Rechtsgeschichte, Romanistische Abteilung* 106: 81–105.

Collins, Derek. 2008. *Magic in the Ancient Greek World.* Malden, MA: Blackwell.

Delli Pizzi, Aurian. 2011. "Impiety in Epigraphic Evidence." *Kernos* 24: 59–76.

Dreher, Martin. 1983. *Sophistik und Polisentwicklung: Die sophistischen Staatstheorien des fünften Jahrhunderts v. Chr. und ihr Bezug auf Entstehung und Wesen des griechischen, vorrangig athenischen Staates.* Frankfurt am Main: P. Lang.

———. 1995. *Hegemon und Symmachoi: Untersuchungen zum zweiten athenischen Seebund.* Berlin: Walter De Gruyter.

———. 1996. "Das Asyl in der Antike von seinen griechischen Ursprüngen bis zur christlichen Spätantike." *Tyche* 11: 79–96.

———. 2008. "Antwort auf F. S. Naiden." In *Symposion 2007: Vorträge zur griechischen und hellenistischen Rechtsgeschichte*, edited by Edward M. Harris and Gerhard Thür, 139–144. Vienna: Verlag der Österreichischen Akademie der Wissenschaften.

———. 2010. "Gerichtsverfahren vor den Göttern? 'Judicial Prayers' und die Kategorisierung der *defixionum tabellae*." In *Symposion 2009: Vorträge zur griechischen und hellenistischen Rechtsgeschichte*, edited by Gerhard Thür, 301–335. Vienna: Verlag der Österreichischen Akademie der Wissenschaften.

———. 2014. "Die Rechte der Götter." In *Symposion 2013: Vorträge zur griechischen und hellenistischen Rechtsgeschichte*, edited by Michael Gagarin and Adriaan Lanni, 1–26. Vienna: Verlag der Österreichischen Akademie der Wissenschaften.

Gagarin, Michael. 2008. *Writing Greek Law.* Cambridge: Cambridge University Press.

———. 2011. "Writing Sacred Laws in Archaic and Classical Crete." In *Sacred Words: Orality, Literacy, and Religion*, edited by A. P. M. H. Lardinois, J. H. Blok, and M. G. M. Van der Poel, 101–111. Leiden: Brill.

Gauthier, Phillipe. 1996. "Bulletin épigraphique: Institutions." *Revue des études grecques* 109: 568–574.

Georgoudi, Stella. 2010. "Comment régler les *theia pragmata*: Pour une étude de ce qu'on appelle 'Lois sacrées.'" *Metis* n.s. 8: 39–54.

Gernet, Louis. [1938] 1968. "Einführung in das Studium des alten griechischen Rechts." In *Zur griechischen Rechtsgeschichte*, edited by Erich Berneker, 4–38.

Darmstadt: Wissenschaftliche Buchgesellschaft. First published (in French) in *Archives d'histoire du droit oriental* 2: 261-292.

Harter-Uibopuu, Kaja. 2002. "Strafklauseln und gerichtliche Kontrolle in der Mysterieninschrift von Andania." *Dike* 5: 135–159.

Horster, Marietta. 2006. "Die Olivenbäume der Athena und die Todesstrafe." In *Symposion 2003: Vorträge zur griechischen und hellenistischen Rechtsgeschichte*, edited by Hans-Albert Rupprecht, 167–185. Vienna: Verlag der Österreichischen Akademie der Wissenschaften.

Latte, Kurt. 1920. *Heiliges Recht: Untersuchungen zur Geschichte der sakralen Rechtsformen in Griechenland.* Tübingen: Mohr.

Lupu, Eran. 2009. *Greek Sacred Law: A Collection of New Documents (NGSL).* 2nd ed. Leiden: Brill.

Maffi, Alberto. 1982. "Τὰ ἱερὰ καὶ τὰ ὁσία: Contributo allo studio della terminologia giuridicosacrale greca." In *Symposion 1977: Vorträge zur griechischen und hellenistischen Rechtsgeschichte*, edited by Joseph Mélèze Modrzejewski and Detlef Liebs, 33–53. Cologne: Böhlau.

———. 1983. Review of *Il diritto in Grecia e a Roma*, by Mario Bretone and Mario Talamanca. *Quaderni di Storia* 17: 245–260.

———. 2007. "Quarant'anni di studi sul processo greco, I." *Dike* 10: 185–267.

———. 2012. "Diritto (parte greca)." In *Thesaurus Cultus et Rituum Antiquorum (ThesCRA)*, vol. 8, 143–150. Basel: Fondation pour le lexicon iconographicum mythologiae classicae; Los Angeles: Getty Publications.

Magdelain, André. 1995. *De la royauté et du droit de Romulus à Sabinus.* Rome: "L'Erma" di Bretschneider.

Naiden, Fred S. 2008. "Sanctions in Sacred Law." In *Symposion 2007: Vorträge zur griechischen und hellenistischen Rechtsgeschichte*, edited by Edward M. Harris and Gerhard Thür, 125–138. Vienna: Verlag der Österreichischen Akademie der Wissenschaften.

Paoli, Ugo Enrico. [1933] 1968. "Die Wissenschaft vom attischen Recht und ihre Möglichkeiten." In *Zur griechischen Rechtsgeschichte*, edited by Erich Berneker, 39–57. Darmstadt: Wissenschaftliche Buchgesellschaft. First published (in Italian) in *Studi sul processo attico* (Biblioteca iuridica 2). Padova: Cedam.

Parker, Robert. 2004. "What Are Sacred Laws?" In *The Law and the Courts in Ancient Greece*, edited by Edward M. Harris and Lene Rubinstein, 57–70. London: Duckworth.

———. 2005. "Law and Religion." In *The Cambridge Companion to Ancient Greek Law*, edited by Michael Gagarin and David Cohen, 61–81. Cambridge: Cambridge University Press.

Prott, Hans Theodor Anton von, and Ludwig Ziehen, eds. 1896–1906. *Leges Graecorum sacrae et titulis collectae.* 2 vols. Leipzig: Teubner. Reprinted in 1988 with a prefatory note by A. N. Oikonomides by Ares Publishers.

Rigsby, Kent J. 1996. *Asylia: Territorial Inviolability in the Hellenistic World.* Berkeley: University of California Press.

Robertson, Noel. 2010. *Religion and Reconciliation in Greek Cities: The Sacred Laws of Selinus and Cyrene*. Oxford: Oxford University Press.

Rubel, Alexander. 2000. *Stadt in Angst: Religion und Politik in Athen während des Peloponnesischen Krieges*. Darmstadt: Wissenschaftliche Buchgesellschaft.

Scheid, John. 2006. "Oral Tradition and Written Tradition in the Formation of Sacred Law in Rome." In *Religion and Law in Classical and Christian Rome*, edited by Clifford Ando and Jörg Rüpke, 14–33. Stuttgart: Steiner.

Schiemann, Gottfried. 1999. "*Ius.*" In *Der Neue Pauly: Enzyklopädie der Antike*, edited by Hubert Cancik and Helmuth Schneider, vol. 6, 89–99. Stuttgart: Metzler.

———. 2001. "Recht." In *Der Neue Pauly: Enzyklopädie der Antike*, edited by Hubert Cancik and Helmuth Schneider, vol. 10, 804–813. Stuttgart: Metzler.

Schumacher, Leonhard. 2006. *Stellung des Sklaven im Sakralrecht: Corpus der römischen Rechtsquellen zur antiken Sklaverei*. Vol. 6. Stuttgart: Steiner.

Sealey, Raphael. 1994. *The Justice of the Greeks*. Ann Arbor: University of Michigan Press.

Simon, Dietrich V. 1975. "*Ius sacrum.*" In *Der Kleine Pauly: Lexicon der Antike*, edited by Walter Sontheimer, vol. 3, 17–18. Stuttgart: Druckenmüller.

Sokolowski, Franciszek. 1955. *Lois sacrées de l'Asie Mineure*. Paris: Éditions de Boccard.

———. 1962. *Lois sacrées des cités grecques: Supplément*. Paris: Éditions de Boccard.

———. 1969. *Lois sacrées des cités grecques*. Paris: Éditions de Boccard.

Thesaurus Defixionum Magdeburgensis (TheDeMa). Directed by Martin Dreher. http://www-e.uni-magdeburg.de/defigo/wordpress/.

Todd, Stephen C. 1993. *The Shape of Athenian Law*. Oxford: Clarendon Press.

Velissaropoulos-Karakostas, Julie. 2011. *Droit grec d'Alexandre à Auguste (323 av. J.-C.–14 ap. J.-C.): Personnes, biens, justice*. 2 vols. Athens: Centre de recherches de l'antiquité grecque et romaine; Paris: de Boccard.

Versnel, Hendrik. 2002. "Writing Mortals and Reading Gods: Appeal to the Gods as a Dual Strategy in Social Contract." In *Demokratie, Recht und soziale Kontrolle im klassischen Athen*, edited by David Cohen and Elisabeth Müller-Luckner, 37–76. Munich: Oldenbourg.

7 / SUMMARY FINES IN GREEK INSCRIPTIONS AND THE QUESTION OF "GREEK LAW"

Lene Rubinstein

THE MAIN QUESTION TO BE ADDRESSED IN THE PRESENT chapter is the extent to which officials in the Greek poleis were authorized to impose sanctions summarily for offenses of various types, without first having obtained a verdict from a court or a comparable institution that had clearly established the guilt of the offender. The discussion will focus in particular on the epigraphical evidence from communities other than Athens, on some of the methodological problems that this material presents, and, more broadly, on the potential relevance of the epigraphical evidence for summary fines to the wider debate on "Greek Law."

Among Anglophone scholars there has been a perceptible change of approach to "Greek law" as a meaningful concept during the last decade of the twentieth century and the first decade of the twenty-first. Not least because of the work of Michael Gagarin himself, it is now increasingly widely accepted that there were significant structural and procedural similarities between the legal systems of individual Greek city-states, which in other respects—including size, constitutional framework, and local traditions—differed markedly from one another. Yet, as has often been emphasized by Gagarin, the recognition of fundamental structural and procedural principles as "Greek" does not mean that local variations, substantive as well as procedural, were insignificant. In some cases, it may be possible to explain particular variations on a general Greek theme with direct reference to the general political and ideological contexts of the different communities under investigation. For example, in some attested legal systems, the eligibility to sit as judge, at least in certain types of legal hearing, was subject to a property qualification;[1] this in turn may be taken as an indication that the administration of justice in that community operated in a wider aristocratic or oligarchic political context.

However, many questions still remain to be explored further in modern scholarship. One of these is to what extent particular legal institutions, procedures, or principles were shaped or adapted to suit the different political systems that prevailed in individual communities. Is it possible to identify features that were inextricably linked to what may be characterized as "democratic" administration of justice? And likewise, are there any that can be labeled as specifically "aristocratic" or "oligarchic"?

Sometimes we may have reliable evidence to show that a particular community in a particular period operated with a property qualification when manning its courts, or that it permitted important legal disputes to be decided by panels of judges who served for life. Yet these features alone do not necessarily permit firm conclusions to be drawn regarding the broader constitutional framework in which its courts were functioning. If the evidence for Athens had been as patchy as it is for the vast majority of other Greek communities in the archaic and classical periods, the continued existence of the Areopagus Council, with its life-membership and exclusion of the lowest census group, the *thetes* (at least on paper), might quite reasonably have led modern historians to regard the constitution of fourth-century Athens as much less democratic than it actually was.

Conversely, many of the features attested for the administration of justice in classical Athens may in fact have also existed in more narrowly based constitutions, where they would not have been perceived as particularly "democratic," although modern discussions conventionally associate them specifically with a democratic form of government. The difficulty can be illustrated with reference to the modern debate, summarized by Gagarin,[2] on the gradual spread of written law in archaic and early classical Greece, a phenomenon that defies confident constitutional labeling.

In this regard, the legal historian's dependence on Athenian literary sources, and on the Attic orators in particular, presents a serious problem. It is clear from Athenian forensic oratory that the Athenians themselves frequently chose to interpret and represent their legal institutions, processes, and principles as unique manifestations of their own particular form of government, sometimes drawing explicit and unfavorable comparison with the administration of justice in nondemocratic states. There has been a tendency among modern scholars to accept at least some of their claims at face value. But just as it is clear that the existence of an assembly did not in itself make a democracy, so it is also apparent from Pierre Fröhlich's *Les cités grecques et le contrôle des magistrats* that the desire and will to hold officials accountable for their conduct in office through formal legal procedures were not confined to just those communities that can be easily labeled "democratic."[3] Fröhlich's work is among several recent studies on legal and constitutional features of the Hellenistic Greek poleis that have been based on a large body of epigraphical material. Indeed, one of the most significant recent developments in the field of Greek epigraphy has been the creation of electronic facilities that have made a large proportion of the epigraphical evidence for other Greek communities more readily available. As a result, there are now more opportunities for us to assess which aspects of Athenian law and administration of justice may have been peculiarly "democratic" and which of them might be identified as more generally Greek.

I have previously argued that the institution of the volunteer prosecutor (*ho boulomenos*), traditionally associated mainly with the Athenian democratic administration of justice, is one that can be traced across time, space, and constitutional and ideological divides.[4] This in turn calls for a reassessment of the link that is conventionally made between *ho boulomenos* and Athenian-style democracy. The epigraphical evidence suggests that the use of volunteers as agents in various processes of law enforcement may be interpreted more broadly as a characteristic of Greek administration of justice, rather than a peculiarly democratic institution.

The subject of the present chapter, namely the authorization bestowed on officials to impose summary fines without prior authorization from a court or comparable institution, is most naturally characterized as belonging at the other end of the Greek constitutional spectrum. Although there is evidence, most recently discussed by Edward Harris,[5] which shows that even Athenian officials were authorized to impose summary penalties in a variety of contexts, there is almost universal agreement that the Athenians—presumably along with other democratic communities in the classical period—did impose very strict limitations on the sanctions that they could impose without prior reference to a regular *dikastērion* ("popular court"), although it must be noted that the 500 drachmas which the Council of 500 were authorized to impose summarily, at least until the mid-fourth century, would have been a formidable sum for all but the wealthiest residents at Athens.[6] The limitation of the officials' penal authority conforms to the general characterization of *dēmokratia* as a form of government in which the decision-making powers of officials were limited to a minimum. The powers of the board of the Eleven, who were authorized to impose the death penalty on a *kakourgos* ("offender") without trial unless the person apprehended denied his guilt, is normally regarded as a striking exception to this general principle.

But just as the institution of the volunteer prosecutor was arguably not inextricably tied to a democratic form of government, so it may be asked whether summary justice dispensed by polis officials was a particular characteristic of more narrowly based constitutions. The epigraphical material suggests that the phenomenon was probably as widespread as that of volunteer prosecution, and that it should not necessarily be regarded as a characteristic of any particular type of constitution. Moreover, its recurrent application as a practical measure in certain contexts, such as the agora, religious festivals, and other kinds of mass gatherings, points to a remarkable degree of continuity over time. That impression is strengthened further by the notably similar methods by which different Greek communities attempted to reduce the opportunities for officials to abuse their powers, for example, by imposing clear limits on the sanctions that could be imposed or by providing procedural means through which the sanction could be contested and reversed.

The similarities detectable in the inscriptions from a range of communities may in turn provide a further contribution to the debate over the extent to which the legal institutions and administration of justice in different Greek communities were based on shared legal and procedural principles. As is well known, much of the relevant non-Athenian material dates from the Hellenistic period, and here, too, there has been a marked change of direction in modern scholarship over the past three decades. There has been a growing interest in the Hellenistic poleis and their institutions in Mainland Greece, Asia Minor, and the Aegean, with an increased emphasis on evidence that points to social and political continuity rather than drastic change. The approach to the Hellenistic age as a period of gradual evolution rather than revolution has likewise created new opportunities for a reassessment of the development of the administration of justice in the Hellenistic world.

It has long been recognized that there were striking similarities between the legal systems of the Hellenistic poleis, as evidenced, for example, in the vast corpus of manumission documents and by the activities of foreign judges; and the development of a Greek legal *koinē* ("common language") has often been characterized as a direct result of wider geopolitical developments in the Greek world after Alexander. But although it is highly likely that convergence of different Greek legal systems may have accelerated during this period, many of the patterns that can be discerned in the corpus of Hellenistic inscriptions appear in fact to have had a much longer history, often stretching back well into the classical period and even earlier.

As mentioned earlier, the discussion in this paper will include evidence from the Hellenistic period from the late fourth to the middle of the second century BCE as well as evidence from the classical period, and its focus will be mainly on the epigraphical evidence for communities in the Greek world outside Athens. However, when used as evidence for the power and authority bestowed on officials in different Greek communities, the inscriptions are often less than transparent, and they present some important methodological problems, which I shall attempt to set out in what follows. The identification of individual instances where polis officials were authorized to dispense summary justice is often far from straightforward, and it is probable that the attestations on which the present study is based represent only the tip of a much larger iceberg.

When I first began collecting the epigraphical evidence for law enforcement outside Athens in the archaic, classical, and early Hellenistic periods, I expected that the majority of surviving enactments prescribing sanctions for particular offenses would indicate the nature of the process by which the sanctions were to be imposed. However, a systematic survey of the relevant inscriptions yielded a rather different result, which did not conform to my initial expectations. Although many of the relevant inscriptions do contain instructions, sometimes very detailed ones, on how individual offenses should be reported and prosecuted, an even larger number contain no such information at all. Quite apart from the difficulties presented by inscriptions that have not survived in their entirety, and which often break off just at the point where one might expect the procedural instructions to have been set out, a serious problem arises in connection with those inscriptions that specify only offense and sanction, in spite of the fact that they have clearly been preserved in their entirety. One example is the text inscribed on a sacred boundary stone from fifth-century Corinth, which runs: "Inviolable [sacred boundary stone (?)]. Do not trespass. Fine: eight."[7] This is, of course, an extreme example of brevity, and it must be noted that this text is not really a "law," but rather an equivalent to a warning sign attached to the emergency brake in a modern railway carriage. Yet this simple formula is in fact very widespread, even if most of the relevant inscriptions are rather less lapidary than the Corinthian text.

In cases such as this, the legal historian is left to wonder how the legislators envisaged that the offense in question would be detected and reported, who would be authorized to act upon detection, and, most importantly, who was to decide on the question of whether the person accused of having committed the offense was in fact guilty as charged. It might be tempting to look around for parallel examples of similar prohibitions from other poleis that might provide more information on precisely the matters that the Corinthian inscription leaves untold, but this temptation should be resisted. If the historian's main objective is to identify wider patterns of Greek administration of justice across polis boundaries, any attempt to supply missing information by adducing parallels from elsewhere would be begging the question.

The difficulties associated with the identification of procedures and methods of law enforcement are not confined just to the kinds of inscription that specify only offense and sanction without providing any further instructions. They arise also in connection with a significant number of texts that contain instructions relating to the process of *praxis* ("exacting of the penalty"), that is, on how the sanctions were to be executed in practice and by whom.[8] Frustratingly, many of these inscriptions offer no explicit information on what one might expect to have been a crucial intermediate stage between detection and *praxis*—namely, the decision on whether or not the offender had indeed committed the offense at all, let alone on any mitigating circumstances.

Two texts, both of which proceed directly from the specification of offense and sanction to the provision of instructions on the process of *praxis*, may serve as illustrations of the problem. The first is a clause in a much larger inscription from fifth-century Chios that relates to the definition and demarcation of an area known as Lophitis.[9] The clause prohibits the removal, transposing, and defacing of the boundary stones and prescribes a sanction of one hundred staters and *atimia* ("disenfranchisement"):

> If anyone takes down or moves or obscures any of these boundary stones
> to the detriment of the polis, let him owe a hundred *statēres* and let him be
> *atimos*. The *horophulakes* ["overseers of boundaries"] must exact the fine. If
> they do not exact it, they shall owe the fine themselves. The Fifteen shall
> exact the fine from the *horophulakes*. If they do not exact it, they shall be
> accursed.[10]

The inscription clearly states that the *horophulakes* are responsible, under the threat of a penalty, for exacting the fine. What is less clear is whether they were obliged to exact the fine from the offender directly upon detection, or whether *praxis* was to take place only after the offender had been subjected to some kind of legal process decided by a third party, be it a court, a council, or another board of officials.

As is the case with many other similar inscriptions, the difficulty here arises because of the need to distinguish between, on the one hand, the powers and authorization to enforce a verdict (*Vollstreckungsgewalt*) and, on the other, the permission sometimes granted to officials to impose a penalty summarily on their own authority (*Strafgewalt*). Because the Chian *horophulakes* are not otherwise attested as having had the authority to impose summary penalties, Reinhard Koerner inclined toward the view that the role of the *horophulakes* was merely to enforce the outcome of a legal process, the details of which were omitted from the text inscribed on the stone.[11]

Koerner's reconstruction is certainly plausible. If, on the one hand, the main purpose of the inscribed penalty clause was to deter prospective offenders, the inclusion of information pertaining to the process of *praxis* may have been envisaged primarily as a way of enhancing the deterrent by spelling out clearly the actual consequences of a conviction. On the other hand, there is substantial evidence from other Greek communities of many different types of officials being authorized to impose penalties without a prior legal hearing of any kind, as will be made clear in what follows.[12] Consequently, the Chian inscription still leaves open the possibility that the *horophulakes* did indeed have the power (and the obligation) to dispense summary justice. In this instance, the question has to be left open.

The second text, a fourth-century regulation of the sale of wool that was probably passed in Erythrae (*IK Erythrai und Klazomenai* I 15),[13] further illustrates the scale of the problem. The surviving part of the enactment contains three penalty clauses:

> And the traders must weigh the wool, as much as each of them sells, and they must weigh it honestly. If anyone does wrong, let him owe twenty drachmas for each talent (?). The *agoranomos* ("overseer of the market-place") must exact the fine. Let (the trader) sell until midday. He must not bring (the wool) out into the rain. The wool sellers must not sell wool from one-year-old sheep. If anyone does sell, let him be fined two drachmas per day by the *agoranomos*. Neither a wholesale trader nor a retailer must sell either wool or flocks of wool in a raw state to anyone from any other place than from . . . If he sells in any other place, the wool is to be confiscated and he must be fined twenty drachmas; and all the wool sold in another way than by the public scale is to be announced for public auction by the *prutaneis* (a board of officials) . . .[14]

The first penalty clause that prohibits cheating with the scales prescribes that the *agoranomos* is to exact the fine (*prēxasthō*). As in the Chian text, we are left with the major question of who was to impose the sanction and by what procedure. The *agoranomos* must have been the obvious person to discover any tampering with the scales, and he would also be the obvious person present in the marketplace to whom an aggrieved purchaser would have been likely to turn with his complaint. However, if the basic principle applied by Koerner to the Chian text is also adopted in relation to the wool law, it is possible that the verb *prēxasthō* did not indicate that the *agoranomos* had the power to impose and exact the fine solely on his own authority. Rather, it may have indicated merely that he had the authority to execute a judgment passed as a result of a legal process. On that interpretation, the *agoranomos* would have been instructed to exact the penalty only as a result of a legal procedure in which he himself, the defrauded victim, or possibly a volunteer prosecutor had stated the case against the fraudulent vendor and won it. Since the text contains no indication whatsoever of such a legal procedure or, for that matter, the lack of it, any reconstruction must, again, remain conjectural.

However, the formulation of the second penalty clause does suggest that the *agoranomos*'s authority was not limited simply to *Vollstreckungsgewalt*, but that he did have some authorization to impose sanctions directly: "The wool sellers must not sell wool from one-year-old sheep. If anyone does sell, let him be fined two drachmas per day by the *agoranomos*." The passive imperative "let him be fined" (*zēmiousthō*) along with the agent, the *agoranomos*, expressed in a prepositional phrase with ὑπό (ὑπὸ τοῦ ἀ[γορανό]μου), may indicate a process of summary justice, dispensed by the *agoranomos*.

It is perhaps tempting to infer that, if the *agoranomos* was authorized to impose a penalty for the sale of wool from one-year-old sheep, it is also likely that he would have had the authority to impose a summary fine for cheating with the scales. This, in turn, might explain why there is no reference to any legal procedure in the first penalty clause. But unfortunately, this must remain a matter of competing probabilities. The penalty prescribed in the second clause is low, a mere two drachmas per day. This, as will be seen later on, is within the same range as penalties prescribed in other contexts where there can be no doubt that we are dealing with summary fines. By contrast, the penalty prescribed in the first clause is ten times that amount, and presumably the penalty would be even higher if the trader's fraudulent transactions had involved more than the quantity indicated. It is entirely possible—indeed highly likely—that the *agoranomos* would have been empowered to impose summary penalties below a certain amount, while he would have been obliged to seek the authorization of a court in connection with any offense for which the prescribed penalty exceeded that limit. Consequently, as far as the first penalty clause is concerned, the question of the *agoranomos*'s penal authority is impossible to answer definitively.

The same applies to the third penalty clause that prescribes that wool must be sold only in a particular location: "If he sells in any other place, the wool is to be confiscated and he must be fined twenty drachmas." Here there is no mention of the agent of the two passive imperatives (*steresthō*, "let it [the wool] be confiscated," and *zēmiousthō*). The *agoranomos*, a council, or a law court are all equally plausible candidates, and no clue helps the modern reader to choose among them. Instead of specifying the procedure by which the confiscation and imposition of the fine are to be carried out, the law apparently goes straight on to specifying how confiscated wool is to be sold at public auction by the *prutaneis*. So while the wool law provides reasonably solid evidence (though not entirely secure) for the *agoranomos* having the authorization to impose summary fines of two drachmas per day, it remains uncertain if his authorization likewise extended to the imposition of fines of twenty drachmas or more, or to the confiscation of goods without prior reference to a court or similar authority.

The phrasing of the third clause of the wool law is, in fact, anything but untypical. In the epigraphical material from the archaic, classical, and early Hellenistic periods, the most common penalty clauses by far are those in which the offender is either the subject of an active paying or owing verb without further procedural information, or the subject of a passive punishment verb without the specification of the agent. In the majority of these cases, it is impossible to determine whether the penalty in question was to be imposed as the result of a court action, even when the enactment proceeds explicitly to assign an active role to officials in the process of *praxis*, after the specification of offense and sanction.

What compounds the difficulties further is that caution is called for also when it comes to penalty clauses that are phrased with a board of officials as the subject of a penalty verb, such as *kolazein* ("punish"), *epiballein* ("impose a penalty"), and *zēmioun* and *thōan* ("fine") in the active voice, or as agents in corresponding passive constructions, as in the second penalty clause of the wool law discussed above. For in some inscriptions it is possible that the active verb *zēmioun* does not refer to the act of imposing a summary fine, but rather to the *assessment of the severity* of the fine to be imposed for a particular offense, which could not be exacted without the authorization of a court or a comparable institution. This may have applied, for example, in the fourth-century Athenian enactment passed by the *deme* of Piraeus, *IG* II² 1177, lines 12–17, where the *dēmarch* ("chairman of the *deme*") is given the task of proceeding against offenders transgressing the regulation by "bringing the matter before a *dikastērion*, applying the laws that are in force on such matters, after having imposed a penalty (*epibolēn epibalonta*)."[15] Although scholars generally tend to assume that the penalty could be summarily imposed by the *dēmarch*,[16] it is a distinct possibility that the *dēmarch* was obliged to refer the case to a court before the penalty could be executed. No clause in the enactment explicitly states that a court procedure was required only if the offender failed to pay the fine imposed on him.

Similar considerations apply in connection with a clause in the Tegean building regulations *IPArk* 3 = *RO* 60, lines 15–21:

> If anyone joins in opposing the letting of the work or causes damage by destruction in any way, let the *esdotēres* (officials in charge of letting public contracts) impose a fine of whatever amount seems best to them, and let them summon him by herald to *epikrisis* ("judgment"), and let them bring him before a *dikastērion* composed according to the amount of the penalty.[17]

In their discussion of this inscription, Gerhard Thür and Hans Taeuber suggest that, in this instance too, the penal decision of the *esdotēres* may have required the confirmation of a court in a procedure of *epikrisis* before it could be executed.[18] However, in their interpretation, an *epikrisis* initiated by the *esdotēres* was required only if the offender refused to pay as prescribed.[19] If, on the other hand, he accepted their decision and handed over the amount of the fine without compulsion, a legal hearing was not required. Thür and Taeuber support this reconstruction with reference not only to the clause in *IPArk* 3, lines 45–51, but also to numerous parallel examples from other communities. If this is correct, we may conclude that the *esdotēres* were in fact granted significant penal powers without the mandatory involvement of a court—and it is especially striking that the text does not impose an explicit limit on the penalty that the officials were allowed to impose at their own discretion. It cannot be ruled out that the *dēmarch* of Piraeus in *IG* II^2 1177 discussed above was similarly permitted to impose and collect fines from offenders who chose not to contest his decision, but the way in which the penalty clause is phrased means that the question must remain open.

Thus, the occurrence of a punishment verb with an official or board of officials as its logical subject is no guarantee that the penalty in question was to be both summarily imposed and executed without the authorization of a court or a comparable body. However, this should not make us despair completely, for it is possible to isolate a number of features in individual penalty clauses, each of which may contribute to a more secure identification of summary penalties in the inscriptions. It is to these that the discussion will now turn.

It is a characteristic of many contractual agreements between private individuals and a polis, a civic subdivision, a sanctuary, or another type of organization, that the officials in charge of supervising the contractor and his work are instructed to impose and exact fines, including the *hemiolion* (a fifty-percent surcharge). Often the officials are instructed to register such penalties directly as debts owed by the contractor, apparently without first having obtained authorization through a judicial process. A contract relating to the sale of a priesthood from third-century Cos may be cited as a typical example (*IG* XII.4 1 304). Lines 8–15 stipulate that the priestess must pay the price of her contract in three installments at specified times. If she fails to pay by the deadline, the *tamiai* ("treasurers") are to register her with the *praktores* ("exactors of public debts"), who are to exact from her double the amount owed.[20] Penal clauses of this kind, not just for late payments but also for other types of breach of contract, appear with a remarkable degree of consistency in contracts from all over the Greek world.[21]

The penal authority conferred on the officials who supervised such contracts merits further study in its own right and more attention than can be given to it here. In the present context, it must of course be taken into account that there are significant differences between penalties that could be imposed summarily on the basis of a contractual agreement and penalties imposed for legal offenses more generally. That having been said, some of the processes that can be observed in connection with the policing of contractors occur also in connection with other types of summary fines. Thus, a penalty clause from second-century Cyme (*SEG* 33.1039), which prohibits the lighting of fires and the hanging of votive tablets and other dedications from the beams of the buildings in a heroön ("hero shrine"), authorizes the *agoranomoi* and *hieronomoi* ("overseers of sanctuaries") to impose summary fines of up to five staters "without being subject to legal action" (*ontes anupodikoi*), and to exact these fines on the spot "in whichever way they can" (ᾧ ἂν δύνωνται [τϱ]όπῳ). If the officials are unable to collect the money, they are to register the fine as a debt.[22] That the officials were empowered to punish without first subjecting the offender to a legal hearing is beyond doubt in this case. On the other hand, it is highly likely that the officials would have been obliged to refer the case to a court or comparable institution if they believed the offender to be deserving of a more severe penalty than the maximum five staters that they were allowed to impose on their own authority. It is frustrating that the text does not indicate what procedures were to be initiated by the officials in such cases, and the omission of this procedural information again highlights the dangers of arguments from silence when it comes to the possible involvement by the courts in the enforcement of regulations of this type.

That registration of the fine as a debt could sometimes lead directly to the commencement of a process of *praxis* without the prior involvement of a court is clear from the gymnasiarchal law of Beroea. This enactment offers several interesting details on the stages of a process that begins with the detection and reporting of an offense, and leads to the registration of a summary penalty with a board that was authorized to carry out *praxis* (*EKM* 1.Beroia 1.B, lines 29–37). If a gymnasiarch (*gumnasiarchos*, the official in charge of a gymnasium) knowingly allowed certain categories of persons to anoint themselves,[23] he would incur a fine of 1,000 drachmas. The person who had detected him in this offense was to report him to the city's *exetastai* ("auditors" or "examiners"), who in turn were instructed to register the fine with the *politikos praktōr* ("exactor of public debts"):

> If the *gumnasiarchos* knowingly permits any of these aforementioned persons to anoint himself, or if he gives permission in spite of another person having drawn his attention to such an unauthorized person and pointed him out, let him pay 1000 drachmas. In order that the fine should be exacted, the denunciator must hand a written record to the *exetastai* of the polis, and let these register the fine with the *politikos praktōr*. If they do not register the fine, or if the *praktōr* does not exact it, let these people, too, pay the same penalty and let a third of this be paid to the person who has brought the legal action. If the *gumnasiarchos* believes that he has been re-

corded unjustly, it shall be possible for him, having stated his objection within ten days, to be judged in the relevant *dikastērion*.[24]

Here there can be no doubt that the *exetastai* were not only authorized but also obliged to impose the fine and pass it on for *praxis* without first having referred the case to a court. A legal hearing was prescribed only if the gymnasiarch decided to contest the penalty formally. From this it can be inferred that, if the gymnasiarch acquiesced, the fine would simply be imposed and exacted summarily without further ado.

The evidence for summary fines being registered with treasurers, *praktores*, or other relevant boards of officials is not confined to the Hellenistic period. Among the earlier examples is a fifth-century regulation passed by Andros pertaining to pilgrimages to Delphi (*CID* I 7). Here, five men are to be selected from among the delegation and made to swear an oath. The men, who may perhaps best be described as quasi-officials, receive authorization to impose fines of up to five drachmas a day for disorderly conduct by their fellow delegates, along with instructions that they must submit a written record of the penalties to the *boulē*, presumably upon their return.[25] It is probable, though not by any means certain, that the *boulē* was the body that would be responsible for actually exacting the fines, once the delegation had returned home.

Generally, a prescription that an official or board of officials was to proceed directly to registering the offender formally as a debtor may often be interpreted as an indication that the officials in question had the power to dispense summary justice. However, caution is called for here. There are several instances where it cannot be ruled out entirely that the registration of the offender as a debtor would have been preceded by a legal hearing of some kind, a hearing that was taken for granted and therefore left implicit in the text of the enactment.

An example of this can be found in a regulation from second- or first-century Tymnos (*IK Rhod. Peraia* 201, lines 12–18 = Bresson [1991] no. 102), which contains a penalty clause very similar to that found in the Cymaean enactment (*SEG* 33.1039) discussed above. In the enactment of Tymnos, the *hierothutēs* ("sacrificing priest") in charge of a stoa is instructed to register with the *hierotamiai* ("treasurers of sacred funds") anyone who affixes objects to the roof or architraves of the stoa with nails as owing a sacred fine of a hundred drachmas:

> It shall not be permitted to anyone to affix anything either to the roof or to the architraves. If anyone does anything in contravention of what stands written, let the *hierothutēs* and the *damosios* ("public servant") and any

other member of the deme who wishes prevent him. And if he does not comply, let them also register him with the *hierotamiai* as owing a penalty of one hundred drachmas to be sacred to Apollo, and let them remove what has been affixed.[26]

The plural verb "let them register" (*apographontō*) strongly suggests that the instruction was issued not only to the *hierothutēs* in his official capacity, but also to the volunteer who had tried in vain to prevent the offense, as well as to the *damosios*, who was most likely of unfree status.[27] But although it seems perfectly plausible that the *hierothutēs*, the *damosios*, and any deme-member acting as a volunteer would have been allowed to initiate a registration of the penalty without first obtaining a verdict in court, it is highly unlikely that the *hierotamiai* would have been authorized to act directly on the denunciation and exact the penalty from the alleged offender without some form of legal hearing, not least if the denunciation had been made by an unfree individual.

When it comes to the procedure that the *hierotamiai* were required to follow upon denunciation, the text is silent. At least two different scenarios are possible. The *hierotamiai* may have had the authority to question the alleged offender and themselves decide upon the question of his guilt. Alternatively, they may have been required to refer the case for a hearing before a third party, perhaps themselves acting as prosecutors *ex officio*, or else presiding over the hearing with the *hierothutēs* or the volunteer denunciator conducting the prosecution. Although it is impossible to tell how the *hierotamiai* were supposed to proceed upon receiving a denunciation made by a volunteer or by the *damosios*, the Tymnian regulation constitutes an important warning: the instruction issued to a board of officials that they must follow up a denunciation with the registration of the alleged perpetrator as owing the penalty does not in itself show conclusively that the penalty was to be summarily imposed.

However, in the examples from Cyme, Beroea, and Andros discussed earlier, there are other features which may allow a more secure identification of the penalties as summary, and which also recur in other inscriptions. Of these, the three most important ones are:

1. An explicit indication of the limit of the fine that a relevant board of officials was authorized to impose without reference to a court or comparable institution. Such indications often, but not always, make it clear that the board could exercise a certain amount of discretion. This feature is attested in the Cymaean regulation, as well as in the enactment from Andros.

2. An explicit reference to the officials' authorization with the adjective *kurios* or *krateros* ("authorized") or with the adverb *kuriōs* ("authori-

tatively"). The adjective *kurioi* is found in an Andrian enactment that granted penal authority to five members of the delegation to Delphi, who were required to swear an oath before taking on their duties, and who thus occupied a position as quasi-officials for the duration of the journey.

3. An explicit indication that the imposition of a penalty could be subjected to a process of judgment if, and only if, the person on whom it had been imposed objected formally to the sanction. As mentioned earlier, the gymnasiarchal law of Beroea provides a period of ten days within which the gymnasiarch is permitted to contest the fine imposed on him. It is clear *e contrario* that the fine was to be exacted without a prior hearing, if the gymnasiarch chose not to make a formal objection. This is also the model which is assumed by Thür and Taeuber to have been applied in the Tegean building regulation (*IPArk* 3 = *RO* 60) discussed above.[28]

In several texts, two or all three of these features occur together. In these cases it seems certain that the officials in question had the power to dispense summary justice. But even when it occurs on its own, each feature constitutes a strong indication that a legal hearing was by no means mandatory.

The indication of a clear limitation of the penalty that a given official or board of officials was authorized to impose is important evidence for the relationship between the officials and the legal institutions in the communities in which they operated. In some enactments it is made clear that if the official(s) decide that a more severe penalty is called for, the case must be subjected to a legal hearing, be it before a court, a council, or a comparable institution.[29] In such cases, it can be inferred *e contrario* that such a process would not be required, if the official(s) opted for a penalty that did not exceed the maximum as defined in the enactment. But even in texts that do not prescribe the involvement of a court for offenses which were deemed deserving of a penalty in excess of the maximum, the definition of a limit within which the officials were allowed to exercise discretion is in itself a good indication that penalties that fell below this limit could be imposed summarily.[30] That this was indeed the case is clear whenever the definition of the officials' range of discretion is combined with a statement to the effect that the officials in question are to be *kurioi* or *krateroi* when imposing the penalty, or, alternatively, that they are to impose it *kuriōs*.[31]

The *kurios* stipulation is not confined to those enactments that prescribe an upper limit to the officials' discretion; it also occurs in texts that apparently prescribe a sanction fixed by law to be imposed for a particular offense. Thus, in a funerary regulation pertaining to the war dead from mid-fourth-century Thasos, several boards of officials (the *gunaikonomoi* ("overseers of women"), the *archontes* ("officials"), and the *polemarchoi* (a board of high-ranking officials) are each authorized (*karteroi*) to inflict penalties as prescribed by the laws (ταῖς θωαῖς ταῖς ἐκ τῶν νόμων) for violations of any of the prohibitions set out in the previous lines of the enactment.[32]

The cross-reference to existing legislation permits two different interpretations. One is that each of the prohibitions set out in the text (including one pertaining to activities on the day of the *ekphora* [the carrying out of the corpse to the burial ground]), one prohibiting mourning rituals for more than five days, and one pertaining to the ritual performed in connection with the actual burial) was already covered in existing Thasian legislation, and the other, that definitions of the sanctions to be imposed for each offense were to be found there.[33] In that case, the main purpose of the clause in the present text may have been to permit the boards of officials mentioned to impose the penalties on the spot, without seeking the prior authorization of the court. And if so, one reason why such a permission would have been perceived as necessary may have been that the *polemarchoi* (one of the least well-known boards attested in fourth-century Thasos, as pointed out by Hamon)[34] would not normally have been involved in the enforcement of Thasos's funerary legislation. Since they were to play a prominent role specifically in connection with the funerals of fallen soldiers, it may have been regarded as expedient to grant them the same type of penal authority as that which may already have been exercised by the board of *archontes* and *gunaikonomoi* according to existing Thasian legislation.

Another possible interpretation, however, is that the cross-reference ταῖς θωαῖς ταῖς ἐκ τῶν νόμων ("the fines on the basis of the laws") refers not to other statutes regulating funerary practices, but to the laws that defined and limited the remit and authority of each of the three boards of officials, including the severity of the penalties that each board was allowed to impose summarily. Such statutory limits of the penal powers that a board of officials was permitted to exercise are attested not only for classical Athens, but also for other poleis.[35] As far as the Thasian funerary regulation is concerned, the implications of this interpretation would be that the sanction imposed summarily for, say, extending the period of mourning beyond the five-day limit, would have varied according to which of the three boards happened to be notified of the actual offense.

Although it might run counter to our expectations, such an interpretation should not be dismissed a priori: a parallel is provided by a law from second-century Delos (*SEG* 48.1037) which prohibits unauthorized herding within the *perirrhanteria* ("sacred area") of the sanctuary. Instructions are issued to the *hieropoioi* ("temple officials"), the *boulē*, and "all the rest of the officials" to punish the offender "with the penalty which each board of officials is authorized (*kuria*) to impose."[36] The editors of the Delian text, Feyel and Prost, have argued that the main priority of the Delian enactment is to create the maximum deterrent effect.[37] By issuing an authorization to all polis officials, allowing them to intervene directly by imposing summary fines, the community increased the probability that the offender would indeed be caught and made to pay a penalty for his transgression. If this is correct, it in turn suggests that the Delians regarded deterrence as more important than absolute consistency in the penal response to the particular offense in question. It is possible that the same may have applied to the Thasian regulations of the funerals of the war dead; but without further Thasian evidence it is impossible to make a definitive choice between the two alternative interpretations.

When the *kurios* stipulation is found in combination with a penalty that appears to have been within the penal limits as generally defined for each individual board of officials, the stipulation might at first seem redundant. However, in those cases it almost certainly served the purpose of indicating not only that the officials were authorized to impose the penalty on the spot and exact it without a prior legal hearing, but also that the person on whom it was imposed would not be given an opportunity to contest the penalty before its implementation. This is certainly the case in the regulation pertaining to the shrine of Amphiaraus in Oropus, whereby the priest is authorized both to impose a summary fine and to seize immediately the property of the offender, unless the latter agrees to pay up.[38]

The *kurios* stipulation, however, did not necessarily mean that the officials' decision to impose the penalty was irreversible. As demonstrated by Fröhlich, the practice of submitting officials to accounting procedures at the end of their term of office was ubiquitous in the late classical and Hellenistic periods.[39] It must be envisaged that complaints against unjust fines could be made at this point. It is only when the *kurios* stipulation is combined with an immunity clause, stating that the officials are immune from prosecution (*anupodikoi*) and from being audited concerning this act when stepping down from office (*anupeuthunoi*), as in *SEG* 33.1039, cited above, that the officials' ruling may be assumed to have been final.[40]

Although the process of *euthunai* ("auditing") or its equivalents would in many cases have left open the possibility of reversing the officials' decision, the consequences of a summary fine could still be serious, in the interim, for the person on whom it had been unjustly imposed. In those cases where the process of *praxis* was to follow straight after the imposition of the fine, the accused risked having their property seized. Even when *praxis* was not to be carried out instantly but the fine was instead to be registered formally as a debt, the person fined would often face other penalties designed to encourage prompt payment, including the fifty-percent surcharge (the *hemiolion*) or the doubling of the fine, sometimes combined with various forms of *atimia*. The obvious risk that a board of officials might be tempted to abuse their penal power may be one reason why the *kurios* stipulation tended to occur mainly when the summary fine to be imposed was on a modest scale.

One way of tempering the penal authority of the officials, and thus of reducing the risk of abuse, was to provide a procedure by which the person penalized would be able to object formally to the officials' decision before its implementation. Several enactments that permit and instruct officials to impose a penalty on their own authority also prescribe that a hearing must take place, but if and only if the offender maintains that the penalty is being unjustly imposed. Such provisions are attested for numerous Greek cities across different regions. The scope that they offer for a systematic comparison and contrast between the procedures adopted by different communities in different contexts is of significant relevance to the wider debate on the concept of "Greek law."

A general feature that appears to be shared by most of the provisions for procedures by which the officials' decision could be challenged is that the procedure is triggered either by a formal objection to the penalty and the reason for its imposition[41] or by a simple refusal to pay on the part of the person fined, resulting in subjection to a formal legal hearing.[42] In either case, the norm seems to have been that the person fined would have appeared as a defendant in any ensuing legal process.[43] But there are important differences, too, in regard to both the identity of the prosecuting agent and the forum to which the final decision was referred.

Sometimes it was envisaged that the officials who had been responsible for imposing the fine would themselves act as prosecutors in a legal hearing arising from the putative offender's formal objection or refusal to pay. This was almost certainly the case in *IG* IV²1 98 from third-century Epidaurus, where the prosecution against a contractor appears to have been conducted by the *agōnothetēs*, perhaps assisted by the *hellanodikai*, and in *IPArk* 3, lines 17–21 and 45–51, as interpreted by Thür and Taeuber.[44]

More problematic is an enactment from third-century Thasos (*IG* XII *Suppl.* 348) which authorizes a board of officials, the *epistatai*, to impose fines on individuals who beach their ships contrary to the stipulations in the law. The *epistatai* are permitted to collect the fine immediately, provided that the person fined does not object to their ruling. If he does object, the case must be referred to the board of *apologoi* ("auditors"), who are responsible for passing the case on to a court. It is conventionally assumed that the *apologoi* would themselves have been required to plead the case on behalf of the *epistatai*.[45] However, it is possible that the *apologoi* were to be responsible mainly for the formal processing and introduction of the case, and that the *epistatai* would take on the role as prosecutors during the actual hearing.

An altogether different format is found in the Labyadae inscription from fifth- or fourth-century Delphi (*CID* I 9.A, lines 33–44 = *RO* 1). The enactment prescribes a summary fine to be imposed on the *tagoi* ("officials") for receiving the *apellaia* (a sacrifice) on unauthorized days, and provides for a hearing before the assembly (*halia*) if the *tagoi* object formally to the penalty. However, the task of prosecuting the *tagoi* is left to a volunteer prosecutor (*ho chrēzōn*), rather than to the board of incoming *tagoi* who may well have been responsible for exacting the fines from their predecessors.[46]

The involvement of a volunteer prosecutor seems also to have been envisaged in *SEG* 50.1195, lines 32–38, from third-century Cyme, in connection with the enforcement of a provision that prohibits the sale or hypothecation of arms donated by Philetaerus to the city. Anyone who wishes (*ho thelōn*) is invited to apprehend the person involved in such a sale or hypothecation and to bring him before the board of *phularchoi* ("tribal officials"). If the person apprehended denies his guilt, the *phularchoi* are to decide the case (*krinet[ō]san*), most likely with the denunciator stating the case against the defendant. In this case, the involvement of the volunteer does not in itself indicate a type of process that we might associate with democratic justice, not least because the personnel judging the merits of the objection were also directly responsible for receiving the denunciation and for exacting the penalty if they found against him.[47]

A similar process of judgment, in which the very same officials authorized to impose the penalty are also to decide any subsequent dispute with the person fined, appears to have been envisaged in *IK Erythrai und Klazomenai* II 510 from third-century Clazomenae. Here the personnel in charge of policing a land-leasing contract, with authorization to impose a fine on a contractor defaulting on his rent and to expel him from the land, were also in charge of the process of *epikrisis*, in case the contractor objected to their decision.[48] Such a setup very likely made the position of the defendant more precarious than if he had been entitled to be judged by an independent body. However, before this procedure is dismissed as mere window dressing, along with the procedure prescribed in *SEG* 50.1195, it should be taken into consideration that such hearings may still have limited the scope for abuse of the summary powers bestowed on *individual* members of the boards in question. An individual member of a board, if acting alone, might be tempted to abuse his summary powers for his own private and illegitimate ends (for example, by pocketing the rent paid by the tenant). His colleagues, however, would have a personal interest in preventing this, not least if the board was held collectively liable for offenses committed by its individual members.[49] The opportunity for the person fined to present his objections before the board in its entirety may have gone some way toward addressing the problem, and it may therefore have constituted a significant deterrent against malpractice and embezzlement. That having been said, it is hardly a coincidence that most attested procedures dealing with objections to summary fines involved an outside third party, be it a council, an assembly, or a regular court. What is more, in some cases stipulations to the effect that the case itself was to be processed and introduced by a different board provided a further check on the officials' power.[50]

In those cases where enactments explicitly provided for a procedure by which a summary penalty might be reversed as a result of a legal hearing before a third party, it might be objected that these should not really be counted as examples of summary justice. For it might be assumed that most offenders would have had an obvious incentive to insist on a hearing, rather than simply accepting the officials' decision and paying the fine without any further ado. Yet, in many instances the choice available to the putative offender was not necessarily an easy one, because many such provisions for appeal attached a tangible financial risk to a defendant's objection. If they simply refused to pay the fine in the hope that a subsequent legal hearing might result in the penalty being annulled, they risked facing the additional penalty of the *hemiolion* or of a doubling of the original penalty, if the judgment went against them.[51] At Beroea, a person who objected to a summary fine imposed by the gymnasiarch almost certainly faced the loss of court deposits, if the court ruled in favor of the gymnasiarch,[52] and would possibly also have been required to pay the *hemiolion* that would otherwise have been imposed on the gymnasiarch if the latter had been found to have punished without justification. Likewise, it is probable that an individual who objected to the imposition of a summary fine by the *neōpoiai* in third-century Samos (*IG* XII.6 169, lines 25–34) would have been required to deposit the salary payable to the court, in the same way (κατὰ ταὐ[τά]) as was prescribed in disputes between private individuals and those authorized to trade in the sanctuary. In these and several other cases, the person fined would have had to weigh the financial risks very carefully against the chances of success in a hearing, before challenging the officials' decision.

Despite the variations discernible in the material discussed so far, the structural similarities do suggest that the procedural measures by which individual communities attempted to combine the advantages of granting penal authority to officials with measures that served to limit the scope for potential abuse may be characterized as "Greek." However, more compelling as an argument in favor of "Greek law" as a viable analytical concept is a well-attested alternative procedure by which a summary fine might be contested and reversed:

the oath. The use of the oath as a definitive means of settling a legal dispute is often regarded as a phenomenon mainly of the archaic and early classical periods. Nevertheless, its association with summary justice seems to have been not only remarkably consistent across different regions but also remarkably durable.

In many attested cases, the oath is designated *exōmosia* ("oath of disclaimer"). The term is well known from classical Athens. There it is normally associated with an oath by which a person would be able to absolve himself from a duty that had been imposed on him, or that he had assumed voluntarily, without incurring the penalty that would otherwise have resulted from his failure to carry it out. This basic application is also apparent in some of the non-Athenian material. In the examples that will be discussed here, the oath is prescribed as a means of deciding a question of fact, which in turn will release the swearer from the penalty that would otherwise have been imposed and exacted from him. To mention but a few examples: In the Labyadae inscription from fifth- or fourth-century Delphi, *CID* I 9.D, lines 2–24 = *RO* 1, fines are prescribed against anyone who acts in breach of certain regulations pertaining to a number of festivals, but if an offender objects to an imposed fine, release can be gained by swearing the customary oath of *exōmosia*.[53] In *LSAM* 45 = *SEG* 15.677 from fourth-century Miletus, an individual worshipper who fails to pay the priestess of Artemis her share as prescribed will incur a summary fine and be registered as a debtor; however, if he or she swears an oath of *exōmosia* before the *boulē* to the effect either that he has not sacrificed or that he has provided the priestess with her portion (*gerea*), the penalty will be reversed.[54] *FD* III.3 238, lines 16–19 = *LSCG Suppl.* 44 (from second-century Delphi), obliges young men to participate in the torch-races if selected by the *hagemones* ("leaders") and imposes a fine of ten silver staters on anyone who refuses to take part as prescribed. However, if the contestant asserts by means of an *exōmosia* that he is either unable (*adunatos*) to participate or outside the relevant age bracket (*presbuteros*), he will escape the fine and another contestant must be registered in his place.[55] In the gymnasiarchal law of Beroea, a man selected by the gymnasiarch to act as a judge in the contest of *euexia* ("bodily vigor") will incur a summary fine of ten drachmas unless he declares himself unable (*adunatos*) to comply by swearing the *exōmosia*, and this also applies to the boy or youth who has been appointed *lampadarchēs* ("leader of the torch-race") by the gymnasiarch.[56]

Common to several of the attested examples is the fact that the oath was the only prescribed procedural means by which an individual who had taken on a contractual obligation or who had been selected for a particular task would be able to avoid a summary fine for noncompliance. In these cases it appears that the *exōmosia* effectively functioned as an alternative to a legal hearing by which a summary penalty might be appealed. Thus, while the aforementioned regulations from Delphi and Beroea grant a release from the summary fine to the person swearing to be *adunatos*, the elected financial administrators of the foundation of Aristomenes and Psylla in second-century Corcyra were required to submit to a decision by the council and assembly, if they declared that they had been unable to carry out their duties as prescribed and that they were therefore not liable to the fine.[57]

A similar contrast can be drawn between, on the one hand, a third-century Euboean enactment pertaining to contractors who have agreed to compete in a number of festivals on the island (*IG* XII.9 207 + p. 178, lines 52–54 = Le Guen 2001, no. 1) and, on the other, a second-century regulation passed by the Association (*koinon*) of Dionysian Artists in Ionia and the Hellespont (*IK Iasos* 152 = Le Guen 2001, no. 53). The former prescribes summary penalties to be imposed on artists who fail to honor their contractual obligations in a polis belonging to the Euboean confederacy. However, the enactment permits the oath of *exōmosia*, by which a defaulting contractor may escape the fine if he asserts that he had been prevented from participating for legitimate reasons.[58]

The latter, *IK Iasos* 152 = Le Guen 2001, no. 53, likewise imposes summary fines—in this instance payable to the *koinon* of Dionysian artists—on members who have been selected to perform for free at the Dionysia in Iasos and who have failed to comply.[59] In this enactment, however, there is no provision that permits an artist from stating formally in an oath of *exōmosia* that he or she had been legitimately prevented. Instead, it provides that an artist must make a case before the assembled *koinon* if claiming that the absence had been due to illness or bad weather and justifies release from the penalty. The assembly will in turn decide the case by a vote, based upon a rational assessment of the evidence provided by the artist during the hearing.[60]

Yet, the application of the *exōmosia* at Euboea should not be interpreted simply as a relic from an earlier age, a relic that had been kept merely as a concession to tradition. In lines 61–62 of the Euboean enactment, a retroactive clause makes the oath of *exōmosia* available also to those contractors who have incurred penalties before the passing of the present law, stating explicitly that they may be released from the earlier penalties by this means.[61] This may be taken to suggest that the *exōmosia* had so far not been available to contestants fined for breach of contract in each individual member state of the Euboean confederacy, and therefore that the introduction of the *exōmosia* as a means of reversing such summary penalties was an innovation in this context. Even if the clause was based upon existing practice as it may have prevailed in each of the participating poleis, its introduction in the present enactment was evidently the result of a conscious and rational decision on the part of those who had framed the law.

The text does not indicate which procedure, if any, the *exōmosia* had replaced, let alone what may have motivated the Euboeans to introduce or extend its application. It is possible that the *exōmosia* was provided as a means of obtaining release from summary penalties because the enactment itself was concerned mainly with the organization of a number of important religious festivals. It is certainly the case that the classical and Hellenistic examples of the use of the oath in connection with summary fines are found most frequently in enactments and contracts that concerned religious ritual (including festivals and sacrifices) or the administration of sanctuaries (including the cultivation of sacred land). It is conceivable that a certain degree of conservatism in these areas of legislation may have contributed to the survival of the oath as a means of establishing a particular fact, which would then lead to a definitive settlement of any controversy arising from the imposition of the summary fine.

Even so, one should not overlook the fact that there sometimes seem to have also been sound, practical reasons for definitively settling questions of fact by means of a formal oath. For example, if a dispute turned on whether or not a summary fine should be imposed because a bereaved family had exceeded the restrictions on grave goods when burying their deceased relative, the *exōmosia*, as prescribed in a set of Delphian funerary regulations, seems an eminently sensible alternative to actually digging up the corpse.[62] Likewise, it may well have been perceived as an almost impossible task to establish on the basis of reliable evidence whether a tenant farmer should incur a summary fine for not having applied the quantity of manure as specified in his contract. Thus, the use of the oath to settle that question in *IG* XII.7 62, lines 22–25 = *RO* 59, which pertains to the leasing of sacred land in fourth-century Arkesine, may have been conceived of first and foremost as a realistic and satisfactory alternative to a formal hearing.

Indeed, the application of the oath in these and other, similar situations as a very practical measure where facts could not easily be established may have contributed to its survival throughout the Hellenistic period and beyond. To be sure, there is Hellenistic evidence that points to an awareness that the oath itself might be abused, just as it is the case for fourth-century Athens.[63] Thus, the second-century gymnasiarchal law of Beroea envisages a situation where a person, wishing to be released from his duty as *lampadarchēs* without having to pay the penalty of fifty drachmas, is exposed (*elenchtheis*) by the gymnasiarch and the youths of the *gymnasion* as having misused the *exōmosia*.[64] In this case, he will have to pay the fifty-drachma fine and discharge his duties as *lampadarchēs* as instructed—this, in effect, means that his sworn statement can be overturned if the gymnasiarch so decides. It is nevertheless striking that the Beroean law prescribes a countermeasure to be applied if the swearer is suspected of having sworn the oath falsely, rather than abandoning the use of the *exōmosia* altogether.

If a certain degree of conservatism may have contributed to the survival of the oath as a formal means of dispute settlement, particularly in legislative areas pertaining directly or indirectly to religious ritual, festivals, and the administration of sanctuaries, this does not in itself make it less relevant to the question of Greek law more broadly defined. A considerable proportion of the epigraphical evidence for legal procedures and institutions in the Greek world outside Athens relates to festivals, leases of sacred land, sacrificial rituals, foundations, and temple administration. The connection between Greek legal systems in their various manifestations and religious ritual and practice, including the use of the oath, represents an area where much research remains to be done, especially for the third and second centuries and later. Such investigations are likely to add further evidence that may inform the debate not only on phenomena that may point to important continuity over time, but also on the question of the unity of Greek law as it operated in communities that in other respects, not least ideological and constitutional, may have differed significantly from each other. It is to this question that I shall now return, in the hope of offering some conclusions on the basis of the material which I have surveyed so far.

Most of the evidence for the use of summary penalties in the classical and Hellenistic periods that I have been able to identify does not suggest that there was a firm connection between summary justice, administered by polis officials and sanctuary personnel, and particular types of political constitution. Although it might have been expected that the penal authority granted to such officials would have constituted a preferred alternative to mandatory and adversarial legal hearings in nondemocratic jurisdictions, the evidence does not seem to point to such a constitutional link. Rather, a case can be made in favor of seeing the decision to grant summary penal powers to officials as primarily a practical measure, adopted by democratic and nondemocratic communities alike, in areas where volunteer prosecution or prosecution by officials would not have been perceived as a realistic method of ensuring enforcement of the community's laws and regulations.

There is currently a broad consensus—though not by any means unanimity—among modern scholars that wherever a Greek community relied mainly on volunteers to initiate legal actions against alleged offenders, there was a risk that the actual enforcement of the laws would be uneven and patchy. This is likely to have been the case not least when the victim of a crime was the community as a whole rather than a specific individual or group of individuals. If the initiative to launch a prosecution for a specific offense rested with the volunteer, a lawbreaker with a high political profile and numerous resourceful enemies could, *ceteris paribus*, expect to be exposed to a higher risk of denunciation than the one who lived in relative obscurity and had managed to stay on good terms with his community. In some types of legislation, not least enactments targeting political offenses at a high level, volunteer prosecution may nevertheless have been perceived as broadly satisfactory. Political rivalry and personal enmity combined with the potentially high level of publicity surrounding, for instance, an act of treason or an unlawful decree proposal may have been seen as providing sufficiently strong incentives for capable volunteer prosecutors to step forward.

In other areas of legislation, however, the incentives may not have been perceived as strong enough for this mechanism to work with a tolerable level of efficiency. There, the unreliability of a process of law enforcement that depended primarily on individual initiative may have been seen as far more of a problem. For it was not only high-profile crimes committed by high-profile individuals that could be potentially detrimental to the community as a whole: less spectacular offenses committed by people who did not enjoy a place in the limelight could still, cumulatively, have very unfortunate consequences for the collectivity. One did not have to be a prominent citizen with equally prominent and ambitious enemies in order to dump rubbish in public places, pollute the water supply, or let one's goats destroy a sacred grove. Likewise, as far as control of the marketplace is concerned, the threat of volunteer prosecution may not have been seen as providing a satisfactory level of deterrence for the regulations to be respected. Markets and trading were not the preserve of permanent residents in the community, let alone of high-profile citizens, but often attracted people from beyond the local area. The incentives for a volunteer to go to the trouble and risk of initiating a prosecution against a foreigner or small-scale citizen trader were very likely quite low.

In his discussion of the mechanisms of law enforcement in classical Athens, Harris draws attention precisely to the marketplace and other public spaces, and to the army, as areas controlled by legislation in which various Athenian officials appear to have been given an important role in the initiation of law enforcement procedures.[65] In some of the examples discussed by Harris, the Athenian officials concerned very clearly had powers to impose penalties summarily. In other instances, however, their authorization appears mainly to have been that of initiating prosecutions in response to particular offenses committed within their area of jurisdiction.

As I have argued earlier in this chapter, it is often difficult to distinguish between the two on the basis of the epigraphical material, and this observation applies both to the Athenian and to the non-Athenian evidence. Yet the distinction itself is important. If an enactment instructed—and sometimes even compelled—officials to initiate legal actions against offenders within their own areas of jurisdiction, this may have helped to reduce the unevenness in the actual enforcement of the laws, inconsistency which might otherwise have presented a serious problem if the decision to prosecute had been left entirely in the hands of volunteers. Nevertheless, the mandatory referral of such cases for a hearing before a third party, be it a court, a council, an assembly, or even another board of officials, would still have provided a significant check on the officials' powers. And it is precisely this restriction of the officials' penal authority which is normally assumed to have been an important priority in democratic systems such as the Athenian one.

Granting officials the power to impose summary penalties that could subsequently be executed *without* a prior legal hearing is quite a different matter. This is true even in those cases where the legislation did offer procedures by which the penalty might be contested and ultimately reversed. As mentioned earlier, it seems frequently to have been the case that to refuse to abide by the officials' decision to impose the sanction meant exposing oneself to a financial risk (often in the form of the *hemiolion* or the doubling of the fine, sometimes coupled with court fees and deposits), if the case was referred to a legal hearing and the ruling went against you. Where such deterrents applied, the scope for the officials' abuse of their penal authority would have been considerably increased. Individual officials may have faced a greater temptation not only to abuse their power against their personal enemies,[66] but also to embezzle the money instead of passing it on to the appropriate treasury in those cases where they themselves were authorized to exact the fines. It must be noted here that such abuse on the part of the city's officials would almost certainly have been perceived as undesirable not only in communities that chose to label themselves as *dēmokratiai*, but also in those with more narrowly based political constitutions.

Yet, despite these dangers, numerous Greek communities, democratic and nondemocratic alike, bestowed this type of summary power on their officials in a variety of contexts, without requiring that each of their individual penal decisions be subjected to a legal hearing and confirmed by a verdict before execution. There may be several reasons why different Greek communities, regardless of constitution, were prepared to tolerate this risk. Some of these reasons were most likely practical rather than ideological.

In the non-Athenian epigraphical material, the evidence for summary justice dispensed by officials recurs with considerable frequency in enactments devised to keep public mass gatherings under control,[67] to protect the physical infrastructure of the polis and its sanctuaries,[68] and to maintain order in the agora.[69] This is hardly a coincidence.

As far as political and religious mass gatherings are concerned, these are likely to have presented real practical problems of safety even in very small poleis, not least when combined with the consumption of alcohol in connection with certain festivals. In this area, summary justice dispensed by officials is well attested, probably for good reasons, one of which was its speed of implementation. Moreover, the officials' authorization to issue summary fines may in itself have served an important symbolic purpose, not unlike their carrying a whip or a staff (*rhabdos*) which, as highlighted by Bresson,[70] sometimes served as a physical symbol of the officials' coercive powers.[71] For example, if a fistfight broke out between two or more participants, the threat of prosecution and trial, whether initiated by a volunteer or by an official, would not necessarily have constituted an adequate deterrent that could prevent a trivial brawl from turning into something far more serious and destructive. Often the boards of officials who had the duty to keep the gatherings under control were instructed to prevent (*kōluein*) disorderly behavior, or to force (*anagkazein*) or order (*keleuein*) the participants to act in accordance with their instructions. If, on encountering participants who refused to comply, the officials were permitted only to scribble down a summons on a piece of papyrus and wave it at the offender, it is unlikely that they would have been able to keep order in an efficient way. The main deterrent against unruly behavior in such situations may have been not the actual sanction as specified in a piece of legislation as much as the physical presence of officials who were empowered to issue penalties on the spot. And it is highly likely that the participants' compliance with their instructions depended to a significant extent on the respect generated precisely by the officials' penal authority. This is likely, also, to have been the reason why the Andrians bestowed summary penal powers on selected members of their delegation to Delphi (*CID* I 7): the physical absence of the delegation from the polis's legal institutions and officials probably made this deterrent desirable.

This consideration may also explain the permission given to officials to impose summary fines for deliberate attempts to undermine their authority while they were exercising their official duties. Thus a list of fines from fourth-century Pordoselene/Nasos (*IK Adramytteion* 36) lists two summary penalties imposed by the board of *basileis* (a board of high-ranking officials) and the *agoranomos*, respectively: the former on a person who had used abusive language (*kak[ōs ei]pe*; B, lines 14–21) against an official ([*to]n archonta*) during a festival; the latter on a man who apparently had used abusive language against the *agoranomos* in the agora (A, lines 18–21).[72] Parallels to this can be found not only in classical Athens (with the case of the "unruly soldier" in Lysias 9 being among the more famous examples),[73] but also, for example, in the gymnasiarchal law of Beroea.[74]

As for small-scale offenses committed by traders in the agora—as well as the type of low-level destructive behavior that, if unchecked, could cause significant damage to streets, buildings, water supply, and vegetation—summary penalties make practical sense not only because of the speed with which they could be imposed, but also for reasons of economy. Often an individual offense would not have been on a scale that would have made the full extent of a proper prosecution and court hearing a viable proposition. Even where the unsuccessful litigant, whether prosecutor or defendant, was required to pay the salary of the judges manning the court,[75] the courts' time was still a limited resource. If the offense was a minor one, the resources needed for a court hearing may well have outweighed the potential benefits of a conviction, not least because a modest penalty was likely to have very little effect in terms of general deterrence. By contrast, summary justice, dispensed by officials, was not only swift but also cheap. Its financial and practical advantages were almost certainly as evident to those who passed laws in a democratic setting as to those who legislated in an aristocratic or oligarchic political context.

It is true that many of the attested penalties that could be imposed by officials and exacted without a prior legal hearing were on a rather modest scale. And so it could be argued that they do not in themselves challenge the fundamental notion that the imposition of sanctions was in principle the preserve of the popular courts, and that it was first and foremost the courts that were responsible for the actual process of law enforcement in democratically governed communities.

However, from the point of view of the vast majority of ordinary citizens, matters may have looked very different indeed. First, while a fine of, say, ten drachmas may have been an utterly trivial sum to someone among the wealthy citizens who populate the speeches of the Attic orators, such a sum may have represented a serious problem for those who eked out a living as small-scale traders or subsistence farmers. Second, the types of offense for which summary penalties appear frequently to have been imposed were precisely those which ordinary members of the community would have been most likely to commit when going about their daily business in the agora and in the streets, when grazing their flocks of goats and sheep, when performing their military duties, and when participating in communal religious and political activities. Their main personal encounter with the administration of penal justice in their community was more likely to have been in the guise of various officials who were empowered to impose penalties on the spot, rather than panels of judges deciding their cases in court, regardless of the form of government that was in place in their communities.

The attractiveness of summary justice in a variety of contexts did of course have to be balanced against the risk that an official might abuse his penal authority, as mentioned earlier. It is clear from a wide range of inscriptions that this type of behavior was indeed a cause for concern. However, the elaborate accounting procedures applied to officials in oligarchies as well as democracies may have been perceived as offering some protection against abuse, especially when combined with the permission granted to the person fined to formally challenge the justification for the penalty.

It is of course possible that different communities at different times varied in regard to the zeal with which they tried to balance the advantages of summary justice with its obvious drawbacks, and that democratic administrations of justice may have devised procedures of appeal and accounting that would have made it both easier and more affordable for ordinary people to challenge the officials' decisions. As mentioned earlier, the epigraphical evidence suggests that even oligarchic poleis took a keen interest in controlling this aspect of their officials' behavior, if only to ensure that fines were imposed as prescribed and did not end up in individual officials' private pockets. And just as the desire to control the officials' behavior may have been motivated more by pragmatic and financial considerations than by specific ideological concerns, so the permission granted to officials to punish without a prior legal hearing can readily be linked not to a particular form of government, but rather to particular areas of legislation where that kind of deterrent served an obvious practical purpose. Above all, the similarities in legal procedures and principles that can be identified in the classical and Hellenistic inscriptions discussed here provide a strong argument in favor of "Greek Law" as a meaningful analytical concept in modern debates on crime and punishment in the ancient Greek world.[76]

NOTES

1. See, e.g., *IK Erythrai und Klazomenai* I 2.A, lines 13–18 (Erythrae, first half of the fifth century). The enactment appears to have been concerned with legal actions directed against polis officials, and the fact that the property qualification is spelled out, along with prescriptions for the total size of the dicastic panel, may suggest that the prescriptions were not universally applicable across the entire Erythraean administration of justice but were specific to the particular type of legal action to which the enactment pertained.

2. Gagarin 2008: 67–74.

3. Fröhlich 2004.

4. Rubinstein 2003.

5. Harris 2007.

6. See, e.g., Rhodes 1981: 537–542.

7. *Corinth* 8.1 22: [hόρος?] | [hιερὸς?] | ἄσυλος. | μὲ καται|βασσκιέτο. ζαμίια· IIIIIII. All translations in this chapter are the author's.

8. For a general discussion of *praxis* clauses in inscriptions from outside Athens, see Rubinstein 2010.

9. On this inscription, see in particular Faraguna (2005), who argues that while the text cited on side A of the stele relates to the demarcation of Lophitis, sides B, C, and D are concerned with the sale of confiscated property by the Chian polis.

10. Koerner 1993, no. 62.A, lines 8–21: ἢν τίς τινα τῶν ὅρων τούτων ἢ ἐξέληι ἢ μεθέληι ἢ ἀφανέα ποιήσει ἐπ' ἀδικίηι τῆς πόλεως ἑκατὸν στατῆρας ὀφειλέτω, κάτιμος ἔστω· πρηξάντων δ' ὀροφύλακες· ἢν δὲ μὴ πρήξοισιν, αὐτοὶ ὀφειλόντων· πρηξάντων δ' οἱ πεντεκαίδεκα τὸς ὀροφύλακας· ἢν δὲ μὴ πρήξοισιν, ἐπαρῆι ἔστων.

11. Koerner 1993: 233–234: "Of the institutions that are mentioned in the inscription, only the King had the power to impose sanctions; the rest had only to collect the fines and thus had only the authority to enforce them (. . .) The inscription contains no information on the denunciation of the offender or on criminal procedure; nor is the recipient of the fine mentioned. However, this was certainly the polis" (author's translation).

12. I discuss some of this evidence in Rubinstein 2012: the relevant epigraphical material spans the entire period from the earliest archaic evidence to the mid-second century and beyond.

13. The inscription is regularly attributed to Erythrae by modern scholars, but the possibility that it was passed in Chios cannot be ruled out.

14. *IK Erythrai und Klazomenai* I 15: [κ]αὶ ἔρια ἵστ[ασθαι τοὺς ἐμπο]λέοντας ὅσα ἂ[ν ἕκαστος ἐμπο]λῆι, ἵστασθαι [δὲ ἀδόλως· ἢν δὲ] ἁμαρτάνηι ὀφε[ιλέτω δραχμὰς] εἴκοσι κατ' ἕκασ[τον τάλαντον·] πρηξάσθω δὲ ὁ ἀγορ[ανόμος· πω]λείτω δὲ μέχρι μεση[μβρίης.] ὑετίων δὲ μὴ ἐχφέρ[ειν. τῶν ἐ]πετέων προβάτων τ[οὺς ἐριοπώ]λας ἔρια μὴ πωλεῖν· ἢ[ν δὲ πωλῆι,] ζημιούσθω ὑπὸ τοῦ ἀ[γορανό]μου ἡμέρης ἑκάστης [δραχμαῖς] δύο. εἴρια μηδὲ γνά[φαλλα ἐκ πό]κου μὴ πωλεῖν τὸν ἔ[μπορον μη]δὲ τὸν μετάβολον μ[ηδενὶ ἄλλο]θεν μηδαμόθεν ἢ παρ[ά . . . . . .]λης· ἢν δέ που ἄλληι [πωλῆι?, στε]ρέσθω τῶν ἐρίων κ[αὶ ζημιού]σθω δραχμαῖς εἴκ[οσι καὶ πᾶ]σα ἀποκηρύσσετ[αι ὑπὸ πρυτά]νεων ἢ ἄλλως πω[λεομένη ἢ ἀπὸ] τοῦ ταλάντου [---] διὰ τινα [. . .]ν[---].

15. *IG* II² 1177, lines 12–17: ἐψηφίσθαι Πειραιεῦσιν, εἰάν τίς τι τούτων παρὰ ταῦτα ποεῖ ἐπιβολὴν ἐπ[ι]βαλόντα τὸν δήμαρχον εἰσάγει[ν] εἰσ τὸ δικαστήριον χρώμενον τοῖς νόμοις οἳ κεῖνται περὶ τούτων· ("Let it be decided by the demesmen of the Peiraieus that if anyone does any of this in contravention of this enactment, the demarch must bring him before a court after having imposed a penalty, applying the laws that are in force on these matters.")

16. See, e.g., Whitehead 1986: 396.

17. *IPArk* 3 = *RO* 60, lines 15–21: εἰ δ' ἄ[ν] τις ἐπισυνίστατοι ταῖς ἐσδόσεσι τῶν ἔργων ἢ λυμαίνητοι κατ᾽ εἰ δέ τινα τρόπον φθήρων, ζαμιόντω οἱ ἐσδοτῆρες, ὅσαι ἂν δέατοί σφεις ζαμίαι, καὶ ἀγκαρυσ[σόν]τω ἰν ἐπίκρισιν καὶ ἰναγόντω ἰν δικαστήριον τὸ γινόμενον τοῖ πλήθι τᾶς ζαμίαυ.

18. Thür and Taeuber 1994: 38–39.

19. Thür and Taeuber 1994: 32.

20. *IG* XII.4 1 304, lines 8–15: κα[ταβολὰς] δὲ ποησεῖται τοῦ εὐρέματος τρεῖς, τὰν μ[ὲν πρά]ταν ἐμ μηνὶ Καρνείωι τῶι ἐπὶ Χαρμίδα, τὰν δὲ δ[ευτέρα]ν ἐμ μηνὶ Γεραστίωι τῶι μετὰ μόναρχον Χαρμίδα[ν τὰν δ]ὲ τρίταν ἐμ μηνὶ Ἀλσείωι ἐπὶ τοῦ αὐτοῦ μον[άρχου· α]ἰ δέ κα μὴ καταβάληι τὰν καταβολὰν ἐν τῶι χρόν[ωι τῶι γ]εγραμμένωι ἀπογραψάντω αὐτὰν τοὶ ταμ[ίαι τοῖς] πράκτορσι πράξασθαι διπλάσιον. ("She must pay the price fetched at auction in three installments, the first in the month of Karneion during the year when Charmidas is *monarchos* [a high-ranking official], the second in the month of Gerastion in the year of Charmidas's successor as *monarchos*, and the third in the month Alseion in the office period of the same *monarchos*. If she does not pay her installment at the time specified in writing, let the treasurers register her with the collectors [*praktores*] for the collection of double the amount.")

21. Compare, e.g., a third-century regulation for the lease of land belonging to the sanctuary of the Muses in *I Thespies* 55, lines 17–24; *IG* VII 3073, lines 2–5 (the *naopoioi* ["temple officials"] are instructed to carry out *praxis* and to register the contractor as debtor only if they are unable to retrieve the money owed); *IG* XII 7 515, lines 37–39 (the *boulē* ["council"] is to register as a debtor a tenant who has failed to pay his *prokatabolē* ["installment"] on time and who has incurred a fine of 200 drachmas as a result); *ID* 503, lines 30–40 (if the *hieropoioi* declare themselves unable to exact arrears of *misthos* ["pay"] along with the *hemiolion*, they are to register the contractor and his guarantors as debtors); *IK Ilion* 5, lines 24–30 (the *agōnothetai* ["overseers of festivals"] have imposed a fine of one hundred drachmas on a contractor, Menecrates, son of Dionysius of Ilion, which they have declared themselves unable to exact. At that point they proceeded to register him formally as a debtor). For a brief general discussion of fines imposed in connection with building contracts in Epidauros, Delos, and Delphi, see Feyel 2006: 337–339.

22. *SEG* 33.1039 = *IK Kyme* 13.VI, lines 80–87: μηδενὶ δὲ ἐξέστω ξύλα κάειν μή[τε] ἐν τῷ ναῷ μήτε ἐν τῷ προνάῳ μηδὲ ἐν ταῖς στοαῖς ταῖς ἀνατιθεμέναις ὑπὸ Ἀρχίππης μηδὲ πίνακας μηδὲ ἄλλο ἀνάθεμα μηθὲν ἔστω ἐκ τῶν δοκῶν κρίμνα[σαι]. εἰ δὲ μή, κωλυέτωσαν τὸν τούτων τι ποιοῦντα ο[ἱ ἱ]ερονόμοι καὶ οἱ ἀγορανόμοι, [ᾧ] ἂν δύνωνται τρόπῳ, καὶ ζημιούτωσαν ἕως στα[τ]ήρων πέντε, ὄντες ἀνυπόδικ[οι], καὶ πραξάτωσαν τὴν ζημίαν ᾧ ἂν δύνωνται [τρ]ό[π]ῳ, καὶ τὰ διάφορα ταῦτα ὑπάρχειν εἰς τὴν ἐπισκευὴν τοῦ ἱεροῦ. ἐὰν δὲ μὴ δύνωνται πρᾶξαι, ἀναγραψάτωσαν, καὶ μηθὲν ἦσσον ὁ βουλόμενος τὸν τούτων τ[ι] ποιοῦντα κωλυέτω ἀζήμιο[ς]. ("It shall not be permitted for anyone to burn wood in the inner sanctuary or the front hall or the stoas dedicated by Archippe, or to hang pictures or any other votive from the beams. Otherwise, let the *hierono-moi* and the *agoranomoi* stop the person doing any of this in whichever way they can,

and let them fine him up to five staters without being subject to legal action, and exact the fine in whichever way they can, and this income is to be earmarked for the repair of the sanctuary. If they are unable to exact, they must register [the fine], and anyone who wishes is equally to stop, without the risk of a sanction, the person doing any of this.")

23. The law lists slaves, freedmen or their descendants, the physically impaired, prostitutes, those engaging in trades associated with the agora, as well as persons who were drunk or afflicted by madness. See Gauthier and Hatzopoulos 1993: 78–87, for a detailed commentary on this clause.

24. *EKM* 1.Beroia 1.B, lines 29–37: ἐὰν [δ]ξ τινα ὁ γυμνασίαρχος ἐάσῃ ἀλείφεσθαι τῶν διασαφουμένων εἰδώς, [ἢ] ἐνφανίζοντός τινος αὐτῶι καὶ παραδείξαντος, ἀποτινέτω δραχμὰς [χ]ιλίας· ἵνα δὲ καὶ εἰσπραχθῆι, δότω ὁ προσαγγέλλων ἀπογραφὴν τοῖς ἐξε[τ]ασταῖς τῆς πόλεως, οὗτοι δὲ παραγρα-ψάτωσαν τῶι πολιτικῶι πράκτορι. ἐ[ὰν] δὲ μὴ παραγράψωσιν, ἢ ὁ πράκτωρ μὴ πράξῃ, ἀποτινέτωσαν καὶ οὗτοι τὸ ἴσον [ἐπ]ίτιμον καὶ τῶι ἐγδικασαμένωι διδόσθω τὸ τρίτον μέρος. ἐὰν δὲ δοκῇ ἀδίκως [π]αραγεγράφθαι ὁ γυμνα-σίαρχος, ἐξέστω αὐτῶι ἀντείπαντι ἐν ἡμέραις [δ]έκα διακριθῆναι ἐπὶ τοῦ καθήκοντος δικαστηρίου.

25. *CID* I 7.B, lines 4–17: βολὲ δὲ τὸν πλεόντον ἐς Δελφὸ[ς] Ηελέσθο πέντ' ἄνδρας καὶ ὀρκοσάτο. σῖτον δὲ μὲ φερόντο ταύτες ὄνεκα τὲς ἀρχὲς. οἱ δὲ κύριοι ἔστων ζεμιῶσαι τὸν ἀκοσμέοντα μέχρι πέντε δραχ[μέ]ον ἑκάστες ἑμέρες· ὂν δ' ἂν [ζ]ημιόσοσι ἀπογ<ρ>αψάντον ἐν βολὲι. ("Let the council select five men from among those sailing to Delphi and administer an oath to them. They are not to receive an allowance for this office. They shall be authorized to impose a fine of up to five drachmas a day on the one who is acting in a disorderly fashion. They must register, in the council, the person whom they fine.")

26. *IK Rhod. Peraia* 201, lines 12–18: μὴ ἐξέσ[τω δὲ μ]ηθενὶ μηδὲ ποθαλ[οῦ]ν μηθὲν μήτε ποτὶ τὰν στέγαν μήτε ποτὶ τὰ [ἐπι]στύλια· εἰ δέ τίς κα π[ο]ῇ τι παρὰ τὰ γεγραμμένα, κωλυόντω α[ὐτὸ]ν ὅ τε ἱεροθύτας καὶ ὁ δαμόσιος καὶ ἄλλος ὁ χρῇζων τῶν συγ[δ]αμετᾶν· τὸν δὲ μὴ πιθόμενον καὶ ἀπογραφόντω ποτὶ τοὺς ἱ[ερο]ταμίας ὀφίλοντα ἐπίτιμον ἱερᾶς Ἀπόλλωνος δραχμὰς ἑκατό[ν, κα]ὶ ἀναιρεύντω τὰ ποθαλωθέντα.

27. Bresson 1991: 110.

28. Thür and Taeuber 1994: 38–40.

29. This is attested for fifth-century Athens (*IG* I³ 82, lines 24–28), where the *hieropoioi* who are responsible for keeping order during a *pompē* ("sacred procession") are authorized to impose penalties of up to fifty drachmas and to register the fines; if they deem that the offender is deserving of a more severe penalty, they must refer the case to a court. A similar function is entrusted to an elected board of *epimelētai* ("overseers") in *SEG* 30.61, from fourth-century Athens; here the indication of the maximum limit of the summary fine that they are allowed to impose has been lost. In *I.Oropos* 277, lines 9–17, from fourth-century Oropus, the priest of Amphiaraus's shrine is authorized to impose fines of up to five drachmas for offenses committed in the sanctuary and to decide disputes between individuals of up to three

drachmas. Cases involving more than those amounts are to be referred to a court. It seems most likely that this provision is to be applied in connection both with offenses that directly affected individual victims and with offenses that were committed against the sanctuary itself, if the latter were found to call for a penalty in excess of the five drachmas that the *hiereus* ("priest") could impose on his own authority. In *IG* XII *Suppl.* 150, lines 10–15 = *LSCG Suppl.* 83, from second- or first-century Astypalaea, the *prutaneis* may impose penalties up to a limit that seems to have been defined in relation to their office generally. If the conventional restoration of the text is accepted, they were obliged to refer the case to the *boulē* if they found that a heavier sanction was called for: εἰ δέ τίς κα πομπεύσας μὴ θύσηι τῶι Διονύσωι ἐν τῶι γεγραμμένωι χρόνωι, ἐναρόν τε αὐτῶι ἔστω καὶ οἱ πρυτάνεις ζαμιωσάντω αὐτόν, ὅσσωι κύριοί ἐντι, [ἢ εἰς βου]λὰν παραγόντω· ἁ δὲ βουλὰ ζαμιωσά[τω, ὅσσωι κυρία] ἐστί. ("If anyone who has participated in the procession does not sacrifice to Dionysus within the stipulated time limit, this shall occasion a curse on him, and let the *prutaneis* punish him with a fine of as much as they are authorized to impose or let them bring him before the *boulē*. The *boulē* shall punish him with a fine of as much as they are authorized to impose.")

30. See, e.g., *SEG* 33.1039, lines 84–87 (Cyme, second century), *CID* I 7 (Andros, fifth century), *IG* XII.5 569, lines 6–8 (Carthaea, third century), *IG* XII.5 647, lines 25–26 = *LSCG* 98 (Coresia, third century).

31. See, e.g., *CID* I 7.B, lines 10–15: οἱ δὲ κύριοι ἔστων ζεμιῶσαι τὸν ἀκοσμέοντα μέχρι πέντε δραχ[μέ]ον ἑκάστες ἐμέρες ("They shall be authorized to impose a fine of up to five drachmas a day on the one who is acting in a disorderly fashion"); *I.Oropos* 277, lines 10–11: ζημιούτω ὁ ἱερεὺς μέχρι πέντε δραχμέων κυρίως ("Let the priest impose a fine up to five drachmas authoritatively"); *IG* XII.5 569, lines 6–8: κύριος ἔστω ὁ ἐπιμ[ελ]ητὴς τὸν μὲν ἐλεύθερον ζημιῶν [ἄχρ]ι δέκα δραχμῶν, τοὺς δὲ π[αῖδα]ς τοὺ[ς ἐ]λευθέρους καὶ τοὺς οἰκέτας πληγαῖς κολάζων ("The overseer shall be authorized to impose a penalty of up to ten drachmas on a free man, and to punish free children and slaves with lashes"); *IG* XII.5 647, lines 25–26 = *LSCG* 98: ὃς δ' ἂμ μὴ παρῆι τῶν νεωτέρων δυνατὸς ὤν, κύριος ἔστω αὐτὸν ζημιῶν μέχρι δραχμῆς ("If any of the young men is not present, although he is able, the *gumnasiarchos* shall be authorized to fine him up to ten drachmas").

32. *SEG* 57.820 A, lines 1–7 (*cf. LSCG Suppl.* 64 = *Nouveaux choix d'inscriptions grecques* no. 19 = Pouilloux 1954: 371–378, no. 141): [- - - - -] μηδὲν ὁ ἀγορηνόμος περιοράτω τῆι [ἡ]μέρηι ἧι ἂν ἐχφέρωνται πρὶν τὴν ἐχφορὰν γενέσθαι· πενθικὸν δὲ μηδὲν ποείτω μηδεὶς ἐπὶ τοῖς ἀγαθοῖς ἀνδράσιν πλέον ἢ ἐν πέντε ἡμέραις· κηδεύειν δὲ μὴ ἐξέστω· εἰ δὲ μή, ἐνθυμιστὸν αὐτῶι ἔστω καὶ οἱ γυναικονόμοι καὶ οἱ ἄρχοντες καὶ οἱ πολέμαρχοι μὴ περιορώντων καὶ θωιῶντες καρτεροὶ ἔστων ἕκαστοι ταῖς θωαῖς ταῖς ἐκ τῶν νόμων· (". . . nor may the *agoranomos* allow it on the day when the dead are carried to the grave, before the *ekphora* has happened. No one must display mourning for the brave for more than a period of five days. It shall not be permitted to bury the dead [*sc.* with a private ceremony]. Otherwise, it shall weigh on his conscience, and the *gunaikonomoi* and the *archontes* and the

polemarchoi must not permit it, and each board shall be authorized to inflict the fines on the basis of the laws.") For a discussion of the text as a whole, see Fournier and Hamon 2007.

33. This is the interpretation adopted by, e.g., Bernhardt (2003: 266) and Frissone (2000: 132–133).

34. Hamon 2010: 312.

35. See, e.g., *IG* XII *Suppl.* 150 = *LSCG Suppl.* 83, cited n. 29, where the *prutaneis* are instructed to impose a penalty within the legal limit that applied to them generally (καὶ οἱ πρυτάνεις ζαμιωσάντω αὐτόν, ὅσσωι κύριοί ἐντι) or else refer the case to the *boulē*.

36. *SEG* 48.1037, lines 5–8: ζημιοῦσθαι δὲ αὐτοὺς καὶ ὑπὸ τῶν ἱεροποιῶν καὶ ὑπὸ τῆς βουλῆς καὶ ὑπὸ τῶν λοιπῶν ἀρχόντων τῆι ζημίαι ἧι ἑκάστη κυρία ἐστὶν ἡ ἀρχὴ ζημιοῦν.

37. Feyel and Prost 1998: 466–467.

38. *I.Oropos* 277, lines 10–11: ζημιούτω ὁ ἱερεὺς μέχρι πέντε δραχμέων κυρίως καὶ ἐνέχυρα λαμβανέτω τοῦ ἐζημιωμένου. Compare, e.g., *I.Scythiae Minoris* II.2 col. I, lines 19–20, from second- or first-century Tomoi, where the military officers (*hegemones*) are authorized to impose fines of up to ten *arguroi* (a unit of coinage) per day and to exact them in whichever way they can, without any risk of being subjected to a legal action.

39. Fröhlich 2004.

40. This interpretation of the immunity clause is suggested by, e.g., Feyel and Prost (1998: 467) in relation to *LSCG Suppl.* 53, lines 16–17; *ID* 502.A, line 12; and *ID* 509, lines 25–27, all from third-century Delos. However, it is probable that the immunity clause relates specifically to the process of *praxis* itself, and that its main purpose in these and other cases is to ensure that the officials who are responsible for collecting the fines will not be deterred by the risk of subsequent legal actions from using coercion when carrying out their duty. On this, see Rubinstein 2010: 200–203.

41. E.g., *EKM* 1.Beroia 1.B, lines 29–37 (ἀντειπεῖν); *SEG* 50.1195, lines 32–38 (ἀντιλέγειν); *IG* XII.6 169, lines 31–34 (ἀντειπεῖν); *EKM* 1.Beroia 1.B, lines 102–108 (ἐὰν δέ τις φήσῃ μὴ δικαίως ἐζημιῶσθαι); *IG* XII.6 172, lines 6–10 (ἐὰν δὲ ἀδίκως ἐζημιῶσθαι φῆι); *CID* I 9.A, lines 31–44 = *RO* 1 (ἀμφιλέγειν); *IG* XII *Suppl.* 348, lines 1–5 (ἂν δέ τι ἀμ[φ]ι[σβ]ητῆτ[αι]); *IK Erythrai und Klazomenai* II 510, lines 3–7 (ἐὰν δέ τι ἀμφισζβητῆται).

42. This appears to have been envisaged in *IG* IX.1² 706.A, lines 3–6, where the archon who expels a Narykaian envoy is liable to a fine of fifteen drachmas, but must pay double "if he is convicted in a legal action." On this clause, see Wilhelm (1984: 418–419), who draws attention to parallels in Plato's *Leg.* 762b and elsewhere for the principle "daß ein Vergehen härter bestraft wird, wenn sich der Schuldige nicht zu sofortiger Anerkennung seiner Straffälligkeit und Leistung der Buße versteht." A similar principle seems to have applied in McCabe, *Teos* 41, lines 66–69, where the *tamiai* who fail to comply with their obligation to lend money or to pay the teachers as prescribed incur a fine of 2,000 drachmas each, but double the amount if they are convicted in a legal action (cf. also lines 53–57, where a fine of 10,000 drachmas appears

to have been doubled if the person fined was subjected to trial and his culpability confirmed by a court). In *IG* IV²1 98, a contractor operating in Epidaurus, who had incurred a summary fine of 500 Alexandrian drachmas imposed by the *agōnothetēs* and the *hellanodikai* ("chief judges at the games"), and who had had 200 drachmas deducted from his pay (*misthos*), was either unable or unwilling to pay the remaining 300 drachmas. He was summoned before the *boulē*, who ruled that the fine had been correctly imposed (καὶ ἐπέκρινε αὐτὸν παρεόντα ἁ βουλὰ δικαίως ἐζαμιῶσθαι). The outcome of the legal process was not only that the contractor and his guarantor were obliged to pay the 300 drachmas outstanding, but also that the *hemiolion* was charged on that amount. As pointed out by Thür (2002: 331), the participle παρεόντα indicating the presence of the contractor during the hearing before the council makes sense only if it is assumed that he appeared as defendant, rather than as prosecutor.

43. This is what is argued by, among others, Thür and Taeuber (1994: 39–40). There are some instances where this cannot be determined with certainty. It remains a possibility that persons fined by the *neōpoiai* ("temple officials") for offenses in the Samian Heraeum (*IG* XII.6 169, lines 32–34) may have acted as plaintiffs and the *neōpoiai* as defendants; see, however, Thür and Taeuber 1978: 223, which maintains that it would have been the *neōpoiai* who acted as prosecutors. Some uncertainty also remains in connection with the clause in *IG* XII.6 172, lines 6–10, which provides an opportunity for a person to object to a fine imposed by the *prutaneis* for refusing to be seated with his *chiliastus* (a division of the citizen population) in the Samian assembly. Neither of the Samian enactments prescribe a penalty to be imposed on the officials, if the court rules that the fines have been imposed unjustifiably. This supports the view that it would have been the officials who initiated the subsequent legal actions. By contrast, a similar clause in the gymnasiarchal law of Beroea (*EKM* 1.Beroia 1.B, lines 102–108) prescribes that if the person objecting to a fine imposed by the gymnasiarch wins the legal action, the gymnasiarch is required not only to pay him the *hemiolion*, but also to pay the *epipempton* and *epidekaton*. The latter were presumably court deposits of twenty percent (the *epipempton*) and ten percent (the *epidekaton*), respectively, that had been paid by the person who had challenged his decision. This has led Gauthier and Hatzopoulos (1993: 136) to conclude that the gymnasiarch appeared as defendant rather than prosecutor.

44. Thür and Taeuber 1994: 38–40.

45. See Fröhlich (2004: 196–198). The conventional restoration of the clause is as follows: ἂν δέ τι ἀμ[φ]ι[σβ]ητῆτ[αι], [δικασάσθων οἱ] ἀπόλογοι παρὰ δικασταῖς αὐτοῖς· τὴν δὲ καταδίκ[η]ν [παραδόντων τ]ο[ῖ]ς ἐπιστάταις· οἱ δὲ ἐκπρηξάντων. ἂν δὲ μὴ ἐκπρήξωσι[ν, αὐτοὶ ὀφειλόντω]ν. ἂν δὲ οἱ ἀπόλογοι μὴ δικάσωνται ἢ μὴ παραδῶσιν τοῖς [ἐπιστάταις, ὑπ]όδικοι ἔστωσαν τοῖς εἰσι[οῦ]σιν ἀπολόγοις. ("If he has any objection, let the *apologoi* bring the case before a court on behalf of the *epistatai*. They must hand over the verdict to the *epistatai*. The latter must exact the penalty. If they do not exact it, they shall owe the fine themselves. If the *apologoi* do not bring the case before a court or do not hand over the verdict to the *epistatai*, they shall be held to account by the board of *apologoi* who succeed them.")

46. This may be suggested by the clause in *CID* I 9.C, lines 10–15, where the

tagoi are given responsibility for exacting the penalty from the person who offends against the *nomos* and for paying over half the fine to the individual who has successfully brought the prosecution.

47. *SEG* 50.1195, lines 36–38: αἱ δέ κε ἀντι]λέγωισ[ι] κρινέτ/[ω]σαν οἱ φύλαρχοι καὶ τὰν ζαμίαν πραξάσθωσαμ παρὰ τῶ ἐνόχω ἐόντος πρ[άξεος ἐοίσας ἐκ τῶν ὑ]παρχόντων καὶ τῶ σώματος κὰτ τὸν νόμον τὸν ὑβριστ[ή]ριον. ("If they object, let *phularchoi* judge and let them exact the fine from the person who is guilty, with *praxis* permitted both from the property and the person according to the law on outrage.")

48. *IK Erythrai und Klazomenai* II.510: ἐὰν δὲ μὴ [ἀπο]διδῶι [πάσας τὰς ἀπο]φορὰς ἐν τοῖς χρόνοις τοῖς εἰρημένοις, [τὸ διπλάσιον ἀ]ποτείσει, καὶ ἄπεισιν ἐκ τοῦ [χω]ρίου ἔ[χων ὅσα ἂν ἡμε]ῖς θέλωμεν· ἐὰν δέ τι ἀμφισζβητῆται, [τὴν κρίσιν ἐπ]ικρινούμεθ᾽ ἡμεῖς· ὁ δὲ μισθωσάμε[νος πρὸς ὅ] τι ἂν ἐκ κρίσεως γένηται, ἐγγυητὴν [δὲ παρέξει] ἀρεστὸν τοῖς μισθώσασιν· ("If he does not pay all the rents due by the deadlines stipulated, he shall pay double and he shall vacate the land, taking as much with him as we wish. If he has any objection, we shall decide the case. The tenant shall provide a guarantor acceptable to the lessors for the amount that may be payable as a result of the decision.") On the use of the term *epikrisis* in connection with fines imposed by officials, see Thür 2002: 330–332.

49. See Rubinstein 2012.

50. This is the case, e.g., in *IG* XII.6 169, lines 32–34, where the *exetastai* are to introduce cases over disputed fines, and probably also in *IG* XII *Suppl.* 348, mentioned above (p. 120), where it is possible that the *apologoi* may have taken on a dual role both as introducers and as prosecutors in cases referred to them by the *epistatai* (on this possibility, see the discussion in Fröhlich 2004: 197–198).

51. See the examples cited above n. 42.

52. See Gauthier and Hatzopoulos 1993: 136.

53. *CID* I 9.D, lines 2–24 = *RO* 1: α[ἰ] δέ κα ἀμφιλλέγηι τᾶς θωιάσιος, ἐξομόσας τὸν νό[μιμ]ον Ηόρκον λελύσθω. ("If he disputes the fine, he shall be released after he has sworn the customary oath of *exōmosia*.")

54. *LSAM* 45 = *SEG* 15.677: ὃς δ᾽ ἂν ἐκγραφῆι, εἰὰμ μὴ ἐξομόσει ἐν τῆι βολῆι, μὴ θῦσαι ἢ ἀποδοῦναι τὰ γέρεα τὰ γινόμενα, ὀφειλέτω τὴν ζημίην καὶ ἐκπραξάντων αὐτὸν οἱ πράκτορες κατὰ τὸν νόμον. ("If anyone is registered, if he does not swear an oath of *exōmosia* to the effect either that he has not made a sacrifice or that he has paid the due perquisites, he shall owe the fine and the *praktores* shall exact it from him according to the law.")

55. *FD* III.3 238, lines 16–19 = *LSCG Suppl.* 44: εἰ δέ τ[ις], τῶν ἀγεμόνων καταγραψάντων τοὺς ἐν ἁλικίαι, μὴ θέλοι πειθαρχεῖν δυνατὸς ὤν, πράκτιμο[ς ἔ]στω τῶι ἀγεμόνι καὶ τοῖς ἄλλοις λαμπαδισταῖς ἀ[ρ]γυρίου δέκα στατήρων ἰδίαι καὶ ἐν ταῖς ἱερ[ο]μηνίαις· εἰ δὲ φαίη ἀδύνατος εἶμεν ἢ πρεσβύτερος, ἐξομοσάσθω, οἱ δὲ ἀγεμόνες ἄλλον ἀντ᾽ αὐ[τ]οῦ καταγραψάντω· ("Once the *hagemones* have registered those in this age group, if anyone refuses to comply although he is able, he shall be subjected personally to *praxis* of a fine of ten silver staters by the *hagemōn* as well as by the *lampadistai* [participants in the torch race] even during the

sacred months. If he claims not to be able or to be too old, let him swear the oath of *exōmosia*, and let the *hagemones* register someone else in his place.")

56. *EKM* I.Beroia I.B, lines 48–54, 74–78 (second-century Beroea).

57. *IG* IX.1 694, lines 66–72: εἰ δὲ οἱ αἱρεθέντες ἐπὶ τὰν χείριξιν τοῦ ἀργυ-ρίου μὴ ποιήσαιέν τι τῶν γεγραμμένων, εἰ μὴ ἐκδανείσαιεν τὸ ἀργύριον κα-θὼς γέγραπται δυνατοὶ ἐόντες, ἀποτ<ε>ισάντω ἀργυρίου Κορινθίου μνᾶς τριάκοντα καὶ τὸ κεφάλαιον ὅ κα παραλάβ[ω]ντι παραδόντω, εἰ δὲ μή, δι-πλῆ ἀποτ<ε>ισάντω τὸ κεφάλαιον. περὶ δὲ τοῦ ἀδυνάτου βουλὰ καὶ ἁλία ἐπιγινωσκέτω. ("If those who have been elected to administer this money fail to carry out any of the tasks stipulated, if they do not lend the money as stipulated although they are able they shall pay thirty minas of Corinthian silver and they shall hand over the capital which they received; otherwise they shall pay double the amount of the capital. The council and assembly shall decide on the question of inability.")

58. *IG* XII.9 207 + p. 178, lines 52–54 = Le Guen 2001, no. 1: ὑπὲρ ἐξω[μ] οσιῶν· ἐξωμοσίαν δὲ εἶναι τοῖς τεχνίτα[ις] τοῖς λιποῦσί τι τῶν ἔργων αὐτοῖς παραγενομέν[οις ε]ἰς τὴν πόλιν οὗ ἂν λίπωσι τὸ ἔργον ἐντὸς τοῦ χειμῶνος ἐν ἐγμήνω[ι· π]ρ]ότερον δὲ μὴ εἶναι ἐξη<ι>ρῆσθαι· παρόντων τ[ῶν] διδόντων τὰ ἔργα· ἐὰν δέ τις τῶν τεχνιτῶν τῶν λαβόντων τὰ ἔργα ἐ[ν Ε]ὐβοίαι ἀγωνίζηται ἔν τινι πόλει ἐξ ἧς μὴ [ἔστιν αὐτῶι] παραγενέσθαι εἰς τοὺς χρόνους ἐν οἷς οἱ ἀγῶνές εἰσιν ἐν [Εὐ]βοίαι, γινέσθω αὐτῶι ἡ ἐξωμοσία. ("Concerning oaths of *exōmosia*. There shall be an oath of *exōmosia* for those contractors who have failed to honor their obligations if they personally present themselves in the polis where they failed to honor their obligations during the six months of winter. It shall not be possible to be released before that, with those who let the contracts being present. If any of the artists who have taken on contracts for work in Euboea competes in a polis from where it is not possible for him to be present at the dates when the contests take place in Euboea, the *exōmosia* shall be available to him.")

59. For a discussion of the penalty clause in this enactment, see Aneziri 2003: 194–195. She emphasizes that, in this instance, the individual artists selected to per-form had no contractual obligation toward the polis of Iasos, and that this is the rea-son why the penalty for nonattendance is imposed and exacted by the *koinon* rather than by the officials in charge of the festival organization at Iasos, which would otherwise have been the norm. For a different interpretation, see Velissaropoulos-Karakostas 2011: 401–402, which maintains that the artists selected for performance in Iasos will enter into a contractual relationship with the latter.

60. Cf. Aneziri 2003, no. D13.

61. *IG* XII.9 207 + p. 178, lines 52–54 = Le Guen 2001, no. 1: ἐὰν δέ τινες τῶν [πρό]τερον ἐζημιωμένων ἐν ταῖς πόλεσιν τεχνιτῶν πρὸ τοῦ τὸν νόμον κυρωθ[ῆναι βούλ]ωνται ἐργολαβεῖν τὸ Εὐβοϊκὸν ἔργον, εἶναι αὐτοῖς ὅταν παραγένωνται ἐξομοσαμένοις ἀφεῖσθαι τῶν πρότερον ζημ[ιῶν]. ("If any of those artists who have previously incurred fines before this law was ratified wish to take on Euboean contractual work, it shall be possible for them, when they present themselves, to be released from their previous penalties once they have sworn the oath of *exōmosia*.")

62. *CID* I 9.C, lines 19–29 = *RO* 1: Ηόδ' ὁ τεθμὸς πὲρ τῶν ἐντοφήιων· μὴ πλέον πέντε καὶ τριάκοντα δραχμ[ᾶ]ν ἐνθέμεν, μήτε πριάμενον μήτε Ϝοίκω· τὰν δὲ παχεῖαν χλαῖναν φαωτὰν εἶμεν. [α]ἰ δέ τι τούτων παρβάλλο[ι]το, ἀποτεισάτω πεντήκοντα δραχμάς, αἴ κα μὴ ἐξομόσηι ἐπὶ τῶι σάματι μὴ πλέον ἐνθέμεν. ("This is the law about grave goods. One must not inter items of a value above thirty drachmas, neither purchased nor supplied from the household. The thick cloak must be gray. If any of these stipulations are violated, the transgressor must pay fifty drachmas, unless he swears in an oath of *exōmosia* upon the grave to the effect that he has not interred more [than permitted].")

63. See, e.g., Dem. 19.123–127, in which Demosthenes alleges that Aeschines had persuaded his brother and a doctor to swear a false *exōmosia* to the effect that Aeschines was ill and therefore prevented from discharging his duties as an envoy elected by the assembly.

64. *EKM* 1.Beroia 1.B, lines 78–81: ἐὰν δὲ μὴ λαμπαδαρχῆι ἢ μὴ ἐξομόσηται, ἀποτινέτω ὁ αἱρεθεὶς δραχμὰς πεντήκοντα καὶ ὁμοίως ἀλειφέτω καὶ λαμπαδαρχείτω. ὡσαύτως δὲ καὶ ἐὰν ὁ ἐξομοσάμενος φανῇ μὴ δεόντως ὀμωμοκέναι, ἐλεγχθεὶς ὑπὸ τοῦ γυμνασιάρχου καὶ τῶν νέων, ἀποτινέτω δραχμὰς πεντήκοντα καὶ ὁμοίως ἀναγκαζέσθω τιθέναι τὸ ἄλειμμα καὶ λαμπαδαρχεῖν. ("If he does not serve as *lampadarchēs* nor swears an oath of *exōmosia*, the person elected must pay fifty drachmas and still supply the oil and serve as *lampadarchēs*. Likewise also if a person who has sworn the oath of *exōmosia* is exposed by the *gumnasiarchos* and the young men as having clearly sworn it inappropriately, he must pay fifty drachmas, and he shall still be compelled to provide the oil and serve as *lampadarchēs*.")

65. Harris 2007.

66. This complaint is made, famously, by the speaker of Lysias 9.10 in relation to a summary fine imposed on him by the board of generals. He alleges (9.7) that this was also the opinion of the *tamiai* with whom the generals registered the penalty, and that the *tamiai* decided (*ekrinan*) that the penalty should be regarded as invalid (*akuron*). The process by which the generals registered the fine with the *tamiai*, who were responsible for entering it formally as a debt to the treasury, bears a marked resemblance to the provisions in the gymnasiarchal law of Beroea (*EKM* 1.Beroia 1.B, lines 102–108): having decided not to exact the penalty themselves, the generals entered the penalty on a whitewashed board (*leukōma*) which they handed over to the *tamiai* (9.6) upon expiry of their office. The *tamiai* looked into the reason for the complaint (on the problems with this passage, see Todd 2007: 614) and concluded that the generals had abused their penal powers. Yet the speaker appears still to have been registered as owing the fine.

67. See, e.g., *IG* XII.9 189 = *LSCG* 92 = *RO* 73 (festival, Eretria, fourth century), *IG* XII.6 172 (assembly, Samos, third century), *IK Ilion* 52 (festival, Ilion, second century), *EKM* 1.Beroia 1 (gymnasium, Beroea, second century).

68. There are numerous examples: see, e.g., *IG* XII Suppl. 232 (sanctuary, Karthaia, third century); *OGIS* 483 = *SEG* 13.521 (streets, fountains etc., Pergamum, second century); *SEG* 42.785 = Duchêne, *La stèle du port, Études Thasiennes* XIV, Paris 1992 (Thasos, fifth century); see also *IK Byzantion* S3.A, lines 4–7 (Selymbria,

third century), in which a summary fine of 500 (?) drachmas appears to have been imposed by a board of *stratēgoi* ("military commanders") on a person who had either damaged or removed timber and doors belonging to a fortifying structure.

69. See, e.g., *ID* 509 (summary penalty is to be imposed on *ateleis* [persons granted tax exemption] who violate the general provisions of the law on sale of wood and wood products; Delos, third century), *IK Erythrai und Klazomenai* I.15 (Erythrae [?], fourth century), *IK Adramytteion* 36 (Pordoselene/Nasos, fourth century). In *IK Byzantion* S3.B, lines 2–5 (Selymbria, third century), a board of *agoranomoi* have imposed a fine of ten drachmas on a trader (or perhaps a fisherman) who, if the text has been restored correctly, has beaten up a rival and either appropriated or in some way damaged his wares.

70. Bresson 2008: 29–30.

71. In *IK Ilion* 52, the persons elected to keep order during the festival are authorized to punish disorderly participants with their *rhabdos* (there is no indication that they were allowed to use this only against unfree individuals or children), and to impose fines of a specified amount (which has not been preserved on the stone) on persons who refused to comply with their instructions. See further the discussion in Gauthier and Hatzopoulos 1993: 65–68.

72. The list of penalties explicitly identifies fines that had been imposed as the result of legal actions. However, some entries do not record that a legal hearing had taken place, but state only the fines themselves, the names of the persons fined, and the officials who had imposed them, as well as their stated reason for having done so. In such cases, the entries must relate to summary fines rather than to penalties imposed by a court or comparable institution.

73. See also Dem. 21.32–33, with MacDowell 1990: 250–252. MacDowell draws attention to a similar attestation in [Arist.] *Pr.* 952b28–32 and notes that although Aristotle may have had Athenian legislation in mind, his comment does not correspond exactly with Athenian legislation. Here it must be noted that Aristotle's remark may refer to a general principle that applied in the legislation of several different communities: ἔτι δὲ παραπλήσια τούτοις πολλὰ φαίνονται νενομοθετηκότες, οἷον καὶ ἐὰν μέν τις ἄρχοντα κακῶς εἴπῃ, μεγάλα τὰ ἐπιτίμια, ἐὰν δέ τις ἰδιώτην, οὐδέν. ("Moreover, they appear to have passed much legislation similar to this, including for example large penalties if anyone verbally abuses an official, but no penalty if anyone verbally abuses an ordinary citizen.") For a recent discussion of the protection offered to officials against verbal abuse by Athenian legislation, as well as reflections on the summary fine at issue in Lys. 9, see Todd 2007: 591–593.

74. *EKM* I.Beroia I.B, lines 39–41: μὴ ἐξέστω δὲ τὸν γυμνα[σί]αρχον ἐν τῶι γυμνασίωι κακῶς εἰπεῖν μηθενί, εἰ δὲ μή, ζημιούτω αὐτὸν δρα[χ]μαῖς πεντήκοντα. ("It shall not be permitted for anyone verbally to abuse the *gumnasiarchos* in the *gumnasion*; otherwise let the *gumnasiarchos* punish him with a fine of fifty drachmas.")

75. This was the case, e.g., in Samos (*IG* XII.6 169, lines 30–34) and in Delos (*ID* 509, lines 18–27). On the latter, see Vial 1984: 149–151.

76. I should like to express my gratitude to Leverhulme Trust for a research fel-

lowship (2004–2006), during which the empirical work on many of the inscriptions underpinning this article was carried out. I should also like to thank the two anonymous referees for their comments and suggestions, and above all Paula Perlman for her invitation to contribute to the present volume.

REFERENCES

Aneziri, Sophia. 2003. *Die Vereine der dionysischen Techniten im Kontext der hellenistischen Gesellschaft: Untersuchungen zur Geschichte, Organisation und Wirkung der hellenistischen Technitenvereine*. Stuttgart: Steiner.

Bernhardt, Rainer. 2003. *Luxuskritik und Aufwandsbeschränkungen in der griechischen Welt*. Stuttgart: Steiner.

Bresson, Alain. 1991. *Recueil des inscriptions de la Pérée Rhodienne, Pérée intégrée*. Paris: Les Belles Lettres.

———. 2008. *L'économie de la Grèce des cités*. Vol. 2, *Les espaces de l'échange*. Paris: Armand Colin.

Faraguna, Michele. 2005. "Terra pubblica e vendite di immobili confiscati a Chio nel V secolo a.C." *Dike* 8: 89–99.

Feyel, Christophe. 2006. *Les artisans dans les sanctuaires grecs aux époques classique et hellénistique à travers la documentation financière en Grèce*. Athens: École française d'Athènes.

Feyel, Christophe, and Francis Prost. 1998. "Un règlement délien." *Bulletin de correspondance hellénique* 122.2: 455–468.

Fournier, Julien, and Patrice Hamon. 2007. "Les orphelins de guerre de Thasos: Un nouveau fragment de la stèle des Braves (ca. 360–350 av. J.-C.)." *Bulletin de correspondance hellénique* 131.1: 309–381.

Frissone, Flavia. 2000. *Leggi e regolamenti funerari nel mondo greco*. Vol. 1, *Le fonti epigrafiche*. Galatina: Congedo.

Fröhlich, Pierre. 2004. *Les cités grecques et le contrôle des magistrats (IVe–Ier siècle avant J.-C.)*. Geneva: Droz.

Gagarin, Michael. 2008. *Writing Greek Law*. Cambridge: Cambridge University Press.

Gauthier, Philippe, and Miltiadis B. Hatzopoulos. 1993. *La loi gymnasiarchique de Beroia*. Athens: Centre de recherches de l'Antiquité grecque et romaine; Paris: de Boccard.

Gounaropoulou, Loukretia, and Miltiadis B. Hatzopoulos. 1998. *Epigraphes katô Makedonias: Metaxu tou Vermiou Orous kai tou Axoiou Potamou*. Vol. 1, *Epigraphes Veroias*. Athens: Hypourgeio Politismou, Ethnikon Hidryma Ereunōn; Paris: de Boccard.

Hamon, Patrice. 2010. "Études d'épigraphie thasienne, III: Un troisième fragment de la Stèle des Braves et le rôle des polémarques à Thasos." *Bulletin de correspondance hellénique* 134.1: 301–315.

Harris, Edward M. 2007. "Who Enforced the Law in Classical Athens?" In *Sym-

posion 2005: Vorträge ʒur griechischen und hellenistischen Rechtsgeschichte, edited by Eva Cantarella, 159–176. Vienna: Verlag der Österreichischen Akademie der Wissenschaften.

Koerner, Reinhard. 1993. *Inschriftliche Gesetʒestexte der frühen griechischen Polis: Aus dem Nachlass von Reinhard Koerner*. Edited by Klaus Hallof. Cologne: Böhlau.

Le Guen, Brigitte. 2001. *Les Associations de Technites dionysiaques à l'époque hellénistique*. 2 vols. Nancy: Association pour la diffusion de la recherches sur l'antiquité.

MacDowell, Douglas M. 1990. *Demosthenes, Against Meidias* (Oration 21). Oxford: Clarendon Press.

Pouilloux, Jean. 1954. *Recherches sur l'histoire et les cultes de Thasos*. Vol. 1, *De la fondation de la cité à 196 avant J.-C*. Paris: de Boccard.

Rhodes, Peter J. 1981. *A Commentary on the Aristotelian* Athenaion Politeia. Oxford: Oxford University Press.

Rubinstein, Lene. 2003. "Volunteer Prosecutors in the Greek World." *Dike* 6: 87–113.

———. 2010. "Praxis: The Enforcement of Penalties in the Late Classical and Early Hellenistic Periods." In *Symposion 2009: Vorträge ʒur griechischen und hellenistischen Rechtsgeschichte*, edited by Gerhard Thür, 193–215. Vienna: Verlag der Österreichischen Akademie der Wissenschaften.

———. 2012. "Individual and Collective Liabilities of Boards of Officials in the Late Classical and Early Hellenistic Periods." In *Symposion 2011: Vorträge ʒur griechischen und hellenistischen Rechtsgeschichte*, edited by Bernard Legras and Gerhard Thür, 329–354. Vienna: Verlag der Österreichischen Akademie der Wissenschaften.

Thür, Gerhard. 2002. "Entscheidung in Bausachen aus Kerkyra (IG IX 1², 4, 794)." *Zeitschrift der Savigny-Stiftung für Rechtsgeschichte, Romanistische Abteilung* 119: 326–339.

Thür, Gerhard, and Hans Taeuber. 1978. "Prozessrechtlicher Kommentar zur 'Krämerinschrift' aus Samos." *Anʒeiger der philosophisch-historischen Klasse, Österreichische Akademie der Wissenschaften* 115, Sonderheft 12: 205–225.

———. 1994. *Prozessrechtliche Inschriften der griechischen Poleis: Arkadien (IPArk)*. Vienna: Verlag der Österreichischen Akademie der Wissenschaften.

Todd, Stephen C. 2007. *A Commentary on Lysias, Speeches 1–11*. Oxford: Oxford University Press.

Velissaropoulos-Karakostas, Julie. 2011. *Droit grec d'Alexandre à Auguste (323 av. J.-C.–14 ap. J.-C.): Personnes, biens, justice*. 2 vols. Athens: Centre de recherches de l'Antiquité grecque et romaine; Paris: de Boccard.

Vial, Claude. 1984. *Délos indépendante (314–167 avant J.-C.): Étude d'une communauté civique et de ses institutions*. Athens: École française d'Athènes.

Whitehead, David. 1986. *The Demes of Attica, 508/7–ca. 250 BC: A Political and Social Study*. Princeton: Princeton University Press.

Wilhelm, Adolf. 1984. *Abhandlungen und Beiträge ʒur griechischen Inschriftenkunde*. Ser. 2, vol. 1, *In den Jahresheften des Österreichischen Archäologischen Institutes (1898–1948)*. Leipzig: Zentralantiquariat der Deutschen Demokratischen Republik.

8 / SOFT LAW IN ANCIENT GREECE?

Julie Velissaropoulos-Karakostas

THE GENERAL THEME OF THIS BOOK, "ANCIENT GREEK LAW in the 21st Century," may be viewed from a variety of perspectives: for example, the incorporation of ancient Greek law in modern university curricula and its usefulness; the state of modern research on ancient Greek law; the question whether access to and use of primary sources, especially papyri and inscriptions, are essential; and the ways in which ancient Greek law could be made more attractive to young, or not so young, practitioners of law. The topic I set out to present, "soft law" in ancient Greece, falls under the last heading, which focuses on how the research scholar, in performing the role of a university teacher, can draw ancient Greek law into public view in a modern space, thus improving its "visit-ability."

For the historians of ancient Greece, this process is far less burdened with the dangers of anachronism. For example, in the field of economics, even if the teacher draws a parallel between economic crises in the ancient world and the economic predicaments of modern states, it is unlikely that any historian would seek in antiquity an equivalent of the International Monetary Fund. For legal scholars, however, the ground is slippery. Reliant upon contemporary legal terminology, we often do not even ask ourselves whether and to what extent ancient Greek terms, such as *echein kai kratein* or *kurieuein*, can be accurately rendered with modern terms such as "ownership" and "property" or, even more so, with their Latin equivalents *proprietas* and *dominium*.

Besides the fact that modern legal terms are not always suitable to render legal relationships and conditions encountered in antiquity, the modern legal scholar engaged in the study of ancient Greek law is also faced with a pleasant—at least for some of us—surprise. As modern European legal regimes move away from some of the imperatives of Roman law, ancient Greek law becomes more relevant.[1] In the case of the above-mentioned concept of ownership, the acknowledgement of inherent restrictions to the rights of the owner for the benefit of common use brings modern ownership closer to the ancient Greek concept of property than to the *proprietas* or *dominium* of classical Roman law. Even the modern propensity to absorb contract law into the mainstream of tort law[2]—which is unthinkable in the context of the contradistinction between tort and contract, whether in its original Roman context or in more recent versions—allows us to recognize the parallel with the ancient Greek concept of *blabē* ("damage"), which constituted the common foundation of liability whether in tort or contract.[3]

I. SOFT VERSUS HARD LAW

Our modern inquiry into the possible existence in antiquity of soft law—that is, rules which do not originate in the legislative bodies authorized by the constitution to formulate and enact rules of law—forms part of a subconscious tendency to salvage ancient Greek law from relative obscurity. Traditionally associated with international law,[4] the notion of soft law appears with increasing frequency in domestic legal regimes as well as in the context of the European Union. The concept of soft law comprises quasi-legal instruments, such as guidelines, codes of conduct, codes of practice, declarations, and recommendations. As Anna di Robilant points out:

> In its broadest scope, the formula "soft law" labels those regulatory instruments and mechanisms of governance that, while implicating some kind of normative commitment, do not rely on binding rules or on a regime of formal sanctions. First developed in the sphere of public international law, the formula has spread to other fields, becoming a buzzword in the professional vocabulary of private international lawyers, E.U. lawyers and sociologists of law. The notion of soft law reflects two major trends in the globalization of law: the striking multiplication of producers of law and, in turn, of bodies of law and the privatization of legal regimes.[5]

Opponents of the very notion of soft law claim that both the fact that it does not originate in state legislative bodies and the lack of sanctions attendant upon its violation preclude its classification as law. Proponents of soft law counter this argument by asking why we obey laws, while only persons we would regard as defiant have to be coerced to conform to its commands.[6] Do we obey because of the penalties it imposes, or because of the fear generated by these impending penalties, the threat they pose, or the sense of shame and guilt these penalties are capable of arousing? In short, do we obey laws because of the *emotions* they trigger? The answer is only partly yes. Most laws and the relevant jurisprudence are respected even though their intended subjects are not fully aware of their existence and content. Furthermore, the authority of a law does not derive exclusively from its enforceability or the penalties it imposes, which, in any case, are not the sole criteria for the classification of a rule as law. The fact that the violation of a rule does not entail sanctions cannot mean that compliance with the rule is not intended or expected. International regulations on genetically modified products and many of the regulations on the protection of the environment are common examples of rules without sanctions.

The contemporary endeavor to harmonize the private law of European states has brought the soft- versus hard-law debate to the forefront of legal inquiry among European-law and comparative or private international lawyers, as well as legal sociologists and legal historians.[7] The quest for the historical origins of soft law has led some historians to the *lex mercatoria* (medieval "merchant" or "commercial law")[8] and others to late nineteenth- and early twentieth-century theories of social law and legal pluralism.[9]

The danger of anachronism inherent in the attempt to identify legal rules in ancient Greece that correspond to modern soft law, or even in seeking concepts analogous to legal pluralism or customary forms of law of the kind, breadth, and longevity of the *lex mercatoria*, is clear. Nevertheless, this is exactly what I wish to attempt, with the reservation that the object of my inquiry is not the construction of a genealogy of soft law, but rather the identification of related phenomena affirming the view of Gilmore that the development of institutions is not always linear.[10]

The *lex mercatoria* of the late Middle Ages and the Renaissance provides a good starting point. Some legal historians maintain that its origins should be traced to the Roman *ius gentium* ("law of nations" or "international law") and commercial practice in the context of the Roman Empire.[11] The Roman Empire, at least in its eastern, Greek-speaking part, having come into contact with the local populations, may have adopted pre-existing maritime practices applicable in commercial relations between different Aegean islands, including Rhodes. The only element of the so-called Rhodian maritime law that has come down to us—and this thanks to Roman jurists—is the practice of *iactus*, the jettison of cargo at sea in order to save the vessel, and the apportionment of damages to the shippers whose cargo was saved.[12] Demosthenes refers to the jettison of cargo and the contract of a maritime loan in his oration *Against Lacritus*,[13] without, however, associating them with the laws, customary or other, of a specific Greek city. It is plausible to assume that the rules of maritime law attributed by the Romans and later by the Byzantines[14] to the island of Rhodes, existed in the time of Demosthenes as customs but not as legal rules with specific origins.

On the one hand, customs and practices like those applied by Mediterranean merchants and navigators are certainly among the instruments of soft law; but on the other hand, soft laws are not necessarily customary regulations. Their common characteristics are, first, that they do not emerge from an official legislative body, and second, that they can be transformed into hard-law regulations.

It is generally accepted that soft laws are often unwritten rules that international powers follow; they become hard laws when a need arises for more effective enforcement. Some treaties negotiated during the Hellenistic period suggest that this was also true of international relations among the Greeks. Written agreements contracted by the parties were preceded by negotiations in good faith with the expectation that the commitments would be respected or that they would be transformed into written hard law. The *homologia* ("agreement"), or meeting of the minds, that resulted from the preliminary phase in negotiating an international treaty, although not binding in a strict legal sense, carried strong political weight. In order to provide more effective enforcement, the international *homologia* had to be formulated as a decree and approved by the assemblies of the interested parties. In other words, in order to be fully binding, the commitments included in an international *homologia* had to be transformed into hard-law regulations.[15]

2. MOST JUST JUDGMENT

I think no one would seriously doubt that in fifth- and fourth-century Athens and the cities that followed its form of government, the only sources of law with legally binding force were the *nomoi* ("laws") and the *psēphismata* ("decrees"). An apparent deviation from the positivistic attitude of the Athenians is recognizable where there is a gap in the law that required the judge to make a decision according to his "most just judgment" (*gnomē dikaiotatē*) or on the basis of his "own and true opinion" (*gnomē te heautou*).[16] The provision that individuals may be called upon to fill in the gaps in a law is to be found not only in the oath of Athenian jurors,[17] but also in the fourth-century oath of jurors at Eressus[18] and a fourth-century law of the Delphic Amphictyony from Athens.[19]

In the third and second centuries BCE, the expression "most just opinion" (*gnomē dikaiotatē*) or its equivalent is found in the oath of the Cnidian arbitrators who were called upon to settle a dispute between Temnos and Clazomenae;[20] in the oath of the gymnasiarchs from Beroea,[21] who, though deprived of adjudicatory jurisdiction, had powers of coercion; and in a heavily damaged honorary decree from Carystus, the reconstruction of which seems solidly founded.[22] Finally, we note the mention of "most just opinion" in the decree of Ptolemy Philadelphus, which was produced in 226 BCE before the court of Crocodilopolis.[23] This unique royal act introduces a hierarchy of rules of law, placing royal legislation at the very top of the pyramid, followed by civic laws (*politikoi nomoi*), which are probably customs that Greeks attribute to the legislation of a Greek city, and finally the most just opinion of the judge, should the first two categories be lacking.

The legal regimes of the Hellenistic kingdoms widened the range of producers of law by bestowing on judges and arbitrators the right to issue decisions and by granting officials such as gymnasiarchs and children's gymnastic trainers (*paidotribai*),[24] who had powers of coercion, the right to exact penalties. Even though this widening concerns only gaps in the pre-existing rules of law, the recourse to the "most just opinion" and not to the analogous application or the extensive interpretation of existing law remains significant. I believe it expresses the end of an era during which respect for the law (*nomos*) had to be declared by every means available, including the entrenchment of its monopolistic authority. This era begins in the late archaic period;[25] culminates in classical Athens, where it finds its most potent expression; and enters its final stage in the age of Alexander the Great (late fourth century), with the regions of the Greek world entering this phase at different times and with varying intensity.

3. CUSTOM

The question of the place of custom among the sources of law in ancient Greece is intertwined with the problem of the existence of soft law.[26] It appears that in classical Athens there was no scope for customary law, except in religious worship and, more importantly, in sea transport and navigation. Nevertheless, fourth-century authors were perfectly conscious of the fact that certain rules of law were not included in the written laws of the state. Plato holds that the unwritten legal rules (*agrapha nomima*) are not identical with the written statutes laid down by the ancestors,[27] while Aristotle acknowledges the existence of unwritten law and draws a distinction between laws (*nomima*) and customs (*ēthē*).[28] Demosthenes, for his part, distinguishes between *grapta nomima*, which are written laws, and *agrapha nomima*, which he equates with human customs.[29]

References to customary law become more frequent during the Hellenistic period; their applications include, among others, determination of the content of the judges' oath,[30] the location of display of honorary decrees,[31] and sacred sanctions enjoined by the priests and priestesses of Delian Apollo on those who abducted slaves with the intention to export them from the island.[32]

4. GLOBALIZATION AND SOFT LAW

Navigation and sea transport, where the development of customary law was favored, are activities involving both fellow and foreign citizens. I think this is the point where acceptance, even by fairly reluctant Europeans, of the notion of soft law intersects with acceptance by the ancient Greeks of sources of law outside state-generated rules of law. From the time of Alexander the Great, legal relations between citizens of different communities in the eastern Mediterranean are frequent, while, *mutatis mutandis*, a certain kind of "globalization" is reflected in fields such as the administration of justice, family law, and, to an even greater extent, contracts. This is the period when a legal *koinē*, as it has been named by the historians of Hellenistic law, is created, a phenomenon parallel and analogous to the development toward a common Greek dialect (*koinē* Greek). The intensification in the movement of persons and goods was the consequence not of economic change, or at least not exclusively, but rather of a shift in political and social thinking. It not only permitted but also rendered necessary the acceptance of sources of law that did not originate solely in rules of law created by the competent legislative bodies.

Contemporary legal literature on hard and soft law addresses how hard and soft law are used as alternatives, as well as how they can interact in complementary ways. Despite their differences, legal positivists, rationalists, and constructivists converge on the alternative use of hard and soft law and their bilateral, mutually complementary function.[33] In their recent study, Gregory Shaffer and Mark Pollack present a further aspect of this relation in the field of international law:

> . . . that international hard- and soft-law instruments (or, for that matter, any legal instruments that vary in their soft- and hard-law characteristics) serve not only as alternatives or complements, but often as antagonists. Hard and soft legal norms can be antagonistic in a conflict-of-laws sense.[34]

The contract for a loan between the city of Arkesine on Amorgos and the lender Praxicles, a citizen of Naxos, provides an example from the early Hellenistic period (*IG* XII 7 67B, c. 325–275 BCE) of the antagonistic relationship between hard- and soft-law tools. In the entrenchment clause of the contract, the Arkesinians stipulate several sources of authority that potentially would be capable of altering the terms of the contract had this specific clause not been included: another law (*nomos*) or decree (*psēphisma*), a resolution (*dogma*), and a decision of a general or a magistrate. By enumerating the acts of public authorities through which the content of the contract could be altered, the contracting parties, in this case the city and the noncitizen lender, indirectly acknowledge the normative character of legal rules elaborated by bodies other than the popular assembly and the council.

The contract between the city of Arkesine and Praxicles encapsulates the element of alienage, given that the lender did not possess the status of citizen or, as far as we know, of metic (a legitimately domiciled foreigner). If the lender had been a citizen of Arkesine, the entrenchment clause would have taken the form of *mēden autēs kuriōteron* ("nothing [is to be] more authoritative than this [sc. the agreement]") without enumerating particular sources of authority,[35] since it is doubtful that non-state-generated rules were binding upon the Arkesinians in their relations with one another.

The letter that Eumenes II, king of Pergamum, sent to the guild of Dionysiac artists at Teos sometime during the period between 179 and 159 BCE provides another example suggesting that the notion of soft law in the Hellenistic period was accepted in negotiations involving the element of alienage—this time of a king (Eumenes), a polis (Teos), and a collective of individuals (the guild of Dionysiac artists) who were neither the subjects of the king nor, as far as we know, citizens of the polis (*IvP* I 163). The guild was headquartered at Teos until the middle of the second century BCE, when Teos forced its members to leave the city.[36] Prior to the expulsion of the guild from Teos, Eumenes attempted to reconcile the guild and the city by proposing the conclusion of a treaty (*sunthēkē*), which, however, failed in its purpose. The letter concerning the relations between the guild and the city of Teos announces the arbitration of Eumenes in response to embassies sent to him by the guild and Teos. Having taken into account both sides, Eumenes renders his decisions on a variety of matters.[37] In the final part of his letter, the king of Pergamum confers the status of law on the speech drafted by his envoy and the proposals articulated by the representatives of the two parties.

CONCLUSION

These two examples, the first coming from the city of Arkesine and the second from a Hellenistic monarch, do not furnish any evidence that outside of international relations there was scope for the acceptance of a sort of soft law that would be applicable in the relations between fellow citizens alongside the "hard law" of *nomos* (statute) and *psēphisma* (decree). The same should be admitted in the case of poleis adhering to the classical form of government that were subsequently incorporated into Hellenistic monarchies. Statutes and (even more so) decrees continue to be the only ways of creating rules of law that regulate the relations between citizens. Nevertheless, two significant changes take place in this period. First, especially in new cities, these decrees must be in agreement with the rules of law created through the exercise of royal authority. Second, with regard to cities that either lay outside the territory of Hellenistic kingdoms or were already established when incorporated into those kingdoms, pre-existing laws were adjusted to the new needs that resulted from the intensified movement of persons and goods. International treaties, foreign judges and arbitrators (*metapemptoi dikastai*), notarial practices, the acceptance or toleration of customary law, and, more generally, the multiplication of producers of law may be regarded as practical means of managing affairs. The use of these tools resulted in the creation of the Hellenistic legal *koinē*, the common private law of the eastern Mediterranean that was never codified, though some of its provisions were transformed into hard law.

Is it plausible, without fear of anachronism, to speak of globalization and the consequent emergence of soft law(s) from the time of Alexander's successors onwards? I think it is, with two provisos: first, that we acknowledge that the region to which our concept of globalization applies is limited to and coincides with the eastern part of the Mediterranean basin; and second, that we admit that hard law never managed to satisfy the needs of multicultural societies like those of the Hellenistic East, even when they endorsed the dominant mode of cultural expression. Even in the context of monocultural societies, as in the case of traditional cities, the consequences of being different would never have the same intensity or meet with the same opposition as in fifth-century Athens.

NOTES

1. See especially the recent work of Barta 2011: passim.
2. Gilmore 1995: 102–103.
3. Wolff 1961: 91, 129; 1966a; 1966b; 1968b. Cf. Behrend 1970: 141; Herrmann 1975.
4. For the recent literature, see Shaffer and Pollack 2010: 706–799. See also Mörth 2004; Falkner et al. 2005.
5. di Robilant 2006: 499–500.
6. Flückiger 2009.
7. di Robilant 2006: 499–500.
8. Pampoukis (1996: 65–73) rejects the origin of the medieval *lex mercatoria* in the Roman *ius gentium*.

9. di Robilant 2006: 499.

10. Gilmore 1995: 102–103.

11. di Robilant 2006.

12. Kreller 1921; Martino 1937; Osuchowski 1950; Rougé 1966: 398; Velissaropoulos 1980: 320–321.

13. Dem. 35.11: Σωθέντων δὲ τῶν χρημάτων Ἀθήναζε, ἀποδώσουσιν οἱ δανεισάμενοι τοῖς δανείσασι τὸ γιγνόμενον ἀργύριον κατὰ τὴν συγγραφὴν ἡμερῶν εἴκοσιν, ἀφ᾽ ἧς ἂν ἔλθωσιν Ἀθήναζε, ἐντελὲς πλὴν ἐκβολῆς ἧς ἂν οἱ σύμπλοι ψηφισάμενοι κοινῇ ἐκβάλωνται ("If the goods reach Athens safely, the borrowers will pay the accruing money to the lenders in accordance with the agreement within twenty days of their arrival at Athens in full—apart from any *jettison* which the fellow-voyagers vote to make jointly" [trans. MacDowell 2004]).

14. Ashburner 1909.

15. For this process, see, e.g., the arbitration by the Achaean League of the dispute opposing Megalopolis and Orchomenos, after 235 BCE (*Syll.*³ 490, line 9): ἐμμε[ν]εῖν ἐν τᾶι στάλαι καὶ τᾶι ὁμολογίαι καὶ τῶι ψαφίσματ[ι] ("to abide by the [text inscribed on the stele], the *homologia*, and the decree"). The *homologia* is distinct from the text inscribed on the stele and the decree (*psēphisma*) that ratified it. It (the *homologia*) designates the informal engagements of the parties, reproduced, in whole or in part, in the written text inscribed on the stele and in the decree. The same distinction is implied in the treaty between Miletus and Herakleia, c. 180 BCE (*Milet* I 3 150, lines 27–28): τάδε συνέθεντο καὶ ὡμολόγησαν Μιλήσ[ιο]ι καὶ Ἡρακλεῶται ("the Milēsioi and the Herakleōtai approved these terms and agreed"); and the treaty between Ilion and the cities participating in the celebrations for Athena Ilias in 77 BCE (*IK Ilion* 10, line 1): Σύμφωνον καὶ ὁμόλογον ταῖς πόλεσιν ὑπὲρ τῆς πανηγύρεως ("the feast agreed upon and admitted between the cities"); lines 4–5: τάδε ἐποιήσαντο ἐν ἑαυτοῖς ὁμόλογα καὶ σύμ[φ]ωνα παραγενόμενοι εἰς τὸ ἱερὸν τῆς Ἀθηνᾶς ("having thus admitted and agreed upon [between them], they arrived at the temple of Athena"). See Velissaropoulos-Karakostas 2011, 2:215–216.

16. Triantaphyllopoulos 1968; 1985: 221–222.

17. Harrison 1971: 48.

18. Jurors' oath from Eressus, late fourth century BCE (*IG* XII.2 526, γ side. iii, lines 12–20 = RO 83): [Ν]αὶ δικάσσω τὰν [δίκαν | ὅ]σσα μὲν ἐν τοῖς [νό|μ]οισι ἔνι κατ τοὶ[ς νό|μο]ις, τὰ δὲ ἄλλα ἐκ [φιλο|π]ονίας ὡς ἄριστα κ[αὶ | δ]ικαί<ο>τατα· καὶ τιμάι[σ]ω, αἴ κε κατάγνω, ὀρθῶ[ς] | καὶ δι<καί>ως· οὕτω ποιήσω | ναὶ μὰ Δία καὶ Ἄλιον. ("I shall judge the case, as far as it lies within the laws, according to the laws, and in other regards industriously, as well and as justly as possible, and if I condemn I shall assess rightly and justly. I shall do this, by Zeus and Helios" [trans. Rhodes and Osborne 2003: 411, 413].)

19. Law of the Delphic Amphictyony, 380/379 BCE (*SEG* 28.100 = *IG* II² 1126, lines 3–4): Δικα[ξῶ τ]ὰς δ[ίκ]ας ὥς κα δ[ικ]αιοτάτα[ι] γ]νώμα[ι, τ]ὰ μὲγ γε[γρ]αμμ[ένα - - - τὰ δὲ ἄ]|γρα[πτα κ]ατὰ(γ) γνώμαν τὰν αὐτοῦ καὶ [ο]ὐ κερδαγῶ τᾶν δ[ικ]ᾶν οὐ[δεμᾶι - - -] ("I will give judgments according to the most

just opinion, for those matters written - - -, for those unwritten, according to my own opinion and I shall not get any profit from the trial").

20. Herrmann 1979 = *SEG* 29.1130bis (B); Ager 1996: 186–192, Case 71.II, lines 28–31.

21. Gauthier and Hatzopoulos 1993; *EKM* 1.Beroia 1.A, lines 26–34.

22. *IG* XII 9 2, lines 2–7: [τοὺ]ς π<ϱο>βού[λους] | [παϱ]έχοντας παϱ᾽ αὐ[τῶν ἐπαινέσαι αὐτὸν | ἐπὶ τῆι π]ϱοαιϱέσει <ἧ>ς <ἔχ>[ων δια|τελε]ῖ πϱὸς πάν[τας τοὺς - - - | - - -] δικ<ά>ζων γνώ[μηι τῆι δικαιοτάτηι ("The *probouloi* ["magistrates"] from their own means are to praise him for his goodwill which he demonstrates to all the [- - -] judging with most just opinion").

23. *P.Gurob* 2.40–2.45.

24. For the authority of *paidotribai* to enforce penalties, see the donation of Eudemos of Miletus, 200/199 BCE (*Syll.*³ 577, lines 37–40): παιδοτϱίβας καὶ | τοὺς τὰ γϱάμματα διδάξοντας, οὓς ἄϱιστα [. . .] τῶν παίδων ἐπι|στατήσειν καὶ μηδεμᾶι φιλοτιμίαι παϱὰ τὸ δίκαιον πϱοσνέμοι τὴν | αὐτοῦ γνώμην ("gymnastic trainers and schoolteachers who will best look after the boys, and who declare their opinion without unjust partisanship").

25. Gagarin 1986: 121; Gagarin 2008: 76-89.

26. On the place of custom among the sources of law, see Wolff 1968a; Mélèze Modrzejewski 1966, 2011: 22; Welles 1934: 329; Triantaphyllopoulos 1985: 59–62 n. 27. For the use of the terms *ethos* ("custom") and *ethismos* ("accustoming") in papyri, see Schmitz 1970.

27. Pl. *Leg.* 793A: τὰ καλούμενα ὑπὸ τῶν πολλῶν ἄγϱαφα νόμιμα ("what are called unwritten laws by many") are not identical with [τοὺς] πατϱίους νόμους ("the ancestral laws").

28. Arist. *Eth.Nic.* 8.13.5; 10.9.14.

29. Dem. 18.275: Φανήσεται ταῦτα πάντα οὕτως οὐ μόνον τοῖς νομίμοις, ἀλλὰ καὶ ἡ φύσις αὐτὴ τοῖς ἀγϱάφοις νομίμοις καὶ τοῖς ἀνθϱωπίνοις ἤθεσιν διώϱικεν. ("Not only will our laws reveal all these principles, but nature herself established them in *unwritten laws* and in *human customs*" [trans. Yunis 2005].)

30. *IvP* I 163.B.III, lines 4–10: [- - - τοῦ] | ὅϱκου, ὃμ πϱότεϱον εἴθιστο τ[οὺς δικαστὰς ὁϱ]|κίζεσθαι, πεϱιέχοντα δικάσ[ειν κατά τε τοὺς] | νόμους καὶ τὰς ἐπιστολὰς τ[ῶμ βασιλέων καὶ] | τὰ ψηφίσματα τοῦ δήμου, κ[ϱίνω ὡς καὶ ἐν] | πολλοῖς ἔτεσιν ἔμπϱοσθε. ("The oath, which it was formerly common for the judges to swear, with the content to deliver judgments according to the laws and the letters of the kings and the decrees of assembly, [I determine also (to be valid)] for many years in the future.") Cf. Wilcken 1912: 393-394 no. 334, lines 7–8 (244/243 BCE): καὶ κε[χει]ϱογϱαφήκασι τὸν εἰθισμένον | ὅϱκον τοσούτου μεμισθῶσθαι ("and they have declared by the usual written oath so much to be the rent").

31. *Syll.*³ 939, lines 9–14; *SEG* 3.468, lines 13–14.

32. *IG* XI.4 1296.A, lines 1–2 (c. 250 BCE): [τ]άδε ἐπεύχονται ἱεϱεῖς τε καὶ | ἱέϱειαι κατὰ τὰ πάτϱια ("the priests and priestesses curse as follows according to ancestral custom").

33. See, e.g., Shaffer and Pollack 2010: 707–708: "The existing law and social science literature on hard and soft law can be divided into three camps: legal positivist, rationalist, and constructivist. All three of these camps address how hard and soft law are used as alternatives, as well as how they can interact in complementary ways; but they each have different starting points. Legal positivists tend to favour hard law and view hard and soft law as binary terms. For them, hard law refers to legal obligations of a formally binding nature, while soft law refers to those that are not formally binding but may nonetheless lead to binding hard law. Rationalists, in contrast, contend that hard and soft law have distinct attributes that states choose for different contexts. They also find that hard and soft law, in light of these different attributes, can build upon each other. Constructivists maintain that state interests are formed through socialization processes of interstate interaction which hard and soft law can facilitate. Constructivists often favor soft-law instruments for their capacity to generate shared norms and a sense of common purpose and identity, without the constraints raised by concerns over potential litigation. Regardless of their views about the strengths and weaknesses of hard and soft law as alternatives, all three schools examine how hard and soft law can serve as mutually supporting complements to each other."

34. Shaffer and Pollack 2010: 708.

35. For this type of entrenchment clause, see Dem. 35.13, 39, and Gagarin in this volume, pp. 43–44.

36. Le Guen 2001, 2: 33; Aneziri 2003.

37. *IvP* I 163.II.C, lines 2–9: finances of the festival; II.C, lines 9–15: the division of authority between the magistrates of the guild and those of the city; III.B, lines 1–4: the requirement that the guild's officials be bound by the laws of the city wherein a festival was being held; III.B, lines 4–9: the proper oath of the judges of the joint court; and III.C: the drawing up, ratification, and conclusion of a new agreement, which should be flexible enough to admit modification.

REFERENCES

Ager, Sheila. 1996. *Interstate Arbitrations in the Greek World, 337–90 BC*. Berkeley: University of California Press.

Aneziri, Sophia. 2003. *Die Vereine der dionysischen Techniten im Kontext der hellenistischen Gesellschaft: Untersuchungen zur Geschichte, Organisation und Wirkung der hellenistischen Technitenvereine*. Stuttgart: Steiner.

Ashburner, Walter. 1909. *Νόμος Ῥοδίων Ναυτικός* [The Rhodian sea-law] Oxford: Clarendon Press.

Barta, Heinz. 2011. *"Graeca non leguntur?": Zu den Ursprüngen des europäischen Rechts im antiken Griechenland*. Vol. 2.1. Wiesbaden: Harrassowitz.

Behrend, Diederich. 1970. *Attische Pachturkunden: Ein Beitrag zur Beschreibung der μίσθωσις nach den griechischen Inschriften*. Munich: C. H. Beck.

di Robilant, Anna. 2006. "Genealogies of Soft Law." *The American Journal of Comparative Law* 54.3: 499–554.

Falkner, Gerda, Oliver Treib, Miriam Hartlapp, and Simone Leiber. 2005. *Complying with Europe: EU Harmonisation and Soft Law in the Member States*. Cambridge: Cambridge University Press.

Flückiger, Alexandre. 2009. "Pourquoi respectons-nous la *soft*-law? Le rôle des émotions et des techniques de manipulation." In *Rationalité des émotions: Un examen critique; XIVe séminaire interdisciplinaire du Groupe d'Étude "Raison et rationalités,"* edited by Pascal Bridel, 73–103. Geneva: Droz.

Gagarin, Michael. 1986. *Early Greek Law*. Berkeley: University of California Press.

———. 2008. *Writing Greek Law*. Cambridge: Cambridge University Press.

Gauthier, Phillipe, and Miltiadis B. Hatzopoulos. 1993. *La loi gymnasiarchique de Beroia*. Athens: Centre de recherches de l'Antiquité grecque et romaine; Paris: de Boccard.

Gilmore, Grant. 1995. *The Death of Contract*. Edited by Ronald K. L. Collins, 2nd ed. Columbus, OH: Ohio State University Press.

Harrison, A. R. W. 1971. *The Law of Athens*. Vol. 2, *Procedure*. Oxford: Clarendon Press.

Herrmann, Johannes. 1975. "Verfügungsermächtigungen als Gestaltungselemente verschiedener griechischer Geschäftstypen." In *Symposion 1971: Vorträge zur griechischen und hellenistischen Rechtsgeschichte*, edited by Hans Julius Wolff, Joseph Mélèze Modrzejewski, and Dieter Nörr, 321–332. Cologne: Böhlau.

Herrmann, Peter. 1979. "Die Stadt Temnos und ihre auswärtigen Beziehungen in hellenistischer Zeit." *Mitteilungen des Deutschen Archäologischen Instituts, Abteilung Istanbul* 29: 239–271.

Kreller, Hans. 1921. "Lex Rhodia: Untersuchungen zur Quellengeschichte des römischen Seerechts." *Zeitschrift für das gesamte Handelsrecht und Konkursrecht* 85: 257–367.

Le Guen, Brigitte. 2001. *Les Associations de Technites dionysiaques à l'époque hellénistique*. 2 vols. Nancy: Association pour la diffusion de la recherche sur l'antiquité.

MacDowell, Douglas M., trans. 2004. *Demosthenes, Speeches 27–38*. Austin: University of Texas Press.

Martino, Francesco de. 1937. "Note di diritto romano: Lex Rhodia." *Rivista di diritto della navigazione* 3: 335–347.

Mélèze Modrzejewski, Joseph. 1966. "La règle de droit dans l'Égypte ptolemaïque: État des questions et perspectives de recherches." In *Essays in Honor of C. Bradford Welles*, edited by Alan Samuel, 125–173. New Haven, CT: American Society of Papyrologists.

———. 2011. *Droit et justice dans le monde grec et hellénistique*. Warsaw: Faculty of Law and Administration, Warsaw University.

Mörth, Ulrika, ed. 2004. *Soft Law in Governance and Regulation: An Interdisciplinary Analysis*. Cheltenham, UK: Edward Elgar.

Osuchowski, Wacław. 1950. "Appunti sul problema del iactus in diritto romano." *Ivra: Rivista internazionale di diritto romano e antico* 1: 292–300.

Pampoukis, Haris P. 1996. *The Lex Mercatoria as Applicable Law in International Contractual Obligations* (in Greek). Athens: Sakkoulas.

Rhodes, Peter J., and Robin Osborne, eds. and trans. 2003. *Greek Historical Inscriptions: 404–323 BC*. Oxford: Oxford University Press.

Rougé, Jean. 1966. *Recherches sur l'organisation du commerce maritime en Méditerranée sous l'empire romain*. Paris: SEVPEN.

Schmitz, Hans-Dieter. 1970. "Tὸ ἔθος und verwandte Begriffe in den Papyri." PhD diss., University of Cologne.

Shaffer, Gregory C., and Mark A. Pollack. 2010. "Hard vs. Soft Law: Alternatives, Complements, and Antagonists in International Governance." *Minnesota Law Review 94*: 706–799. Republished as *University of Minnesota Law School Legal Studies Research Paper Series* 09–23.

Triantaphyllopoulos, Johannes. 1968. "Le lacune delle legge nei diritti greci." In *Antologia giuridica romanistica e antiquaria*, vol. 1, 51–62. Milan: Giuffrè.

———. 1985. *Das Rechtsdenken der Griechen*. Munich: C. H. Beck.

Velissaropoulos, Julie. 1980. *Les nauclères grecs: Recherches sur les institutions maritimes en Grèce et dans l'Orient hellénisé*. Geneva: Droz; Paris: Minard.

Velissaropoulos-Karakostas, Julie. 2011. *Droit grec d'Alexandre à Auguste (323 av. J.-C.–14 ap. J.-C.): Personnes, biens, justice*. 2 vols. Athens: Centre de recherches de l'Antiquité grecque et romaine; Paris: de Boccard.

Welles, C. Bradford. 1934. *Royal Correspondence in the Hellenistic Period: A Study in Greek Epigraphy*. New Haven, CT: Yale University Press.

Wilcken, Ulrich. 1912. *Grundzüge und Chrestomathie der Papyruskunde* 1.2. Leipzig and Berlin: Teubner.

Wolff, Hans Julius. 1961. *Beiträge zur Rechtsgeschichte Altgriechenlands und des hellenistisch-römischen Ägypten*. Weimar: Böhlaus.

———. 1966a. "La structure de l'obligation contractuelle en droit grec." *Revue historique de droit français et étranger* 44: 569–583.

———. 1966b. "Debt and Assumpsit in the Light of Comparative Legal History." *The Irish Jurist* 1.2: 316–327.

———. 1968a. "Gewohnheitsrecht und Gesetzesrecht in der griechischen Rechtsauffassung." In *Zur Griechischen Rechtsgeschichte*, edited by Erich Berneker, 99–120. Darmstadt: Wissenschaftliche Buchgesellschaft.

———. 1968b. "Die Grundlagen des griechischen Vertragsrechts." In *Zur griechischen Rechtsgeschichte*, edited by Erich Berneker, 483–533. Darmstadt: Wissenschaftliche Buchgesellschaft.

Yunis, Harvey. 2005. *Demosthenes, Speeches 18 and 19*. Austin: University of Texas Press.

9 / FROM ANTHROPOLOGY TO SOCIOLOGY:
NEW DIRECTIONS IN ANCIENT
GREEK LAW RESEARCH

Adriaan Lanni

ONE MAJOR TREND IN THE PROLIFERATION OF SCHOLARLY monographs, translations, commentaries, and edited collections on Greek law at the end of the twentieth century was the influence of modern anthropology. Influential ethnographies such as Gluckman on the Barotse or Bohannan on the Tiv became commonplaces in bibliographies, and the scholarly focus on Athenian legal process and dispute settlement mirrored the work of Laura Nader, one of the most influential anthropologists of the twentieth century.[1] In this chapter, I briefly discuss how anthropological approaches contributed to the study of Greek, and particularly Athenian, law, and then explore whether a turn toward legal sociology might provide new insights. More specifically, I examine whether incorporating some of the contemporary methods in the sociology of law—particularly law and economics and social norms theory—might generate fruitful avenues for future research. Many, but not all, of my examples relate to Athenian rather than Greek law because most of the law and society work so far has focused on Athens, but my conclusions are equally applicable to Greek law more generally.

It may be helpful at the outset to flesh out a bit more clearly what I mean by a turn to sociology. The line between anthropology and sociology is by no means a clear one, and the two fields often overlap. Although one can find counterexamples to every distinction I am about to list, here are some broad-brush generalizations. First, subject: it used to be said that legal anthropology studies legal systems of so-called "primitive" societies or indigenous peoples, while legal sociology investigates the legal systems of "advanced" societies, though social anthropologists now regularly study modern societies as well.[2] Second, methods: ethnographies and closely observed individual case studies are the most common approach in anthropology, while contemporary legal sociology tends to operate at a higher level of abstraction and generalization, using modeling or quantitative empirical studies. Third, emphasis: in explaining the differences between different legal systems, anthropologists tend to focus on the unique culture of each society—its belief system and values—while sociologists tend to focus more on differences in the operation of institutions and social structures that both reflect and reproduce those cultural differences. Fourth, assumptions: at least one main strand of anthropology, exemplified by the work of Bohannan,[3] sees each human society as fundamentally unique and is therefore skeptical about the possibilities of comparative insights, while contemporary legal sociologists start with the premise that all human beings are more or less the same and are therefore much more open to applying their methods and insights to multiple societies.

So what would it mean to turn from anthropology to sociology in ancient Greek law research? In the most general sense, I have in mind a shift in emphasis that would put laws and legal institutions back in the foreground of research. The adoption of "process-oriented" approaches, the focus on dispute settlement and informal means of social control, and the emphasis on the cultural values underlying the legal system (for example, the debate over whether Athens was a feuding society), all resulted in de-emphasizing the substantive legal rules and, to a lesser extent, the operation of legal institutions. In following (consciously or not) the anthropologist Nader's dictum to focus on parties and disputes rather than cases and courts,[4] we have largely neglected further research into substantive areas of law and institutional arrangements during the recent renaissance of Greek law. (Of course, there are exceptions, many of which are represented by the contributions to this volume.) To be clear: my goal is not to criticize anthropologically inflected work on Greek law. On the contrary, the use of anthropology was enormously helpful in emphasizing the extent to which Athenian law was embedded in society. It has generated many useful insights. My point is simply that despite the flurry of recent research, there is still a lot of ground left to explore on the relationship between law and society in Greece, particularly by focusing more attention on substantive legal rules and the operation of formal legal institutions.

Michael Gagarin's masterful book, *Writing Greek Law*, shares many features with the turn to sociology I am advocating. Gagarin highlights a feature unique to ancient Greek law: the use of written, publicly accessible legislation combined with an oral, informal procedure.[5] Although he discusses the possible cultural reasons for this arrangement, his account of what makes Greek law unique focuses less on culture and more on the implications of the Greek institutional structure.[6] This emphasis on the operation of institutions, rather than the Greeks' unique culture, opens up the possibility for important comparative work. Gagarin examines how different approaches to writing in legislation and litigation in a variety of societies, including Hammurabi's

Babylon, ancient Rome, and early England, can help explain the important differences between these legal systems.[7]

So far, I have sketched in a very general way how future research into Greek law might benefit from changing its emphasis somewhat to reflect sociological rather than anthropological approaches. In this paper, I focus on a very specific aspect of the turn to sociology, namely, the application to Greek law of social science methods being used to study the operation of contemporary laws and legal institutions. These current methods reflect the generalizations about sociology mentioned earlier: they tend to focus on the incentives created by rules and legal institutions in society, and their basic methods and insights operate at a level of generality that invites application to other societies. I concentrate in particular on two such methods: law and economics, and social norms theory. Before turning to these methods, I will briefly discuss the impact of anthropology on Greek law scholarship at the end of the twentieth century.

I. ANTHROPOLOGY AND GREEK LAW

Prior to the last decade of the twentieth century, there were scattered examples of prominent scholars of Greek law applying concepts from anthropology. Ugo Enrico Paoli and Louis Gernet come immediately to mind as representing a law-and-society approach to Greek law, and Sally Humphreys, whose work often touched on legal topics, consciously imported concepts from anthropology.[8] But it was the 1990 publication of *Nomos: Essays in Athenian Law, Politics, and Society*, edited by Paul Cartledge, Paul Millett, and Stephen Todd, that ushered in the trend toward anthropologically influenced Greek law work in the Anglophone world. In the introductory chapter of *Nomos*, Todd and Millett make a "plea for the study of Athenian law to loosen some of its links with 'law' and to strengthen its links with legal anthropology."[9] More specifically, the piece lists as illustrative three anthropological perspectives that might be of benefit to the study of Athenian law: first, that law and politics are not separate, but part of a continuum; second, the importance of looking beyond the trial to examine the litigants' strategies in the broader dispute, including informal and pretrial institutions; and third, that conflict does not necessarily imply pathology.[10]

In the decade or so following the publication of *Nomos*, several Anglophone Greek law scholars, many of them educated at Cambridge, attempted to implement the approach advocated in the *Nomos* volume. Anthropological influence is most obvious in the work of David Cohen. In *Law, Sexuality, and Society*, Cohen explicitly applies a comparative anthropological model.

He draws links between the normative structures and social practices of ancient Athenian and modern Mediterranean cultures, focusing in particular on notions of gender, privacy, and the public/private distinction.[11] In *Law, Violence, and Community*, Cohen takes a process-oriented approach to Greek law.[12] He sees the trial as just one small part of an ongoing disputing process. In this work, substantive law and institutional detail take a backseat to discussion of the origin of the parties' disputes, the cultural norms related to such disputes, and the parties' strategies before, during, and after trial. For Cohen, understanding the nature of Athenian litigation means first and foremost examining Athenian culture—what he interprets as a feuding society in which Mediterranean notions of honor were central.[13]

While other scholars have not been as thoroughgoing as Cohen in applying a full-blown anthropological model, much of the work by Anglophone scholars at the end of the twentieth century reveals at least some anthropological influence. Most prominent is the process-oriented approach advocated by Nader.[14] The turn to legal process implies not just studying the court resolution of a case, but examining the entire dispute, focusing on the parties. Some examples of process-oriented approaches to Greek law include Todd's focus on procedure in *The Shape of Athenian Law* and Robin Osborne's discussion in "Law in Action in Classical Athens" of the tendency for lawsuits to spawn more lawsuits.[15] The anthropological turn away from formal legal rules and institutions also produced fascinating work on the importance of informal rules and mechanisms of social control, such as gossip and arbitration, a trend exemplified by Virginia Hunter's *Policing Athens*.[16] Finally, much of the anthropologically inflected work on Athenian law attempted to uncover the distinctive cultural beliefs and values reflected in and reproduced by the legal system. I am thinking here of the debate between David Cohen and Gabriel Herman over whether Athenian culture is better characterized as one of revenge or self-restraint; of Danielle Allen's analysis of what she calls the Athenians' distinctive "system of value" underlying its penal decisions; and of Matthew Christ's attempt to understand Athenian notions of litigiousness.[17]

As these examples attest—and there are many more—the anthropological turn in Greek law was remarkably generative, opening up new areas of research. Precisely because this move was an attempt to emphasize the relationship between law and society by expanding the focus beyond the traditional doctrinal and institutional questions, there have been comparatively few attempts to apply a law-and-society analysis to the study of substantive legal doctrines or formal institutional arrangements. I want to turn now to look at what a more sociological approach to Greek law might look like, and think through what some of the potential advantages and pitfalls of this approach might be. As I mentioned at the outset, for the purpose of this chapter I want to focus on two particular socio-legal methods: law and economics and social norms theory.

2. LAW AND ECONOMICS

The economic analysis of law can take many forms; I will discuss just a few examples. Moreover, I will focus on positive law and economics rather than normative law and economics, since this seems much more relevant to the study of the ancient world—that is, I will talk about studies that make descriptive claims about causes and effects of rules and institutions, rather than studies that advocate certain rules or regimes.[18] At the outset, it may be worth correcting a common misconception. Not all scholarship in law and economics adopts the artificial assumptions of perfect rationality and perfect information familiar from neoclassical economics. Much of the work being done today in law and economics tends to fall into the category of new institutional economics rather than neoclassical economics, and to adopt the idea of bounded, not perfect, rationality, or of incomplete information. In fact, many of the most interesting issues in law and economics revolve around situations in which actors cannot pursue their preferences in a perfectly rational way, often because the relevant information is either impossible or extremely costly to obtain. Bruce Frier and Dennis Kehoe have an excellent article in the 2007 *Cambridge Economic History of the Greco-Roman World* that offers an introduction to new institutional economics and its potential application to the Roman world.[19]

One of the central concepts of law and economics that is particularly relevant here is transaction costs, that is, the cost involved in making an economic exchange, over and above the actual price of the good or service purchased. Transaction costs might include the costs relating to locating a vendor, determining the quality of the product, reaching agreement on a price with the other party, and ensuring that the other party carries out his side of the bargain, which could entail bringing a lawsuit.[20] The presence of transaction costs may explain some behavior that might at first seem puzzling: for example, an individual may decide to pay a higher price to someone he trusts and has dealt with before because that kind of deal will reduce information and bargaining costs. One of the more controversial strands of law and economics, especially from the perspective of an historian, is that particular legal rules develop because they are efficient.[21] This sort of approach often attempts to explain particular legal rules or institutional arrangements because they reduce transaction costs or address inefficiencies created by asymmetries in information.

Richard Posner's thesis that many of the private law rules of the Anglo-American common law developed as they did because they are efficient is the most famous example of this approach.[22] Another example of what I will call the functionalist approach is a paper by Daryl Levinson on collective sanctions.[23] He looks at the use of collective sanctions in history and today—from blood feuds and frank pledge to economic sanctions of rogue states in international law and imposing liability on shareholders for tort violations of corporations. He argues that collective sanctions do not stem from a notion of collective responsibility, which many have argued is particularly prevalent in societies that are, for lack of a better word, "primitive." Instead, he provides a functional explanation: innocent group members are punished because they are in the best position to identify, monitor, and control responsible individuals, and can be motivated to respond to sanctions. For Levinson, collective sanctions are "delegated deterrence regimes."[24] Levinson does not discuss the Mytilene debate in Thucydides, or any other evidence from ancient Athens, but one can imagine that he might draw some support from suggestions in Diodotus's speech that at least some Athenians might have been thinking precisely along these lines (Thuc. 3.39–40). On the other hand, this kind of functionalist explanation seems to fall short for some types of Athenian collective sanctions—imposing *atimia* ("disenfranchisement") on descendants not yet born is clearly not a delegated deterrence regime.[25]

Other ways to apply functional law and economics to Athens would be to analyze various aspects of Athenian legal doctrine—inheritance rules, the institution of the *epiklēros* (heiress), any of a number of procedural rules—and explore whether these rules can be explained, at least in part, based on economic efficiency rather than cultural values and other concerns. Frier and Kehoe discuss, for example, how the Roman institution of the slave *peculium* (that is, property committed to the slave's use) promoted efficiency in enterprises run by slaves in a variety of ways.[26] Most notably, the *peculium* gave slaves incentives to run the business well, but the slave-master relationship ensured that slave managers could not open their own competing shop once they had learned the business at their owner's expense.

Of course, functional explanations are very common in all sorts of historical work and are certainly not limited to law and economics. Functionalist law and economics arguments are open to one of the standard critiques of all functionalist explanations: they are circular in the sense that they focus on the effects rather than the cause of the phenomenon under study.[27] But there is a weaker version of the type of functionalist law and economics arguments that I have been describing that may succeed in avoiding this critique: the argument here is not that efficiency is the main, or even a primary, cause of the rule or institution under study, but simply that, whatever the origins of the rule, its efficiency benefits help explain why it persisted rather than being abandoned.

A second strand of law and economics attempts to explain not why certain rules develop, but how rational actors will respond to these rules. One insight from law and economics is that a rule may not have the obvious expected effect because rational actors will incorporate the effects of the rule into their bargains. David Friedman provides an example: a law barring landlords from evicting tenants without six months' notice may initially seem to help tenants and hurt landlords, but over time landlords will simply raise the rent to reflect the cost incurred from the law.[28] The result may actually hurt some tenants because they are forced to pay a premium for this enhanced protection even if they are unlikely to need it. Moreover, landlords may try to prescreen applicants and avoid renting to low-income tenants, making it harder for them to get apartments. It is important to note that this kind of law and economics is not limited to market transactions. One example is a recent paper on the effects of three-strikes laws—that is, laws like the one in California that impose a life sentence if a person is convicted three times for a felony, even if the usual penalty for the third felony is far less severe.[29] The argument in the paper is that three-strikes laws reduce crime rates in the relevant state overall but have two perverse effects: first, they increase serious violent crime, on the theory that criminals with two strikes against them have incentives to do everything possible to avoid getting caught for the third crime, and second, they increase crime in neighboring states, as criminals with previous strikes have incentives to commit their crimes elsewhere to avoid the effects of the rule.[30]

Applying this kind of approach to Athens might involve looking at how rational individuals might have responded to various legal rules, and thinking through how these rules might have changed social and economic interactions. The existing scholarship in this vein includes studies of how Athens's rules for taxation and liturgies promoted certain types of "invisible" assets like money and loans;[31] encouraged easy-to-conceal investments, like scattered properties; and encouraged wealthy rather than poor immigrants.[32] These studies have tended to focus on legal rules that directly affect the economy. There is much more work to be done in analyzing the incentives created by other types of legal rules and institutions. How did litigants respond to the incentives created by various rules relating to bringing frivolous prosecutions? How did the various methods of holding public officials accountable affect how magistrates did their jobs? How did the costs associated with the uncertainties created by jury verdicts and the difficulties of enforcing judgments affect daily life?

One common criticism of law and economics is that it is too abstract and reductionist, namely, that this approach tends to ignore the many other social, cultural, and legal circumstances that might influence the causes and effects of the law or institution. But it is possible to use economic concepts without committing to the reductionism of a traditional economic model. For historians, the fundamental insight of law and economics is that it is worth exploring what incentives laws and institutions create, because they may suggest counterintuitive effects of laws or help explain puzzling phenomena. We don't have to assume perfect rationality or information, or a modern market economy, to recognize that different legal regimes create different incentives, and that absent countervailing cultural forces, the behavior of many Athenians was likely influenced in part by those incentives. I will sketch out one example in the briefest of outlines.[33]

The broad use of evidence in Athenian trials likely compensated for problems of legal enforcement in a private prosecution system. In Athens many public offenses, particularly "victimless" offenses, were probably prosecuted irregularly—not in response to the seriousness or visibility of the infraction, but because the defendant might or might not have happened to have a personal or political enemy willing to serve as a volunteer prosecutor, even though the latter for the most part did not stand to gain financially from any judgment and risked a large fine if he failed to get one-fifth of the jurors' votes. Similarly, offenses committed against victims who lacked the resources to bring suit or to enforce a judgment if they were to win were probably systematically underenforced.

My argument is that the character attacks in our court speeches, particularly attacks for norm violations unrelated to the case itself, served a disciplinary function that helped compensate for legal underenforcement in Athens. As is often pointed out, law court speakers regularly discuss the character and past bad acts committed by their opponent, even when they are unrelated to the charge in the specific case.[34] Scholars disagree about how much this type of character evidence influenced jury verdicts; my own view is that it was a regular and important part of court rhetoric.[35] By permitting any past norm violation to be used against a litigant at trial, the Athenian approach encouraged litigants to uncover and punish their opponents' past violations, even violations unrelated to the charge in the case. Discussion in court of an opponent's norm violations might not only have an effect on the jury's verdict. It would also publicize the offending behavior to hundreds of jurors, which would serve as a form of shame sanction in itself and would also encourage informal social sanctions outside of court.

To the extent that Athenians could anticipate being involved in a court case or public hearing where their character might be an issue, the broad evidence regime would give them incentives to obey laws that were unlikely to be directly enforced and to avoid injuring weak victims who were unlikely to sue them. Athenians could not casually commit victimless crimes or injure those who might be powerless to sue them because these offenses would come back to haunt them if they ever found themselves in court in the future. In this way, the aspects of the Athenian legal system that seem furthest from a "rule of law" in the modern sense may actually have played an important role in inducing compliance with the laws. The argument I just sketched is an example of an attempt to analyze the incentives created by a particular aspect of the court system—the broad evidence regime—and to think through how that kind of incentive structure might affect the enforcement of norms. It is of course very helpful, whenever possible, to include ancient sources that provide anecdotal evidence that at least some ancients were acting in accordance with the predicted incentive effects of the law or institution.[36]

3. SOCIAL NORMS THEORY

The second example of legal sociology I would like to discuss is social norms theory. Though anthropologists and sociologists have been studying social norms and informal means of social control for a long time, it is only in the last fifteen years that social norms theory has made a big splash in legal academic circles. One major strand of social norms theory is the study of how social norms and informal means of social control affect behavior, and the relationship of these mechanisms to formal legal rules and institutions. Lisa Bernstein has studied how the diamond merchants of New York enforce their own norms very effectively without reference to courts or other legal institutions, through the use of private arbitration.[37] I have already mentioned two studies of classical Athens: Hunter's examination of various means of informal social control, like private arbitration and gossip, and Cohen's study of the formal and informal norms relating to adultery and the seclusion of women.[38] Robert Ellickson has studied how cattle ranchers in Shasta County, California, conform to their own sets of informal norms, which are quite different from the legal rules.[39] In particular, Ellickson has argued that informal norms and dispute resolution mechanisms are more likely to be used when the parties have an ongoing, multiplex relationship; when the size of the stakes are low; and when the dispute is not complex. One application of social norms theory might attempt to see if Ellickson's factors help predict when Athenians went to law and when they chose informal means of dispute resolution.

The examples I have provided so far fit just as easily within the rubric of legal anthropology as legal sociology. More recent work on social norms focuses less on ethnographic case studies of the operation of informal mechanisms in a single society, and more on modeling the operation of social norms at a more general level. Some of the questions recently posed include: Can we predict when formal and informal mechanisms will serve as complements to each other rather than as substitutes? Why and how do social norms change over time? When and how are norms internalized?

Let me sketch out in a bit more detail one strand of social norms theory that I think is particularly enlightening for readers unfamiliar with modern legal theory: the "expressive function" of law. Legal sociologists have pointed out that a law's impact is not limited to the direct effect produced by the sanction or incentive created by a law; law can serve a variety of other roles—symbolic, constitutive, and so forth—that have profound effects on society. Some scholars working on modern law have tried to describe some of the mechanisms through which a law may strengthen, weaken, or change social norms and thereby indirectly affect individuals' behavior.[40] To cite a simple example, an antilittering ordinance may have a significant impact even if it is rarely (or never) officially enforced. The law may serve an "expressive function," communicating that the community disapproves of those who litter, and emboldening individuals to enforce the law informally, thereby changing both the norms and behavior surrounding the disposal of trash.[41]

Exploring the expressive function of statutes offers a fruitful new approach for scholars of Athenian law for a few reasons. The expressive function of law may have served an even more important role in ancient Athens than it does today. Laws passed in the Athenian Assembly were comparatively direct, well-publicized expressions of community sentiment, whereas modern legislation gives at best only a noisy signal of popular consensus because of the operation of parties, interest groups, and so forth. Athenian laws were also relatively well publicized: they were passed by the popular Assembly and displayed prominently. Because much modern legislation is technical and largely unfamiliar to the general public, only a small percentage of laws are likely to have an expressive effect. In Athens, by contrast, the expressive function of law was potentially implicated in every decision of the Assembly.

To provide a sense of how attention to the expressive effect of law might change our understanding of Athenian law, I will summarize very briefly case studies of two sets of Athenian statutes whose impact extended well beyond the relatively few cases in which they were enforced through the court system.

In the first case study,[42] I examine the expressive effects of the statute prohibiting *hubris*. This statute was unusual in that it protected slaves as well as free persons (Dem. 21.47). But because slaves did not have standing to bring suits, this law was likely rarely enforced in court. Nevertheless, the *hubris* law played a prominent role in Athenian public discourse because deterrence of *hubris* was thought vital to social stability in the democracy. I argue that the expressive effect of the *hubris* law may explain the Athenians' unusual solicitude toward others' slaves, particularly in the agora ([Xen.] *Ath. Pol.* 1.10–12;

Dem. 9.3; Pl. *Resp.* 563b; Eur. *Ion* 855–856). In this way, the *hubris* law may have reduced violence and promoted security in business transactions.

The second case study concerns laws that barred high-level political participation by male citizens who had previously worked as prostitutes, and the effect these laws may have had on social norms and practices related to homosexual pederasty (Aeschin. 1.28–32, 119, 160–161).[43] According to the current scholarly consensus, these laws reflect an Athenian conception of a private sphere in which homoerotic and other sexual activity was free from regulation so long as it did not infringe on the political life of the city.[44] From this perspective, the law's practical effect was limited to a very small number of elites who might anticipate taking an active role in the city's politics. But my argument is that when the expressive function of the laws is taken into account, the laws may have had a much broader practical impact. Because the line between pederasty and prostitution was blurry at best, an Athenian would likely recognize that the law could be interpreted to include many pederastic relationships. The laws changed the social meaning of homosexual pederasty. Rather than conferring honor by indicating your participation in an elite institution that traditionally produced the city's political leaders, having been an *erōmenos* (subordinate, often adolescent partner in a homosexual relationship) might now detract from your status by marking you as potentially unable to assume positions of power and influence in the democracy. I argue that for this reason the prostitution laws may have changed the norms and practices surrounding homosexual pederasty in various ways, forcing some men into the closet, inducing others to adopt an ideal of chaste pederasty, and provoking resistance in still others, radicalizing them and driving them out of democratic politics.

This study of the expressive effect of laws in Athens illustrates one of the themes of the turn to sociology I began with: refocusing some of our scholarly energy from law court rhetoric to the substance of Athenian statutes. Applications of social norms theory are often less reductionist and more context-specific than studies employing law and economics. But most social norms studies share the assumption that individuals will react in predictable, rational ways to incentives created by formal or informal norms and institutions. In this sense, they are open to some of the same criticisms I have already discussed in relation to law and economics.

CONCLUSION

In sum, I think that a familiarity with the social science methods discussed here is useful for ancient historians. These methods' value comes not so much from directly applying them to Greek law, though some of that type of work might be illuminating; rather, what is more important is that knowledge of these approaches encourages us to pay more attention to the incentives created by norms, laws, and institutions, and to think through how those incentives might affect behavior—without necessarily ignoring the social context or relying on a formal, and inevitably somewhat reductionist, direct application of these methods. In 1985, Moses Finley, quoting Hans Julius Wolff, justly referred to Greek law as "a stepchild in modern study."[45] Since that time, in large part because of the extraordinary work of Michael Gagarin and many of the contributors to this volume, Greek law has become a flourishing field. I have tried to suggest that further advances can be made by exploiting the current work in the sociology of law and by focusing on substantive law and the operation of formal institutions.

NOTES

1. Gluckman 1955; Bohannan 1957; Nader and Todd 1978.
2. For a note on this traditional distinction between legal anthropology and sociology, and its obvious deficiencies, see Todd and Millett 1990: 15 n. 28.
3. For a discussion of Bohannan and relativism, see Donovan 2008: 112–122.
4. See Nader and Todd 1978; Nader and Yngvesson 1973.
5. Gagarin 2008: 1–2, 242–247.
6. Gagarin 2008: 222–224, 244–245.
7. Gagarin 2008: 214–224.
8. Paoli [1930] 1974, [1933] 1974; Gernet 1979, 1982; Humphreys 1978, 1985.
9. Todd and Millett 1990: 14–15.
10. Ibid.
11. Cohen 1991: 35–69.
12. Cohen 1995: 21–24.
13. Cohen 1995: 61–86.
14. See Nader and Todd 1978; Nader and Yngvesson 1973. For discussion, see Donovan 2008: 135–147.
15. Todd 1993; Osborne 1985.
16. Hunter 1994.
17. Compare Herman 2006: 184–216, with Cohen 1995: 87–118. See Allen 2000: 50–72; Christ 1998.
18. For a recent summary discussion of the use of law and economics in legal history, see Klerman 2017.
19. Frier and Kehoe 2007.
20. For an introduction to transaction costs, see Frier and Kehoe 2007: 117–119.
21. There are several ways of defining what is "efficient" in economic terms, but for our purposes a crude definition like "maximizing utility" or "allocating re-

sources in a way that maximizes net benefit" is sufficient. And utility is often defined in terms of wealth, but it does not have to be: it can include moral values and other preferences.

22. Posner 1979.
23. Levinson 2003.
24. Levinson 2003: 373–394.
25. Lanni 2017.
26. Frier and Kehoe 2007: 130–134.
27. Elster 1983: 61.
28. Friedman 1987: 144.
29. Iyengar 2008.
30. Ibid.
31. Cohen 1992: 194–202.
32. Lyttkens 1992: 13–14, 19–20; see also Lyttkens 1997 (arguing that the Solonian law introducing a property requirement for office gave wealthy Athenians an incentive to signal their wealth via publicly visible spending, thereby contributing to the creation of the liturgical system); Kaiser 2007 (applying a game-theory model to analyze the incentives created by the trierarchic system). For a discussion of economic rationalism in fourth-century Athens more generally, see Christesen 2003.
33. For a fuller statement of this argument, see Lanni 2009.
34. Lanni 2006: 46–64.
35. For a discussion of the debate, see Lanni 2009: 693 with n. 4.
36. We do have anecdotal evidence in this particular example, namely statements by litigants that they performed liturgies in the hope that it would help them in any future court cases: Lys. 20.31, 25.13. Similarly, Cohen 1992: 198–202 points to evidence of Athenians keeping much of their property in "invisible" form, presumably to avoid liturgies and taxes.
37. Bernstein 1992.
38. Hunter 1994; Cohen 1991.
39. Ellickson 1991.
40. E.g., Cooter 1998; Lessig 1996; McAdams 1997.
41. McAdams 1997: 400–408.
42. This argument is developed more fully in Lanni 2016.
43. The argument is worked out in more detail in Lanni 2010.
44. Cohen 1991: 229.
45. Todd and Millett 1990: 1.

REFERENCES

Allen, Danielle S. 2000. *The World of Prometheus: The Politics of Punishing in Democratic Athens*. Princeton: Princeton University Press.
Bernstein, Lisa. 1992. "Opting out of the Legal System: Extralegal Contractual Relations in the Diamond Industry." *Journal of Legal Studies* 21.1: 115–157.

Bohannan, Paul. 1957. *Justice and Judgment among the Tiv*. Oxford: Oxford University Press.

Cartledge, Paul, Paul Millett, and Stephen C. Todd, eds. 1990. *Nomos: Essays in Athenian Law, Politics, and Society*. Cambridge: Cambridge University Press.

Christ, Matthew R. 1998. *The Litigious Athenian*. Baltimore: Johns Hopkins University Press.

Christesen, Paul. 2003. "Economic Rationalism in Fourth-Century BCE Athens." *Greece and Rome*, ser. 2, 50.1: 31–56.

Cohen, David. 1991. *Law, Sexuality, and Society: The Enforcement of Morals in Classical Athens*. Cambridge: Cambridge University Press.

———. 1995. *Law, Violence, and Community in Classical Athens*. Cambridge: Cambridge University Press.

Cohen, Edward E. 1992. *Athenian Economy and Society: A Banking Perspective*. Princeton: Princeton University Press.

Cooter, Robert. 1998. "Expressive Law and Economics." *Journal of Legal Studies* 27.S2: 585–608.

Donovan, James M. 2008. *Legal Anthropology: An Introduction*. Lanham, MD: AltaMira.

Ellickson, Robert C. 1991. *Order without Law: How Neighbors Settle Disputes*. Cambridge, MA: Harvard University Press.

Elster, Jon. 1983. *Explaining Technical Change: A Case Study in the Philosophy of Science*. Cambridge: Cambridge University Press.

Friedman, David. 1987. "Economic Analysis of Law." In *The New Palgrave: A Dictionary of Economics*, edited by John Eatwell, Murray Milgate, and Peter Newman, vol. 3, 144–148. London: Palgrave.

Frier, Bruce, and Dennis Kehoe. 2007. "Law and Economic Institutions." In *The Cambridge Economic History of the Greco-Roman World*, edited by Walter Scheidel, Ian Morris, and Richard P. Saller, 113–143. Cambridge: Cambridge University Press.

Gagarin, Michael. 2008. *Writing Greek Law*. Cambridge: Cambridge University Press.

Gernet, Louis. 1979. *Droit et société dans la Grèce ancienne*. New York: Arno. Reprint of the 1955 edition by Sirey.

———. 1982. *Droit et institutions en Grèce antique*. Paris: Flammarion.

Gluckman, Max. 1955. *The Judicial Process among the Barotse of Northern Rhodesia*. Glencoe, IL: Free Press.

Herman, Gabriel. 2006. *Morality and Behaviour in Democratic Athens: A Social History*. Cambridge: Cambridge University Press.

Humphreys, Sally C. 1978. *Anthropology and the Greeks*. London: Routledge and Kegan Paul.

———. 1985. "Social Relations on Stage: Witnesses in Classical Athens." *History and Anthropology* 1.2: 313–369.

Hunter, Virginia J. 1994. *Policing Athens: Social Control in the Attic Lawsuits, 420–320 BC*. Princeton: Princeton University Press.

Iyengar, Radha. 2008. "I'd Rather Be Hanged for a Sheep than a Lamb: The Unintended Consequences of 'Three-Strikes' Laws." *NBER Working Paper Series* 13784.

Kaiser, Brooks A. 2007. "The Athenian Trierarchy: Mechanism Design for the Private Provision of Public Goods." *Journal of Economic History* 67.2: 445–480.

Klerman, Daniel. Forthcoming 2017. "Economics of Legal History." In *The Oxford Handbook of Law and Economics*, edited by Francesco Parisi. Oxford: Oxford University Press.

Lanni, Adriaan. 2006. *Law and Justice in the Courts of Classical Athens.* New York: Cambridge University Press.

———. 2009. "Social Norms in the Ancient Athenian Courts." *Journal of Legal Analysis* 1.2: 691–736.

———. 2010. "The Expressive Effect of the Athenian Prostitution Laws." *Classical Antiquity* 29.1: 45–67.

———. 2016. *Law and Order in Ancient Athens.* New York: Cambridge University Press.

———. 2017. "Collective Sanctions in Classical Athens." In *Ancient Law, Ancient Society: Festschrift in Honor of Bruce Frier*, edited by Thomas A. McGinn and Dennis Kehoe. Ann Arbor: University of Michigan Press.

Lessig, Lawrence. 1996. "Social Meaning and Social Norms." *University of Pennsylvania Law Review* 144.5: 2181–2189.

Levinson, Daryl. 2003. "Collective Sanctions." *Stanford Law Review* 56.2: 345–428.

Lyttkens, Carl H. 1992. "Effects of the Taxation of Wealth in Athens in the Fourth Century BC." *Scandinavian Economic History Review* 40.2: 3–20.

———. 1997. "A Rational-Actor Perspective on the Origin of Liturgies in Ancient Greece." *Journal of Institutional and Theoretical Economics* 153.3: 462–484.

McAdams, Richard H. 1997. "The Origin, Development, and Regulation of Norms." *Michigan Law Review* 96.2: 338–433.

Nader, Laura, and Harry F. Todd., Jr., eds. 1978. *The Disputing Process: Law in Ten Societies.* New York: Columbia University Press.

Nader, Laura, and Barbara Yngvesson. 1973. "On Studying the Ethnography of Law and Its Consequences." In *Handbook of Social and Cultural Anthropology*, edited by John J. Honigmann, 883–921. Chicago: Rand McNally.

Osborne, Robin. 1985. "Law in Action in Classical Athens." *The Journal of Hellenic Studies* 105: 40–58.

Paoli, Ugo Enrico. [1930] 1974. *Studi di diritto attico.* Milan: Cisalpino-Goliardica. First published in 1930 by R. Bemporad e Figlio.

———. [1933] 1974. *Studi sul processo attico.* Padua: Cisalpino-Goliardica. Reprint of the 1933 ed. published by A. Milani.

Posner, Richard A. 1979. "Utilitarianism, Economics, and Legal Theory." *Journal of Legal Studies* 8.1: 103–140.

Todd, Stephen C. 1993. *The Shape of Athenian Law.* Oxford: Clarendon Press.

Todd, Stephen C., and Paul Millett. 1990. "Law, Society, and Athens." In Cartledge, Millett, and Todd 1990, 1–18. Cambridge: Cambridge University Press.

Mogens Herman Hansen

INTRODUCTION

The theme of my contribution is oral law in ancient Greece. It was one of three possible topics I suggested when I was invited to this symposium, and it is the one Michael Gagarin preferred.

The first question is: What is oral law? Oral law is law that has to be remembered because the society in question has no knowledge of writing at all or, alternatively, makes no use of writing in legislation and administration of justice.

In his groundbreaking monograph *Writing Greek Law*, Gagarin distinguishes between the use of writing in legislation and in administration of justice. While already in the archaic period laws were written down, administration of justice was still conducted orally during most of the classical period, and the transition from oral to written culture in court proceedings took place over the course of the fourth century BCE, sometimes even later.[1] This is a very important insight, illuminatingly discussed and convincingly argued in Gagarin's book.

The issue I want to take up here concerns legislation and law in the sense of coercive general rules. What did the Greeks do before they began to write down laws, presumably in the mid-seventh century BCE? Did they have laws passed by the community and remembered by its members? Or did they just have some customs and traditions that cannot be considered a body of laws in the proper sense?

I shall subdivide the issue into two questions. First: is it at all possible to have orally transmitted laws in the proper sense, that is, unwritten general rules passed by a legislator or some legislative assembly, whereafter they are remembered and transmitted to the next generation by all or some of the members of the community? Second: if that is possible, did the ancient Greeks have laws of that kind?

Gagarin suggests a negative answer to both questions. He believes that there is an essential and almost inescapable connection between law and writing,[2] so that oral law in the proper sense does not exist and never has.[3] Medieval Iceland may be an exception.[4] In conformity with this view, he shows that oral law in this sense is unattested in our sources for archaic Greek society.[5]

As to the first question, I take a more favorable view of oral law in general. I believe that in some preliterate societies there have been rules that are similar to the rules we identify as laws in early literate societies. The principal difference seems to be that they were not written down but had to be remembered. As to the second question, I agree that there is no direct evidence that supports the existence of oral laws in archaic Greece, but given the sources we have, we cannot take absence of evidence as evidence of absence.

I. EXAMPLES OF SOCIETIES WITH ORAL LAW

The first and longer part of my contribution will be to provide six examples of societies ruled by orally transmitted laws.

My first, and by far the best-known, historical example of an orally transmitted law code is that of Iceland between 930 and 1117–1118 CE.[6] In 930 the Althing was set up. It was a general meeting held every midsummer at Thingvollr, a plain at the northern tip of Iceland's biggest lake. The Althing was in charge of both legislation and administration of justice for all of Iceland. Administration of justice was conducted in different courts in which the judges were a number of thingmen (*þingmenn*) appointed by the thirty-nine chiefs (*goðar*)—nine from each of the eastern, southern, and western parts of Iceland, and twelve from the northern part. New laws were debated in a general assembly (*Alþingi*) to which all free Icelanders had access, but the laws were passed by the thirty-nine chiefs, chaired by the lawspeaker (*lögsögurmaður*). He was elected for a three-year period and could be re-elected. At least one of the lawspeakers filled the office for twenty-seven years. His principal duty was each year to recite from memory all the rules of procedure for the Althing and the other "things" (assemblies) associated with the Althing, plus one-third of the other laws, so that he would have recited the entire law code in the course of his three-year period of office.[7] The law code was committed to writing in the years 1117–1118. Manuscripts comprising the entire code date from circa 1260.[8] The written version of the code comes to several hundred pages in print but includes both new laws, revisions of earlier laws, and obsolete laws.

Gagarin mentions the Icelandic example briefly in *Early Greek Law* and describes it in more detail in *Writing Greek Law*. He concludes that "medieval Iceland appears to be one of the clearest examples of what many scholars mean by oral law—a fixed set of specific rules preserved and transmitted orally."[9] In his discussion, however, Gagarin focuses on the sagas and on *Njal's Saga* in particular, and he notes, "Serious doubts have been raised, moreover, about the reliability of the sagas as historical sources, and some scholars now dispute the historicity of the picture we have from *Njal's Saga* of the oral preservation of laws."[10]

Gagarin is right that *Njal's Saga* is literature, not law, and that the sagas were written down at least 150 years after the oral transmission of laws had been replaced by a written text. I agree that much of what we read about the administration of justice in *Njal's Saga* is not above suspicion. But what we know about the lawspeaker's recital of the laws at the Althing and the writing down of the laws in 1117–1118 does not stem from the sagas but from Ari's *íslendingabók* (book of the Icelanders) and from the *Grágás*, that is, the written version of the law code.[11] Ari started writing his account in 1122,[12] only four years after the laws were written down, and the section in the *Grágás* about the lawspeaker's annual recitation of the laws seems to have included some rules that had been allowed to stand although they had become obsolete.[13]

Finally, it is worth noting that medieval Iceland was a society in which members of the upper class were literate, and after the year 1000, when the Icelanders in the Althing decided to convert to Christianity, at least the clerics could read their copies of the Latin Bible. But laws still had to be remembered and were not committed to writing until the twelfth century.

The Lombards provide a second example of a codification of laws that previously had been remembered. The Lombards, or Longobards, were a Germanic tribe that in 569 CE under their king Alboin invaded Italy, and within a few decades conquered the Po valley, Tuscany, Spoleto, Benevento, and, eventually, Calabria.[14] The most enterprising of the Lombard kings was Rothair (636–652). He organized a codification of the Lombard laws, and in November 643 he issued the *Edictum Rothari*, a lawbook written in a not very elegant and rather debased Latin. It is organized into 388 articles, each covering between two lines and half of a page. The edict covers a great variety of topics: penal law, family law, property law, and so forth, altogether mostly substantive law, and, surprisingly, very little about the administration of justice.[15] In the Lombard courts, judgment was passed not by elders but by the king's official.[16] For offenses against the state or the king, the penalty was capital punishment and confiscation of property, and it was entrusted to officials to carry it out.[17] According to Paulus Diaconus, *Historia gentis Langobardorum* (written c. 790), the laws had previously been preserved "only by memory and custom,"[18] and this piece of information is confirmed by the edict itself. Article 386 describes how the codification was carried out:

> Seeking out and finding the old laws of our fathers which were not written down, and with the equal counsel and consent of our most important judges and with the rest of our most happy nation (*exercitus*) assisting, we have established the present lawbook containing those provisions which are useful for the common good of all our people. We have ordered these laws to be written down on this parchment, thus preserving them in this edict so that those things which, with divine aid, we have been able to recapture through careful investigation of the old laws of the Lombards known either to ourselves or to the old men of the nation, we have put down in this lawbook.[19]

Article 388 adds that all cases that have not been settled by November 22, 643, the day the edict was issued, shall be settled in accordance with the edict:

> We add this general order lest any fraud be applied to this edict through the fault of the scribes. If any contention arises, no other copies of this code shall be accredited or received except those which have been written and recognized or sealed by our notary Answald who has written this in accordance with our command.[20]

Rothair's edict looks like a roughly organized compilation rather than a proper codification. Thus, it probably provides an even better impression of what oral law can be than the Icelandic *Grágás*, which is preserved only in revised copies written a century and a half after the laws were first committed to writing.

My third example is the Adkeme Milga, the largest ethnic group in the province of Serawe in Eritrea. The Adkeme Milga live in village communities and, until the 1940s, in accordance with a set of orally transmitted laws and customs, which they believe were laid down once and for all by their two eponymous ancestors. Eritrea was an Italian colony from 1890 to 1941, but the Italians did not interfere with the administration of justice in the village communities. In 1942, as a response to the challenges of modern society, a group of chiefs and notables decided to write down their laws and customs. The codification was carried out in 1943–1944 in collaboration with the *debterat*, the traditional custodians of customary law. The result was a two-part volume in Tigrinya, the vernacular language of Eritrea. Part One contains the text of the laws; Part Two is a collection of maxims. The laws are divided into eighty-four numbered chapters comprising 743 unnumbered clauses. There are chapters about family, land rights, debt, inheritance, offenses, procedure in litigation, and so forth. Because the aim was to record the traditional laws, some obsolete rules are included—for example, concerning slavery. There seem to be only a few innovations. The text of the code amounts to approximately 30,000 words. The result was a genuine compilation of customary law. Particularly noteworthy is the absence of European influences. The codification was carried out by the Adkeme Milga themselves, and no anthropologists were involved.[21]

The Inca empire provides a fourth, and in the Americas, the most impressive, example of oral traditions.[22] Without any knowledge of writing, the rulers in Cuzco succeeded for several generations in controlling an empire that stretched from Quito in Ecuador to Santiago in Chile, 4,000 km from north to south. Everything had to be remembered, and the only mnemonic aid at their disposal was the *quipu*, a row of pendant strings with knots. A few hundred *quipus* are preserved, but we do not know any longer how they were encoded and used, only that they were connected in particular with the remembering of numbers.[23] The Inca administration of justice was not focused on the settlement of disputes between opposed parties. In every town there were government officials whose duty it was to have offenders put on trial and punished.[24] There was an enormous hierarchical system of judges, ranging from local judges in all the towns to a central court in Cuzco.[25] The laws were coercive commands issued by the Inca emperor, and the emperors Pachacútec, who ruled from 1438 to 1471, and Topa Inca Yupanqui, who ruled from 1471 to 1493, seem to have been particularly active as legislators.[26] Many of the laws we hear about were penal laws, and some of Draconian severity.[27] The historian Blas Valera (1545–1597) made the following observation about the Inca laws:

> The toil and labours of Numa Pompilius in framing laws for the Romans, or those of Solon for the Athenians, or Lycurgus for the Spartans are less admirable, since these were acquainted with letters and human sciences which showed them how to establish good laws and customs and made it possible for laws to be committed to writing for the use of their contemporaries and for posterity. What is really remarkable is that these Indians, though entirely deprived of these aids and contributions, should have contrived to frame such laws (apart from those referring to their idolatry and errors). Innumerable of these laws are still observed today by the faithful Indians: they are systematised and closely resemble those of the greatest lawgivers. The Indians recorded them distinctly by means of the knots or

threads of different colours which they used for counting, and taught them to their children and descendants so that the laws that were established by their first kings six hundred years ago are still as clearly remembered as if they were but freshly promulgated.[28]

The *quipus* were used to better memorize information about laws, as well as sentences that had to be reported every month to the government in Cuzco.[29] In Cuzco the Inca laws were remembered by specialists, the so-called *amautas*, "philosophers" or "wise men," who also were entrusted with remembering the imperial accounts, the rituals, and the historical traditions.[30]

The fifth example, from Valencia, Spain, stretches from perhaps one thousand years ago until today. Traditionally the economy of Valencia was based on the growing of vegetables in intensively cultivated gardens.[31] Due to drought during the summer period, cultivation depended on irrigation from large reservoirs in which water was stored during winter and spring. There were strict rules regulating the irrigation, and the most important part of the administration of justice in Valencia was connected with disputes between the farmers over irrigation. All such disputes were settled by the so-called water tribunal, the *Tribunal de las Aguas*. The tribunal is attested in 1239 and may reach back to the tenth century. The court meets every Thursday at midday outside the cathedral. It is manned by eight democratically elected judges who have to remember all the complicated rules concerning irrigation. In the sessions, there is no reference to anything in writing and no records are kept. In the 1980s the president of the court instituted the written recording of minutes of the sessions, but after a few years the population began to mistrust the minutes. There were protests, and the taking of minutes was discontinued. The tribunal still exists, but its importance has dwindled since the 1950s, when new large water reservoirs were built behind Valencia.[32]

My final example of oral laws that to some extent have also survived to the present day is the Albanian Kanun. Allegedly this orally transmitted code goes back to Lekë Dukagjini (1410–1481).[33] What we do know from numerous travellers' reports is that the Kanun comprised the laws by which the North Albanians lived in the nineteenth and twentieth centuries.[34] It was transmitted orally from father to son and from generation to generation, and young men who possessed a talent for and an interest in the Kanun prepared themselves for the role of elder later in life.[35] There is no indication, however, that the Kanun was an organized collection of laws that could be recited in its entirety, or that some persons were obliged to know the Kanun, and it was not written down until the early twentieth century, when the Franciscan monk Shtjefën Konstantin Gjeçov (1874–1929) compiled a version of it in Albanian.[36] It appears that what he put down in writing was principally the Kanun of one particular region, that of Mirdita, where the Gjomarkaj clan was the ultimate authority on the law.[37]

Variants are known from other clans in other regions, and there were at least three other versions of the entire Kanun.[38] Furthermore, Gjeçov did not reproduce exactly what he was told by his informants. He seems to have generalized the rules. The organization of all the rules into twelve books, twenty-four chapters, and 1,263 articles is his own, and all the way through he inserted what are obviously his own comments and explanations.[39]

The Kanun covers all aspects of life: church, family, agriculture, property, tort, crimes (including murder), and rules about blood feud, and so forth.[40] The frequent blood feuds are the most discussed aspect of North Albanian society: in the nineteenth and early twentieth centuries, over a quarter of all adult males were killed in them.[41] In spite of its shortcomings, Gjeçov's Kanun is an invaluable source for law and the local administration of justice up to the Second World War. When the communist partisans took over in 1944, the social and political organization of the North Albanian regions took a dramatic turn. The partisans killed about a third of all adult males, principally the leaders of the clans and tribes and many of the elders. "Everyone was lost who could have passed on knowledge of the law, their own history, the working of self-government, and the people's religion."[42] Under Hoxha's regime, the Kanun was suspended and the police succeeded in putting an end to almost all blood feuds.[43] Since the fall of the socialist regime, parts of the Kanun have been revived and are still important in the local administration of justice in northern Albania.[44] Most Albanian families possess a printed copy of Gjeçov's book,[45] but it is not used in the administration of justice or settlement of disputes. To some extent it is still the oral laws as remembered that are in force.[46] The blood feuds have been revived as well, and every year a number of North Albanians are killed in revenge.

Far from all societies have had orally transmitted collections of laws. At the other end of the spectrum are, for example, the Tiv of northern Nigeria. According to Bohannan and Bohannan, "Tiv themselves have never codified their usages into law; in fact, the difference between law and custom is still irrelevant to Tiv."[47] Another example is the Tswana in South Africa, who "have no written or even oral codes setting aside legal rules from all others," and "there is no codified body of law which the courts have to administer."[48] It is worth noting that when these peoples learn to write, they do not develop a desire for having their traditions and legal rules collected and turned into a body of laws. When collections of laws are made, they are drawn up by, for example, missionaries or colonial administrators, who in the process transform the traditional rules and press upon the natives systems of rules which they would not have developed themselves. In nineteenth-century Tahiti, Hawaii, and Tonga, law codes of this type were drawn up by missionary advisers and imposed by native chiefs who had established themselves as kings.[49]

Thus there seems to be a difference between societies like the Tiv and the Tswana on the one hand and, on the other hand, societies like Iceland, the Lombards, and Eritrea. Some preliterate societies had what can reasonably be called a corpus of orally transmitted laws which at a certain point in history were written down and turned into a law code; others seem to have lived without what we would identify as laws, and that applies to both the preliterate and the literate periods. When they learned to write, they did not use script to develop what we would call laws. If or when they acquired a code of laws, it was one imposed by outsiders, not one they developed of their own accord. Where do the ancient Greeks belong?

2. REMEMBERING LAWS

Before I try to answer that question, I shall deal with one general aspect of the issue: the human memory. A condition necessary for having orally transmitted laws is that they can be remembered and passed on without distortion from generation to generation. According to Gagarin, it is unlikely that detailed and complicated regulations could be remembered accurately, and it is also unlikely that such laws could be accurately preserved over long periods by oral transmission from generation to generation. He mentions the longer and more complicated sections of Draco's homicide law (IG I^3 104) as an example of laws which would be difficult to remember and transmit:

> A rule clarifying the situation and specifying the necessary details, would be difficult, however, if not impossible, to compose in a version that could be easily remembered. One would, in effect, have to put the text of Draco's law into Homeric verse, a nearly unimaginable task. And even if one could create a detailed rule in a form that could be easily remembered, it would be nearly impossible to communicate this oral version to a wide audience with all the details intact over time.[50]

I think Gagarin is too pessimistic about what people can remember. In any society there is a small number of persons who possess an extraordinary memory. They can remember an astonishing amount of data and possess total recall for the rest of their lives of what they have once learned. Some of these so-called "savants" suffer from an autistic disorder and are socially dys-functional, but some simply have a prodigious memory without any associated medical condition. In this context I will restrict myself to two examples.

In the 1930s there lived in Leningrad a Russian journalist whom the senior editor of the paper he worked for referred to the famous neurologist Aleksandr Luria, not because he suffered from any disorder, but because the editor found that the journalist's memory was so remarkable that it would be of interest to Luria. Over a number of years Luria tested the journalist and found to his amazement that his subject's memory was unlimited both in the amount of information it could hold and in time. If the journalist was asked to remember several hundred numbers or objects and had just a few seconds to memorize each piece of information, he could reproduce everything without a single mistake. And when Luria several years later asked him whether he remembered, for example, the third session they had had, he would name the date of it, describe the clothing Luria was wearing on that occasion, and repeat all the memory tests to which he had been subjected on that occasion, again without a single error. Luria published the case study in a short monograph which has been translated into many languages, and whose English title is *The Mind of a Mnemonist: A Little Book about a Vast Memory*.[51]

The Russian journalist is a rare example of a mnemonist. But there are today thousands of people who possess what we consider to be an incredible memory. In Islamic seminaries in Pakistan some of the students memorize the entire Koran in Arabic. *Hafiz* is the designation of such a person.[52] The Koran is the size of the New Testament or the *Iliad* and *Odyssey* together, so for a student in Pakistan to know the entire Koran by heart would correspond to an American student knowing the New Testament in ancient Greek by heart. I have met one such student, and he told me that it took him nine months to learn the Koran by heart, but for some other students it had taken up to two years, and many could not do it at all.

In modern Western society these so-called "savants" are marginalized. Their capacity is not of any particular value to society and is mostly treated as a curiosity. But there can be no doubt that in preliterate societies these persons were highly valued and they were among the persons who were entrusted with remembering the history, the rituals, and the laws of the community. What Plato wrote in the *Phaedrus* is true: "The invention of writing has not enhanced people's memory, it has led to forgetfulness and the deterioration of memory" (Pl. *Phdr.* 275a).

We must keep in mind, too, that in preliterate societies not everybody had to remember the laws, only a small group of persons specifically entrusted with this task and specifically trained—the lawspeaker and lawmen in Iceland, the *amautas* among the Incas, and the *debterat* in Eritrea. And they were obviously recruited from among those who possessed a remarkable, perhaps even a prodigious memory. To fill such a post often included the obligation to transmit the knowledge to one's successor.[53] In many advanced preliterate societies, schools were set up for the purpose of providing systematic teaching of classical traditions.[54] Furthermore, in some societies the reciting of a remembered text was entrusted not to an individual but to a group. At the *kuum*, a secret conclave, held by the Kuba in preparation for the recital of the group testimony, the spokesperson is appointed and the testimony rehearsed, so that all are in agreement about it before it is recited in public.[55]

I have not yet come across an example of how laws could be preserved verbatim for several generations, but we have examples of the exact preservation of literary texts. In his classic book *Social Organization*, Robert Lowie notes that the faculty of memory among "primitive" peoples is at times astonishing: "Two renderings of a Hawaiian chant of 527 lines differed only in the omission of a single word; another chant of 618 lines was absolutely identical in the versions independently recorded for Hawaii and on Oahu"—two islands that are 350 kilometers apart.[56]

Finally, we must not forget that laws change in preliterate as well as in literate societies. What we know about early Iceland shows that many laws were changed and new laws added in the course of the two hundred years during which laws were orally transmitted.[57] Similarly, many of the Inca laws were changed, particularly by the Inca Pachacútec.[58]

3. ORAL LAW IN ANCIENT GREECE?

As convincingly argued most recently by Gagarin, the Greeks were a people who cared about laws and legislation, and they did so as far back as the sources go. Most early inscriptions of more than a few words or lines are laws. The oldest are from the mid-seventh century BCE, and among public documents laws dominate the epigraphical record throughout the archaic period.[59] Similarly, in the literary sources for archaic history we hear about famous legislators who compiled collections of laws: Lycurgus, Draco, Solon, Zaleucus, Charondas, Pittacus, and several others. All seem to have been active around 600 BCE, plus or minus a few decades, and most of them wrote the laws they compiled.[60] We know that in Athens both Draco and Solon had their laws written down, and I suppose that that goes for the other archaic legislators as well. Lycurgus seems to be the exception. In archaic Sparta, only a few laws, if any, were written down.[61] Sparta seems to have had oral laws in the archaic period, and written Spartan laws appear only in the classical period.[62] So Sparta may have started to write down laws later than other poleis did, and in this respect—as in several others—Sparta may have been an exception.

Now, what about laws in other early poleis before the age of the great legislators and before the Greeks in the late seventh century began to inscribe their laws on *stelae* and walls of public buildings? Did they have oral laws? I suggested that we ought to distinguish between, on the one hand, peoples like the Tiv and Tswana and, on the other hand, communities like Iceland, Lombardy, and the Inca empire, and we would expect the Greeks to belong in this second category. Yet, there is no evidence of oral law or legislation antedating the written laws. As Gagarin has demonstrated, the evidence we have about *mnemones* ("rememberers") and *hieromnemones* ("rememberers of sacred matters") concerns the administration of justice, not law and legislation.[63]

But, once again, absence of evidence is not evidence of absence. From medieval Denmark, Norway, Sweden, and Iceland we have preserved comprehensive written codes of law that are similar to one another. Only from Iceland do we have an impressive amount of evidence about how these laws were remembered and transmitted orally before they were written down. A few sources show that recitations of laws and eventually their writing down took place in Norway and Sweden too. The Norwegian law of Gulating ("the *thing* held by the people of Gulen," from c. 1100) contains the following paragraph:

> Now we have written down our defense organization and we do not know whether it is correct. But if it is wrong then we shall have the law about our defense duties that existed before and that Atle explained to the men in Gulen, unless our king will accept anything else from us and we all agree in that.[64]

Here we have a direct confrontation between an earlier oral and a later written version of the same law, a law regulating military obligations. Furthermore, the passage reveals a suspicion of written texts that is similar to the one attested in the modern *Tribunal de las Aguas* in Valencia.[65]

In Sweden the oldest of the regional law codes is the Vestgötalag. It is known in two versions, a short version from the beginning of the thirteenth century and a longer and much-revised version from the end of the century. It seems to have been the *Lagman* ("lawspeaker") Eskil Magnusson who was responsible for the writing down of the Vestgötalag in about 1220, and it is presumed that the older and shorter version is the result of his codification.[66]

From Denmark, on the other hand, there is no evidence whatsoever about recitation and oral transmission of laws before they were written down. The presumption is, however, that Denmark had the same institutions and traditions as those known from the other Nordic countries. But in this case all information about oral laws is lost, which is a major obstacle to the study of oral laws. The oral antedate the written laws, and when they are written down, information about them disappears, except in a few cases, like those I mention here. The lack of direct information can sometimes be compensated by indirect information, and with that in mind I return to the issue of oral laws in archaic Greece.

Let us take a look at the oldest law we have preserved, the one from Dreros about the *kosmos* ("chief magistrate").[67] The only provision of this law is that the *kosmos* could not be re-elected for a period of ten years. The law regulates one aspect of his election, but what about all the other rules concerning this official? He probably had to be a citizen of Dreros and not a foreigner. Since Dreros was presumably an oligarchy, there probably was a census requirement and in any case an age requirement. There must have been rules about when, where, and by whom he was elected. And the law we have preserved presupposes that there was a rule prescribing that he was elected for one year. There must also have been rules about the duties he performed. Were all these rules inscribed on a stone which has been lost, or were they written down on papyrus and kept in an archive? Neither, I think, is likely. The presumption is that in the mid-seventh century, all these rules were remembered, and the only one committed to writing was the one concerning the change that was passed by the polis when the citizens of Dreros began using writing for their constitutional rules.

In the mid-seventh century there was no essential difference between the written rule we have preserved on stone and all the other rules about the *kosmos*. But the other rules that were only remembered have been lost forever precisely because they were not written down. Over the course of the archaic and classical periods, the citizens of Dreros undoubtedly passed other amendments of the laws about the election and duties of the *kosmos*, rules which were written down but now are lost.

The law from Dreros is the oldest constitutional rule we have preserved. The other example I want to take up is much later and concerns the Athenian constitution. In support of the view that many constitutional laws were based on oral tradition only, I shall adduce three sources, all related to the period between 413 and 403 BCE, when Athenian debates about the *patrios politeia* ("ancestral constitution") twice resulted in the establishment of an oligarchy.

First, in Dionysius of Halicarnassus we have preserved a fragment of a speech by Thrasymachus in which he discusses the *patrios politeia*: "The *patrios politeia* is causing trouble, although it is very easy to learn about and is the common property of all citizens. For what is beyond our knowledge, we must listen to what is told by old men. For what old men experienced themselves, we can simply ask those who know."[68] In this passage Thrasymachus takes it for granted that knowledge about the *patrios politeia* rests on an oral tradition and can be obtained only by asking and listening.

Second, in 411, when the Athenian assembly debated the constitutional reform proposed by Pythodorus, a certain Cleitophon moved a rider that the elected committee "should also search out the ancestral laws (the *patrioi nomoi*) which Cleisthenes had enacted when he set up the democracy, so that the people might consider these too and deliberate for the best" ([Arist.] *Ath. Pol.* 29.3). The rider shows that there cannot have been an official copy of Cleisthenes's laws to be studied right away by the elected commission. Peter Rhodes's judicious comment on the passage is that "in 411 it was probably not known whether Cleisthenes's laws existed."[69]

In light of Thrasymachus's speech, I am inclined to take this view one step further: by Cleitophon's rider, the elected committee is instructed to search out the ancestral Cleisthenic laws, and that was probably done partly by tracing such Cleisthenic documents that could still be found (namely laws and decrees on specific matters), but principally by questioning older people about what they knew or had heard themselves about the ancestral constitutional practices. It is unlikely, for example, that all the regulations concerning the Cleisthenic organization of the tribes, the trittyes, and the demes were written down and filed somewhere.

Third, in 403, after the rule of the Thirty and the Ten, democracy was restored, and on the proposal of Teisamenus, the Assembly passed a decree of which the first basic section runs as follows: "Let the Athenians be governed as their ancestors (πολιτεύεσθαι . . . κατὰ τὰ πάτρια) and let them use the laws (νόμοις δὲ χρῆσθαι), weights, and measures of Solon and the ordinances (*thesmoi*) of Draco as in former times."[70]

In my opinion it is significant that the reference to the *nomoi* and *thesmoi* is precise and to known texts, whereas the reference to the *politeia* is extremely vague. The presumption is that the Athenians had a traditional democracy, allegedly introduced by Cleisthenes and developed over the course of the fifth century. Some institutions had undoubtedly been regulated by statutes, of which the principal preserved example is *IG* I³ 105, a law regulating the powers of the Council of 500 and the relations between the council and the assembly. From literary sources we know that the Thirty in 403 had Ephialtes's laws about the Areopagus Council removed from the Areopagus and undoubtedly demolished.[71] But many were probably still unwritten, for example, provisions about when a citizen obtained access to the assembly, that citizens over fifty were allowed to speak first, about how votes were conducted, and about when and how magistrates were elected or selected by lot, or the rule that the agenda of a meeting of the assembly had to be posted in public four days in advance.[72] Such regulations may not have been written down until long after they had been imposed, if ever. An obvious parallel is the British constitution.[73] Before the revision of the Athenian laws between 410 and 399, such regulations were probably remembered, yet they had the force of law, and officials as well as private citizens would undoubtedly be prosecuted and punished if they did not follow the rules.

As far as we know, the *axones* ("rotating boards") of Draco and Solon did not include constitutional laws.[74] But the revised Athenian law code drawn up by the *anagrapheis nomōn* ("promulgators of laws") following Teisamenus's decree did include constitutional laws, as is apparent from fourth-century speeches, in particular Demosthenes's speech against Timocrates.[75] After the revision of the laws in 400–399, any valid Athenian law, even one passed in the fourth century, could be referred to as "Solon's law,"[76] for example, the law about the right of citizens older than fifty to speak first in the assembly.[77]

Finally, and most importantly in this context, in 403 in connection with the decision to have a general revision of the laws, the Athenians decided that in future, the magistrates would no longer be allowed to use unwritten laws (*agraphoi nomoi*) in their administration of justice (And. 1.87). What does *agraphos nomos* mean in this context? Gagarin is undoubtedly right in arguing that the term covers written laws passed before the revision but not included in the revised law code.[78] There is no reason to believe, however, that such laws exhausted the category of *agraphoi nomoi*. In his commentary on Andocides's speech, MacDowell states that "this category doubtless includes not only laws which had never been inscribed, but also those which had been inscribed formerly but had since been rescinded (or not reaffirmed in the revision of the laws which began in 410), so that the inscriptions of them had now been obliterated."[79]

Religion is another field where we have some evidence about unwritten law. According to Lysias 6.10, Pericles once advised the Athenians in cases of impiety to apply not only written laws but also the unwritten laws (*agraphoi nomoi*) expounded by the Eumolpidae. In Andocides's speech "On the Mysteries" we learn about a relevant case. In a meeting of the *boulē* held in the Eleusinion, Andocides was accused of having placed an olive branch on the altar of the Eleusinion. His enemy, Callias, declared that according to the ancestral law (*patrios nomos*), the penalty was summary execution. However, supporting Andocides, Cephalus replied that Callias had invoked an ancestral law, but according to a law inscribed on a *stele*, the penalty was a fine of 1,000 drachmas. Furthermore, Callias belonged to the Ceryces (not the Eumolpidae) and was therefore not entitled to expound the law (And. 1.115–116). Apparently the *patrios nomos* invoked by Callias had been replaced by the law written on the *stele*, probably in connection with the revision of the law code, and the regulation that in the future the magistrates were no longer allowed in any matter to apply an unwritten law in their administration of justice.

CONCLUSION

What is the conclusion of my investigation? On the one hand, I agree with Gagarin that in ancient Greece there was indeed a close connection between law and writing that goes back to the early archaic period. I also agree that in the archaic and classical periods there was a contrast between legislation and administration of justice. By and large, while laws—and in particular new laws—began to be written down, judicial procedure was conducted orally and had to be remembered.[80] I also like the idea that in Athens and probably in other poleis as well, there was the same purpose behind having written laws and oral administration of justice—namely, to make law accessible to ordinary citizens.[81] The connection between written laws and democracy is famously stated by Euripides in the *Suppliants* 429–434.[82]

On the other hand, I think that in both books Gagarin is too dismissive of the concept of oral law, which in my opinion is attested in a number of societies and also to some extent in ancient Greece, at least in connection with constitutional law and religious law; and I suggest a modification of the view that there always is a qualitative difference between the written laws and the oral rules that preceded the written ones.[83]

Here a comparison with epic poetry is obvious. Before 1928 no one had thought of the *Iliad* and *Odyssey* as orally transmitted poems. In 1928 Milman Parry showed that the Homeric poems had been orally transmitted before they were written down.[84] His crucial discovery was the parallel with Yugoslavian singers of tales. Today we all know that the *Iliad* and *Odyssey* were oral poems written down much later. And there is a huge literature about oral poetry from all over the world. Strangely enough, no similar comparative study has been undertaken for the oral transmission of laws. To the best of my knowledge, this study is a first attempt. The difference between epic poetry and laws is that two performances of Homer did not have to be identical. The singer would modify his performance in accordance with the composition of his audience. The transmission of laws had to be verbatim just as in the case of religious texts and rituals. I think it is time for scholars to undertake a comparative study of oral transmission of laws,[85] and—inter alia—to investigate the distinction between laws regulating constitutional conventions and laws prescribing general rules of conduct.

1. Gagarin 2008: 1–2, 10–12, 108, 120, 197, 214, 242.

2. Gagarin (2008: 110) rightly points out that "terms like 'writing' (*graphos*, *grammata*) could be used without qualification to designate a written law." But—as he notes as well (34, 91, 110)—an alternative term is *rhetra*, "pronouncement, proclamation," which etymologically indicates orality (Quass 1971: 7–9).

3. Gagarin 2008: 36: "Using the expression 'oral laws' may usefully convey the point that there is a relationship between these oral customs and traditions and later written laws, but at the same time it obscures the important changes that occur when certain rules are written. Thus, I find it more useful to avoid the expression 'oral laws' and speak instead of oral law as existing in the context of orally preserved and transmitted rules." 38: "Not until the invention of writing and its subsequent use in the process of writing legislation did the Greeks create laws for their community that were distinct from their customs and traditions."

4. Gagarin 2008: 6, 8, 27–30, 108.

5. Gagarin 2008: 8, 28, 32, 36.

6. Hastrup 1985: 105–135 (social and political structure) and 205–222 (development of the law). Cf. Dennis, Foote, and Perkins 1980–2000; Sigurdsson 2004.

7. Dennis, Foote, and Perkins 1980–2000, I: 193: "The Lawspeaker is required to tell everyone who asks him what the article of the law is, both here and at his home, but he is not required to give anyone further advice on lawsuits. He is also to recite the assembly procedure every summer and all the other sections so that they are recited every three summers if the majority wish to hear them. Assembly procedure is always to be recited on the first Friday of the assembly if men have time to hear it." See below n. 13.

8. Dennis, Foote, and Perkins 1980–2000, I: 13–16.

9. Gagarin 1986: 10; 2008: 27–30, cf. 8, 108. With reservations, Gagarin accepts it as a possible example of an orally transmitted law code.

10. Gagarin 2008: 29.

11. *Grágás* means "gray lag-goose." Nobody knows why the Icelandic law-code got such an odd name.

12. Hastrup 1985: 216–217.

13. In the mid-thirteenth century the *Grágás* had grown to such size that it would be impossible—even in the course of three years—to have it recited in its entirety. One suspects that the caveats "if the majority wish to hear them" and "if men have time to hear it" are later addenda and that an originally obligatory recitation of all laws when they were orally transmitted had been discontinued when the laws had been written down.

14. Christie 1995: 73–91.

15. For a translation into English of the *Edictum Rothari*, see Drew 1973: 39–130, with introduction, 1–37.

16. Drew 1973: 25–26.

17. Art. 2. prescribes that "he . . . who kills a man by the king's order, shall be entirely without blame" (Drew 1973: 53).

18. Paulus Diaconus, *Historia gentis Langobardorum* 4.42.5–6.

19. Drew 1973: 129.

20. Drew 1973: 130.

21. Duncanson 1949.

22. The best sources are Vega 1961: 96–101, 199–201, 224–227, 261–266, 328–333, 338–339, 355, 391–392, 395–397; Guamán Poma de Ayala 2009: 141–147, sections 182–193.

23. Vega 1961: 331–332.

24. Vega 1961: 99–100.

25. Vega 1961: 98.

26. Vega 1961: 391, 395–396.

27. Topa Inca Yupanqui's laws are summarized in Guamán Poma de Ayala 2009: 141–147, sections 182–193.

28. The passage is quoted by Vega (1961: 262). He had copied and translated it from Blas Valera's treatise in Latin (now lost). Apparently trusting the Indians' traditions, Valera believed that the laws had been transmitted accurately during six hundred years. That is certainly wrong. There is no doubt that the laws were changed every generation, as Valera admits himself. Vega (1961: 391, 395–96) reports, e.g., that Pachacútec, the Inca legislator par excellence, abolished many laws, revised others, and gave many new laws as well.

29. Vega 1961: 98, 226–227, 333.

30. Vega 1961: 331–333.

31. Borrull y Villanova 1831; Glick 1970.

32. "Tribunal de las Aguas de Valencia," *Wikipedia* (Spanish), last modified February 27, 2017, http://es.wikipedia.org/wiki/Tribunal_de_las_Aguas_de_Valencia.

33. Voell 2004: 54–59. See also Tarifa 2008.

34. Voell 2004: 40–44.

35. Voell 2004: 238.

36. The *Kanuni i Lekë Dukagjinit*, composed by Gjeçov, was published posthumously, in 1933. See Voell 2004: 26.

37. See Fox's introduction to Gjeçov 1989: xix.

38. Voell 2004: 51, 106.

39. Voell 2004: 46–49.

40. Voell 2004: 46.

41. Voell 2004: 39.

42. Krasztev 2000: 208.

43. Voell 2004: 107, 114.

44. Voell 2004: 25.

45. Voell 2004: 239.

46. Voell 2004: 52, 238.

47. Bohannan and Bohannan 1953: 43; Gagarin 2008: 18–19.

48. Schapera 1955: 35, 37; cf. Gagarin 1986: 3.

49. *The New Encyclopædia Britannica*, 15th ed. (Chicago 1997). Vol. 25, 242b, s.v. "Pacific Islands."

50. Gagarin 2008: 102, cf. 101; see also 80: "Details in oral texts are unstable and often change with successive readings"; cf. 85. I agree, but we must distinguish between poetic texts, e.g., epics, where every performance was adapted to the audience and the occasion (Jensen 2011: 108–144), and recitals of historical or legal texts.

51. Luria 1987.

52. "Hafiz (Quran)," *Wikipedia*, last modified August 11, 2016, http://en .wikipedia.org/wiki/Hafiz_(Quran).

53. Vansina 1973: 32–33.

54. Vansina 1973: 31.

55. Vansina 1973: 28.

56. Lowie 1950: 202.

57. Hastrup 1985: 208–216; Dennis, Foote, and Perkins 1980: 5.

58. Vega 1961: 391–392, 395–396.

59. Gagarin 2008: 45–66.

60. Gagarin 1986: 51–80; 2008: 44–45; Szegedy-Maszak 1978; Wallace 2009; Hölkeskamp 1999. I share the modification of Hölkeskamp's views in Gagarin 2008: 44–45, 74–75.

61. The only known written document of the archaic period is the so-called Great Rhetra (Plut. *Lyc.* 6.1). In form it is an oracle sent to the Spartan kings from Delphi, and we know from Herodotus (6.57.4) that all oracles from Delphi were filed by the kings and their *puthioi*, the messengers sent by the kings to Delphi whenever the Spartan state put a question to the oracle. The rider to the Rhetra (Plut. *Lyc.* 6.4) purports to be a written amendment issued by Polydorus and Theopompus. If it is genuine, it antedates the law from Dreros and is the oldest of all known Greek laws. But the source may be the exiled king Pausanias's pamphlet on the Lycurgan laws (*FGrHist* 582), in which case its authenticity is doubtful. Cf. Gagarin 1986: 53–54 n. 9; 2008: 93; MacDowell 1986: 3–5; Millender 2001: 127–141; Hansen 2010: xv with n. 15.

62. According to Plutarch (*Lyc.* 13.1), Lycurgus did not have his laws written down. On the contrary, Spartan laws were called not *graphea* but *rhētrai*, "pronouncements" or "sayings," and Plutarch claims that Lycurgus prohibited the use of written laws (*Lyc.* 13.3; [Plut.] *Mor.* 227b). In the classical and Hellenistic periods, however, Sparta had written laws like other poleis (Lyc. 1.129; Plut. *Agis* 5.2, 9.1).

63. Gagarin 2008: 117–121.

64. Holmbäck and Wessén 1946: article 314. Cf. Bagge 2010: 183–184.

65. See p. 177.

66. Holmbäck and Wessén 1946: Inledning xviii–xxxiii, Äldre Västgötalagen 3–200.

67. *ML* 2; *Nomima* 1.81.

68. Thrasym. fr. 1, DK 2: 324.1–6.

69. Rhodes 1981: 376; Hansen 1989: 85–86.

70. Andoc. 1.83. The authenticity of Teisamenus's decree has been questioned by Canevaro and Harris 2012. I am not persuaded. See Hansen 2015.

71. [Arist.] *Ath. Pol.* 35.2. Rhodes 1981: 440; Sickinger 1999: 99.

72. Phot., s.v. πρόπεμπτα; Thuc. 6.8.3.

73. Cf., e.g., the rule that in the House of Commons the members vote by shouting and a division takes place only if the majority cannot be established by voting *viva voce*.

74. Hansen 1989: 82–87.

75. Dem. 24.20–23, 33, 39–40, 42, 45, 50, 54, 56, 59. In this context it is of no consequence whether the inserted documents are authentic or later reconstructions, as argued by Canevaro 2013.

76. Schreiner 1913: 12–60; Clinton 1982: 29; Hansen 1989: 79.

77. Aeschin. 1.23; 3.2.

78. Gagarin 2008: 185.

79. MacDowell 1962: 126. See also Clinton 1982: 35–37.

80. Gagarin 2008: 121, 197.

81. Gagarin 2008: 12, 214.

82. Gagarin 2008: 72, 197.

83. Gagarin 2008: 6.

84. Parry 1971.

85. One of the anonymous referees, for example, has drawn my attention to Caesar's description in *BG* 6.14 of the oral tradition among the Druids.

REFERENCES

Bagge, Sverre. 2010. *From Viking Stronghold to Christian Kingdom: State Formation in Norway, c. 900–1350.* Copenhagen: Museum Tusculanum Press.

Bohannan, Paul, and Laura Bohannan. 1953. *The Tiv of Central Nigeria.* London: International African Institute.

Borrull y Vilanova, Francisco Javier. 1831. *Tratado de la distribución de las aguas del río Turia, y del Tribunal de los Acequieros de la Huerta de Valencia.* Valencia: Benito Monfort.

Canevaro, Mirko. 2013. *The Documents in the Attic Orators: Laws and Decrees in the Public Speeches of the Demosthenic Corpus.* Oxford: Oxford University Press.

Canevaro, Mirko, and Edward M. Harris. 2012. "The Documents in Andocides' *On the Mysteries*." *Classical Quarterly* 62.1: 98–129.

Christie, Neil. 1995. *The Lombards: The Ancient Longobards.* Oxford: Blackwell.

Clinton, Kevin. 1982. "The Nature of the Late Fifth-Century Revision of the Athenian Law Code." In *Studies in Attic Epigraphy, History, and Topography: Presented to Eugene Vanderpool.* Suppl. 19 of *Hesperia,* 27–37. Princeton: American School of Classical Studies at Athens.

Dennis, Andrew, Peter Foote, and Richard Perkins, trans. 1980–2000. *Laws of Early*

Iceland: Grágás; The Codex Regius of Grágás with Material from Other Manuscripts.
2 vols. Winnipeg: University of Manitoba Press.

Drew, Katherine F. 1973. *The Lombard Laws: Translated with an Introduction.* Philadelphia: University of Pennsylvania Press.

Duncanson, Dennis J. 1949. "Sir'at'Adkeme Milga': A Native Law Code of Eritrea." *Africa* 19.2: 141–149.

Gagarin, Michael. 1986. *Early Greek Law.* Berkeley: University of California Press.

———. 2008. *Writing Greek Law.* Cambridge: Cambridge University Press.

Gjeçov, Shtjefën K. 1989. *Kanuni i Lekë Dukagjinit: The Code of Lekë Dukagjini.* Translated and introduced by Leonard Fox. New York: Gjonlekaj Publishing.

Glick, Thomas F. 1970. *Irrigation and Society in Medieval Valencia.* Cambridge, MA: Belknap Press.

Guamán Poma de Ayala, Felipe. 2009. *The First New Chronicle and Good Government: On the History of the World and the Incas up to 1615.* Translated and edited by Roland Hamilton. Austin: University of Texas Press.

Hansen, Mogens Herman. 1989. "Solonian Democracy in Fourth-Century Athens." *Classica et Mediaevalia* 40: 71–99.

———. 2010. "Introduction." In *Démocratie athenienne—démocratie moderne: Traditions et influences,* edited by Alain-Christian Hernández, vii–xxxviii. Vandoeuvres-Geneva: Fondation Hardt.

———. 2015. "Is Teisamenos' Decree (Andoc. 1.83-84) a Genuine Document?" *Greek, Roman, and Byzantine Studies* 56: 34-48.

Hastrup, Kirsten. 1985. *Culture and History in Medieval Iceland: An Anthropological Analysis of Structure and Change.* Oxford: Clarendon Press.

Hölkeskamp, Karl-Joachim. 1999. *Schiedsrichter, Gesetzgeber und Gesetzgebung im archaischen Griechenland.* Stuttgart: Steiner.

Holmbäck, Åke, and Elias Wessén. 1946. *Svenska Landskapslagar: Tolkade och förklarade för nutidens Svenskar.* Vol. 5. Stockholm: Hugo Gebers.

Jensen, Minna S. 2011. *Writing Homer: A Study Based on Results from Modern Fieldwork.* Copenhagen: Det Kongelige Danske Videnskabernes Selskab.

Krasztev, Peter. 2000. "The Price of Amnesia: Interpretations of Vendetta in Albania." In *Albania and the Albanian Identities,* edited by Antonina Zhelyazkova, translated by Maya Dimitrova and Stephen Humphreys, 194–217. Sofia: IMIR.

Lowie, Robert. 1950. *Social Organization.* London: Routledge and Kegan Paul.

Luria, Aleksandr. 1987. *The Mind of a Mnemonist: A Little Book about a Vast Memory.* Translated by Lynn Solotaroff. Cambridge, MA: Harvard University Press. Reprint with new introduction of 1968 publication by Basic Books.

MacDowell, Douglas M. 1962. *Andokides,* On the Mysteries. Oxford: Clarendon Press.

———. 1986. *Spartan Law.* Edinburgh: Scottish Academic Press.

Millender, Ellen G. 2001. "Spartan Literacy Revisited." *Classical Antiquity* 20.1: 121–164.

Parry, Milman. 1971. *The Making of Homeric Verse: The Collected Papers of Milman Parry.* Edited by Adam Parry. Oxford: Clarendon Press.

Quass, Friedemann. 1971. *Nomos und Psephisma: Untersuchung zum griechischen Staatsrecht*. Munich: C. H. Beck.

Rhodes, Peter J. 1981. *A Commentary on the Aristotelian* Athenaion Politeia. Oxford: Oxford University Press.

Schapera, Isaac. 1955. *A Handbook of Tswana Law and Custom*. 2nd ed. London: International African Institute.

Schreiner, Josef. 1913. *De corpore juris Atheniensium*. Bonn: C. Georgi.

Sickinger, James P. 1999. *Public Records and Archives in Classical Athens*. Chapel Hill: University of North Carolina Press.

Sigurdsson, Gísli. 2004. *The Medieval Icelandic Saga and Oral Tradition: A Discourse on Method*. Translated by Nicholas Jones. Cambridge, MA: Milman Parry Collection, Harvard University Press.

Szegedy-Maszak, Andrew. 1978. "Legends of the Greek Lawgivers." *Greek, Roman, and Byzantine Studies* 19.3: 199–209.

Tarifa, Fatos. 2008. "Of Time, Honor, and Memory: Oral Law in Albania," *Oral Tradition* 23.1: 3–14.

Vansina, Jan. 1973. *Oral Tradition: A Study in Historical Methodology*. Translated by Hope M. Wright. Harmondsworth, UK: Penguin Books.

Vega, Garcilaso de la. 1961. *The Incas: The Royal Commentaries of the Inca, Garcilaso de la Vega, 1539–1616*. Edited by Alain Gheerbrant. Translated by Maria Jolas. New York: Avon Books.

Voell, Stéphane. 2004. *Das nordalbanische Gewohnheitsrecht und seine mündliche Dimension*. Marburg: Curupira.

Wallace, Robert W. 2009. "Charismatic Leaders." In *A Companion to Archaic Greece*, edited by Kurt A. Raaflaub and Hans van Wees, 411–426. Malden, MA: Wiley-Blackwell.

22 / THE FUTURE OF CLASSICAL ORATORY

Gerhard Thür

THROUGHOUT MY CAREER IN ACADEMIA I HAVE TAUGHT Roman law, German civil law, and, my favorite, ancient Greek law (epigraphy, papyrology, and Athenian court speeches). In keeping with the focus of this volume, my chapter explores the practical use of classical oratory in education—in law[1] as well as other disciplines—as a challenge of the twenty-first century. I suggest that classical oratory be taught by practicing it in moot courts modeled on Athenian court speeches and procedures. It is my view that the art of communication and persuasion today encompasses not only speaking and writing, but also visual media (which, although nonverbal, one may compare with *atechnoi pisteis*, or "artless proofs," in the classical sense). In the following sections, I focus on the boundary between lying and manipulating the facts. The method of the ancient Greek *rhētōr* ("public speaker") was to "isolate the facts" and combine them into an overall picture that was untrue. I illustrate this using the new Timandrus fragment of Hyperides and Demosthenes's lawsuit against Aphobus. I suggest that for psychological reasons, in Athenian courts the first speaker was in the better position. In conclusion, I argue from practical experience that the "Athenian style" of moot courts is a better way of teaching oratory today than is the imitation of modern trials.

I. INTRODUCTION

Oratory is the art of communication and persuasion, not only by speaking and writing, but also by such visual means as pictures and monuments. Today, in public, business, and private life, we inevitably are confronted with oratory. When one thinks of oratory, one imagines primarily the classical categories of political, court, and commemorative speeches. But only a very few university students will be educated for jobs in politics or law or will have occasion to compose and deliver formal commemorative speeches. However, the field of social communication and persuasion is much broader than these categories suggest. In practical life everybody has to convince an audience, and to be successful one has to use rational as well as emotional elements. How to combine them in an effective way can be learned by practicing classical oratory. For very good reasons rhetoric was the basis of higher education in antiquity.

For didactic purposes, I would prefer to study Athenian court speeches. In Athenian courts, average people spoke to a large audience of average people, and the latter, several hundred lay judges, had to make up their minds—a quick "yes" or "no"—immediately after the parties had spoken. Of course, in modern practice we cannot simply copy Athenian oratory, at least not the arguments *ad personam*. However, from the Athenian court speeches, one can learn all the elements of persuasion. Cicero, the philosophically erudite orator, spoke in person to a more sophisticated upper-class audience. He was confronted with a restricted number of judges, who gave their verdict after hearing several sessions. His speeches are therefore more difficult to explain and to use in teaching oratory. Only very recently have new methods of deconstructing them been found.[2] In my opinion, the ancient rhetorical manuals, the *technai* and *institutiones*, are also of little didactic value today. But the last two points may depend on my personal ignorance; with methods different from mine, dedicated teachers could probably also take advantage of Roman court speeches and general rhetorical theory.

To a significant degree, modern methods of communication and persuasion rely on visual means. Pictures are stronger than words. Does this harm oratory today? Not in my opinion. Instead of deploring our backsliding into speechless barbarism, I would suggest adopting the rhetorical theory and practice of *atechnoi pisteis*. These were prefabricated written documents read aloud to the judges not by the litigants themselves, but by the court secretary. Therefore, they did not belong to the art (*technē*) of rhetorical persuasion; nevertheless, the handbooks taught how to use them in the most effective way. Pictures are nothing other than a means of persuasion outside of oral argumentation. Since antiquity, the task of composing a speech has included the adoption of such means. Indeed, the modern technologies of TV or PowerPoint are meant to persuade (i.e., are used to rhetorical ends). Without going into detail, I only mention two ancient predecessors of these media—coinage and architecture—as studied by Paul Zanker in his *Augustus und die Macht der Bilder*.[3]

One example of modern speechless monumental oratory, nonpolitical at first glance, is the architecture of the Viennese artist Friedensreich Hundertwasser (Friedrich Stowasser), who died in the year 2000. His paintings are perhaps better known, but in his architectural œuvre, Hundertwasser put

FIGURE 11.1. *Hundertwasser House, Vienna 1985: organic "unregulated irregularities."*

FIGURE 11.2. *Hundertwasser garbage incinerator, Vienna 1987: hiding a power plant by "oratory in architecture."*

"diversity before monotony" and replaced a grid system with an organic approach that enabled "unregulated irregularities." He was an enthusiastic forerunner of the environmental movement. From 1983 to 1985, despite fierce criticism, he constructed the "Hundertwasser House," furnished with a total of 250 trees and bushes. Now it is one of Vienna's most visited buildings and has become part of Austria's cultural heritage (fig. 11.1). However, in Vienna there is also another Hundertwasser building. In 1971 a huge garbage incinerator, which also served as a district heating plant, was damaged by fire. After the fire it was difficult to convince the citizens to restore the air-polluting plant in the middle of the city. What were they to do with the structure? The local authority sought help from the famous artist, and in 1987 a new work of art was finally dedicated. The air pollution was the same, but (nearly) everyone praised the new Hundertwasser creation (fig. 11.2). In my opinion this is an extreme example of how rational calculation can trump auspicious emotion. Of course, one cannot find the exact same tricks in classical oratory, but the same psychological effects can be studied there.

2. LIES AND MISREPRESENTATIONS
OF FACT IN GREEK ORATORY

My approach to classical Greek oratory has always been juridical. My interests have been twofold: first, what can we learn about Athenian law from forensic speeches; and second, how can we explain the speakers' procedural strategies based on what we know about Athenian law? These two questions are, of course, linked, but only the second is directly concerned with oratory. From this point of view it is not the formal instruments for composing and embellishing a speech that are important, but rather the overall intellectual structure of court speeches. Surprisingly for a modern lawyer, in an Athenian trial we never hear a party discuss legal questions at the high level of classical Roman jurisprudence or Ciceronian complexity. Statutes quoted by Athenian litigants are mostly clear and (though sometimes used in a distorted way) seem to fit the case exactly, at least as presented in the speech. Usually the facts of the case are in dispute. Facts, not law, are the primary topic of Athenian court oratory. Therefore, when analyzing a court speech, a jurist first has to find out which facts were controversial, admittedly by conjecture. A well-known problem is that, in most cases, only the speech of one party is preserved, leaving us with just one side of the story and no way to check its veracity. Some classicists simply trust—or distrust—the *diēgēsis* or narrative part of the speech. In my opinion this is too formalistic, too trusting in the general rules for a court speech shaped by the rhetorical *technai*.

The questions that need to be asked are: do parties lie in court, and if so, how can we find out what the facts of a case might have been? To answer these questions we have to scrutinize how the *logographers* ("speechwriters") composed the speeches of their clients in order to convince the court. I will give two examples: first, the new Hyperides fragment against Timandrus, and second, Demosthenes's lawsuit against Aphobus. From these one can see that the borderline between "lying" and "manipulating" is blurred.

I would like to start with a few words about the method I have applied since I began working on the *proklēsis eis basanon*, the challenge to torture a slave, some forty years ago.[4] My starting point is the observation that the *logographers*, in order to support their clients' positions, rarely resorted to simplistic lies; instead, they typically created distortions that the audience was largely unable to unravel. They isolated facts that belonged together and, by using psychological links, combined individual aspects of an issue that were true by themselves but perhaps not in combination. The art of lying—or manipulating—involved attributing typical psychological motives to the opponent; there was a broad range of possibilities because a person's actual motives always remained in the dark. Thus, out of a set of facts, the *logographers* shaped an overall impression that was false, but met the needs of their clients' cases. In court the litigants used this technique of portrayal to their advantage by informing the audience in a thorough but guided manner.[5] Through careful preparation of their speeches, plaintiffs, on the one hand, were able to keep their opponents from swaying the jurors with new facts; every relevant fact must be mentioned somewhere in the plaintiff's speech, but not necessarily in a coherent order. The defendants, on the other hand, by exciting high emotions, tried to highlight aspects of the case different from those their opponents presumably would produce. Because of the Athenian system of litigating by speeches composed in advance, there was no room for direct forensic dispute between the parties. The opportunity of checking each other's positions was given in the pretrial meetings of the *anakrisis* ("preliminary hearing") and the official *diaita* ("arbitration"). Here the litigants had to answer each other's questions[6] and disclose all documentary evidence to be used in court.[7] Given the requirements that Athenian law placed on a particular *dikē* ("private lawsuit"), the true state of the conflict (one party's assertion and the other's counterassertion) can successfully be reconstructed out of just one oration through a logical synthesis of the details that the speaker disparately reports—a process I have called "Isolierung der Fakten."[8]

My first example, though fragmentarily preserved in the famous Archimedes palimpsest, is Hyperides's speech against Timandrus.[9] A *sunēgoros* ("co-speaker"), whose name is unknown, is speaking for the young plaintiff Academus, who is calling to account his former guardian, Timandrus, for mismanaging his affairs for thirteen years. The lawsuit was a *dikē epitropēs* ("prosecution for mismanagement of an orphan's estate").[10] In this chapter I will concentrate on the facts. The speaker argues that Timandrus had managed his ward's property in an illegal way (lines 10–16): he did not register the guardianship with the *archon* ("chief magistrate"); he did not have the property leased, which also was to be done by the *archon*;[11] and he prevented a denunciation (*phasis*) intending to lease the property from being filed with the *archon*.[12] Worst of all, he dragged one of the four orphans, the younger girl, away from Athens to his home on the island of Lemnos (lines 25–27). Is it plausible that Timandrus was able to maintain such an illegal position for such a long time? The facts are partly uncontroversial and partly corroborated by witnesses, so they might be recorded correctly. From the comment in lines 3–5, "Yet the laws forbid the guardians to lease the property on their own authority,"[13] I infer that Timandrus will argue in his defense that he himself was lessee of the estate, as was permitted by Athenian law.[14] In this case, at the conclusion of his duty, he was not to be called to account. He only had to pay annual interest to sustain the wards and, at the end of his duty, deliver the capital he had taken over at the beginning of the guardianship.[15] What about the other charges?

The clue to the defendant's argumentation could be the reference to the island of Lemnos. To be appointed as a guardian Timandrus must have been an Athenian citizen; and living in Lemnos he most probably had the status of a cleruch (*klērouchos*, a holder of allotted land in a foreign country who retains his original citizenship). He certainly will argue that he had complied with all of the legal requests mentioned above before the magistrate of the cleruchy in Lemnos. Thus the plaintiff and his witnesses are right that Timandrus did *not* register the guardianship and lease the property *in Athens*. The plaintiff only omitted the essential fact that all this had happened *elsewhere*, that is, on Lemnos. Therefore, the *archon* in Athens evidently had had no reason to accept any *phasis* based on the claim that something was wrong with the guardianship. And the fact that the girl was brought up in Timandrus's house could have been ordered by her father's will.[16]

Through the common psychological explanation in lines 17 and 59—Timandrus's desire for money—the plaintiff glued together all these facts to make the actions seem illegal. And the whole section between these two lines is about the lonesome girl on the faraway island, making the larger part of the fragment mere rhetoric, intended to demonstrate Timandrus's allegedly avaricious character. It really is a pity that the rest of this speech is lost!

My next example is the young Demosthenes's lawsuit against one of his former guardians, Aphobus, consisting of five orations well preserved since antiquity and subject to scholarly discussion for centuries. First, I concentrate on the dispute about Milyas, the foreman of the knife-workshop.[17] By *proklēsis* ("formal challenge"), Aphobus, the defendant, had demanded this man from Demosthenes for *basanos* ("inquiry by torture") to be questioned first about the income of the workshop of thirty minas (27.19–23; 28.12; 29.50), and then about ten talents, the whole amount demanded by Demosthenes (27.50–52, in 29.30 referred to only indirectly). Milyas was asked to confirm or deny that Demosthenes had received all the money. Demosthenes refused the demand to turn Milyas over for torture, holding that the man was no longer a slave but free. And he produced a witness deposition claiming that Aphobus himself by *homologia* ("agreement") "had acknowledged that Milyas was set free by Demosthenes's father."[18] However, in Athens testamentary manumissions were not valid unless an act of public proclamation occurred,[19] which apparently had not yet happened.

How did Demosthenes handle this delicate situation? By "isolating the facts." In section 9 of his first speech against Aphobus (Dem. 29), he seems to be uncertain about the figure of thirty-two or thirty-three knife-makers— a feigned uncertainty regarding Milyas. Not before section 19 does he identify Milyas as "our freedman," depicting him as manager with full authority. In 22, eventually, without saying a single word about Aphobus's *proklēsis*, Demosthenes most probably produces the witness testimony about Aphobus's *homologia*. Then in section 50 he refers to an "unreliable" *proklēsis*, this time without mentioning the name of Milyas. In this way the plaintiff undermined foreseeable conclusions from the *proklēsis* he had rejected, without saying a single word about the *basanos* that the defendant had demanded. From Demosthenes's first speech, throughout the whole *dikē epitropēs* the judges would have remembered that Milyas was a free man and was not to be subjected to torture.

Another topic of this speech, most promising for scholarship even still in the twenty-first century, is the case of Cleobule, Demosthenes's mother. In the following I can only give a brief outline. On his deathbed, her husband, Demosthenes's father (also named Demosthenes), gave her in marriage to Aphobus with a dowry of eighty minas and granted Aphobus the house for a residence (27.5). Aphobus took up residence and, allegedly, received the full dowry (27.16) but "refused" to marry Cleobule. In this sense the audience must have understood the words: μὴ γήμαντος δ᾽ αὐτοῦ τὴν μητέρα τὴν ἐμήν ("[if] he did not marry my mother"; 27.17). Since Demochares, the husband of Cleobule's sister, was interfering in the case, we might come to another conclusion. As Douglas MacDowell in his translation correctly notes,[20] Cleobule left her marital home and moved to the house of her sister. Did *she* refuse to marry Aphobus? It seems likely.[21] Anyway, in court Demosthenes concedes that "a little disagreement" had taken place between Aphobus and Cleobule (27.15). Because Demochares, Cleobule's brother-in-law, was not her *kurios* ("woman's guardian")[22] and her son, Demosthenes, was underage, there was no one to administer her legal interests.[23] Therefore Aphobus, claiming that he had been willing to marry the widow, had good arguments for keeping her dowry, at least until he married another woman, and not providing Cleobule with maintenance (27.15). Did Cleobule incite her son to sue Aphobus first of the three guardians? Most probably she did.[24] Surprisingly, in his *dikē epitropēs* against Aphobus, Demosthenes did not dare praise his mother because "she passed her life in widowhood for her children." He didn't do so until his speech for Phanus in the following *dikē pseudomarturiōn* ("prosecution for false witness"; 29.26), addressing another law court, whose judges were not aware of the speeches in the prior trial. It seems that in his defense against the *dikē epitropēs* Aphobus did not speak very favorably about Cleobule[25]—in vain, as it turned out.

In the first speech against Aphobus there is one more instance of "isolating the facts": emotionally the whole speech is concentrated on Cleobule's dowry. Demosthenes began his account of Aphobus's misdeeds with this point (27.13–18), and his last words were spoken about this dowry (27.69). Imploring the judges for pity, Demosthenes complained about another dowry too: if Aphobus should not be condemned in this trial, he, Demosthenes, never would be able to spend the two talents his father had bequeathed as *proix* ("dowry") to his, the younger Demosthenes's, sister (27.65). Eventually the judges must have forgotten that the co-guardian Demophon, who was provided to marry the girl when she came of age,[26] had cashed the sum in advance, as had been mentioned at the beginning of the speech (27.5). Nevertheless, Demophon refused to marry her. Does this item concern Aphobus? If the sister's dowry really was so important, why did Demosthenes not sue Demophon first? However, Demosthenes may have trapped the judges by the fact that *usually* the mother's *proix* passed to her daughter.[27] *Proix* was an ideal emotional topic to frame sober business interests.

The technique of isolating the facts is used primarily by plaintiffs. They have the opportunity to inform the judges first about the relevant facts of the case, and they benefit from this position. From the first plausible information, the listeners receive psychologically "complex associations" tightly interwoven, especially when backed by emotions. Later, when the defendant is speaking, "associative inhibitions" make it difficult for the audience to understand the facts in a coherent order that is different from the one exposed by the plaintiff.[28] Therefore, in Athenian courts the better rhetorical position was the first word.[29] Giving the last word to the defendant was considered a matter of fairness. And as far as possible, defendants used the *paragraphē* (a "special plea" that the lawsuit was not admissible) to speak first and imprint their points of view on the judges. Moreover, Demosthenes (47.39, 45) reports that in two independent cases concerning *aikeia* ("assault") between two persons involved in a scuffle, both opponents struggled to be *first* to address the court—namely, to be the plaintiff, which indeed seems strange to a modern jurist. As a result, one litigant, Theophemus, accepted the burden of proof to show that his opponent had struck the first blow, but because of his preferable rhetorical position of speaking first, he nonetheless won the case.[30]

Jumping now to the twenty-first century, one may ask whether it makes sense to teach our students the sophisticated art of lying by manipulating an audience. Admittedly, detecting the technique of "isolating the facts" is a rather extreme method for studying classical oratory,[31] combining philological, historical, sociological, and juristic aspects with mass psychology. Searching for the overall intellectual guidelines of court speeches, one cannot benefit much from the ancient *technai* and *institutiones*. Since every actual case preserved in classical court speeches was different, an intensive study of forensic practice is necessary to achieve this goal. A modern lawyer can profit from isolating the facts only in a very restricted way. Today, through cross-examination and forensic dispute, law courts are better equipped for finding the truth than the ancient Athenian *dikastēria* ("popular courts") were. In Athens, in an absolutely passive way, the huge panels of lay-judges were completely dependent on the opponents' speeches, performed in continuous blocks, which were only interrupted by reading aloud short documents. Nevertheless, in present-day penal cases, every prosecutor or attorney-at-law tries in summation to manipulate the jury by exciting emotions in order to stress or reduce the relevance of facts—just as Demosthenes and Hyperides did.

Today the art of isolating the facts and exciting emotionally "complex associations" survives wherever mass psychology is alive, in the fields of politics and economy. This concerns every citizen. As is generally known, in former generations the most successful active players in politics improved their natural abilities by studying classical oratory, and today business executives are trained in "limbic presentation." But a responsible citizen also needs some knowledge of the tools of oratory and mass psychology in order to penetrate political propaganda and commercial advertising. This ability is a welcome by-product of rhetorical education.

The main reason for teaching classical oratory is to furnish intellectual and formal guidelines of perfect self-portrayal in public speaking, and in the same way, in writing addresses and in appearing in visual mass media. All of these techniques can be learned by studying and practicing the classical art of persuasion. For several years I performed Athenian moot courts with my students. My idea was to practice oratory throughout all stages, from *heuresis* ("discovery" or *inventio*) to *hupokrisis* ("orator's delivery" or *actio* / *pronuntiatio*). The didactic aim was to perform cases preserved in classical literature according to the pattern of an Athenian trial: adapting the preserved speech and inventing the opposing plea. Thus we strictly observed the following rules: a written *enklēma* (complaint); disclosure of all documents in an *anakrisis*; a strict time limit in speaking controlled by a *klepsudra* ("water clock"); a prohibition on interrupting the speeches (unless by uproars, *thoru-bos*, in the audience—the speaker has to learn to cope with these); the use of testimony depositions only as short, untimed written documents read aloud; and secret voting immediately after the speeches.

Preparing such a performance (for example, of Lysias 1) in a seminar took a whole term.[32] The first step was analyzing the court speech by all participants: in term papers, several students reconstructed and discussed the legal, historical, and sociological background of the case, the facts presented by the speaker, his legal arguments, and the possible counter arguments of the opponent. Thereby the students also learned how to penetrate manipulations by isolating the facts. Then the rest of the group separated into the roles of jurisdictional staff (presiding magistrate and court secretary) and the two parties, plaintiff and defendant (with supporters on both sides), and both sides, respectively, drafted the *enklēma* and *antigraphē* ("defendant's plea"). The parties separately sketched the outlines of their arguments, checked the *nomoi* ("laws"), and drafted *marturiai* ("testimony" or *inventio*). Later, after the *anakrisis* (in which the litigants formally questioned each other and disclosed their written documents), the speakers attended to composition and style (*dispositio* and *elocutio*). Finally, they learned their speeches by heart (*memoria*) and, at the end of the term, performed the trial (*pronuntiatio*) before a larger public audience, which played the part of judges by secretly voting. Of course, students performing the role of Lysias's client were better off, but the plaintiff and his *sunēgoroi* also composed ingenious speeches.

To conclude the oral presentation of this paper in Austin, Texas, I relied on an *atechnos pistis*, a movie. It was a cut of some fifteen minutes from a one-hour video of the trial against Socrates that was performed by my students in Graz in 2007.[33]

In conclusion here, I want to stress the differences between performing moot courts in the "classical Athenian" way and those following the shape of a "modern" (Anglo-American) trial, even when featuring cases from Greek or Roman law—and the advantages of the former. In Athens, jurisdiction was a matter of direct democracy, where rhetoric played an essential role. In strictly limited time, addressing personally a mass panel of laymen, who immediately after listening to the speeches voted for guilt or innocence, was a great intellectual and emotional challenge for the litigants. This was the matrix of classical forensic oratory. The presiding magistrate was not allowed to interfere or ask questions. Today the presiding judge governs the trial in a different way; he and professional lawyers on both opponents' sides enter mutual legal disputes and question the parties or cross-examine the witnesses.[34] Therefore, a moot court in the modern style emphasizes elements of dialectic rather than rhetoric;[35] here, students are trained more in special legal knowl-

FIGURE 11.3. *Counting the votes in the trial of Socrates, Freiburg, Germany (2007).*

edge rather than in rhetorical argumentation. Moot courts in Athenian style have a more general scope: they do not imply special knowledge of the law but meet the demands of an erudite, responsible citizen of our day. Thus, their place is in legal and classical education as well. Finally, the Athenian style has one more advantage: by interacting with the audience, the litigants have to expose the full case—though seen from different sides—to the listeners, who have an active role and will immediately deliver a judgment. In contrast, moot courts shaped in modern style often are conducted like academic examinations: the presiding professional "judges"—teachers or lawyers—do not decide the case, but rather grade and rank the speakers and teams all competing about the same case. The audience, at the beginning scarcely informed, has—sometimes boringly—an absolutely passive role. This satisfies primarily legal but not rhetorical standards of education.

As in ancient Athens, performing "rhetorical" trials requires some technical equipment.[36] A set for fifty judges seems convenient: fifty *pinakia* (small tablets legitimating the judges, at the beginning, by lot, quickly distributed among the audience); one hundred metal *psēphoi* (tokens used to cast votes to be distributed after the speeches, a set of fifty solid and fifty pierced ones—for "guilty" and "innocent," respectively—in two separate boxes); a *klepsudra*, a metal and a wooden urn (in which to drop the *psēphoi*); and an *abax* (a board for counting the votes). My suggestion is to procure equipment that is commercially available. A booklet explaining where to find and how to use the props, and a professionally recorded video to show how such a trial works, would complete the equipment. The availability of such a mock-trial kit could encourage teachers in classics and legal history to perform "Athenian" moot courts with their students. Last but not least, the translations of and introductions to the Athenian court speeches in the Austin *Oratory of Classical Greece* series edited by Michael Gagarin will be of greatest value for this project.

NOTES

1. See my earlier attempts in this direction: Thür 2006, 2007 (not easily available in the libraries of the United States), and 2014.

2. For example, by Steel 2004.

3. Zanker 2003.

4. Thür 1977.

5. Thür 1977: 255–256. Years later I came to a passage in the psychologizing novel *Crime and Punishment* by the great Russian author Fyodor Dostoyevsky: "But why speak against yourself?" . . . "Because only peasants, or the most inexperienced novices deny everything flatly at examinations. If a man is ever so little developed and experienced, he will certainly try to admit all the external facts that can't be avoided, but will seek other explanations of them, will introduce some special, unexpected turn, that will give them other significance and put them in another light . . . ." (Dostoyevsky 1978: 243). Exactly this method, specified here for criminal examination, was used by the litigants before Athenian courts. See also Marcel Proust about the art of lying: "Elle en détachait un petit morceau, sans importance par lui-même, se disant qu'après tout c'était mieux ainsi puisque c'était un détail véritable qui n'offrait pas les mêmes dangers qu'un détail faux. 'Ça du moins, c'est vrai, se disait-elle, c'est toujours autant de gagné, il peut s'informer, il reconnaîtra que c'est vrai, ce n'est toujours pas ça qui me trahira'" (Proust 1919/1946: 85).

6. See Dem. 46.10. An affirmative answer to such a question could not be contested in court (Dem. 42.12); this—and not "to consent to a contract"—was the original sense of *homologein*. See Thür 1977: 154–158.

7. [Arist.] *Ath. Pol.* 53.2–3 mentions only trials preceded by a *diaita*, but this rule applied to trials preceded by both *diaita* and *anakrisis*. See Thür 2008: 64–66.

8. For the term "isolating the facts," see Thür 1977: 256.

9. For the editio princeps of the whole fragment, see Tchernetska et al. 2007. See now Horváth 2014: 184–188 (with German translation by Herwig Maehler); for the palimpsest more generally, see Netz et al. 2011.

10. So Thür 2010: 11, contra Whitehead 2009: 138–140, 146–148, who holds that after the guardianship was over, the former ward desiring revenge had filed an *eisangelia* either *orphanōn kakōseōs* ("impeachment for the mistreatment of orphans") or *oikou orphanikou kakōseōs* ("impeachment for the mismanagement of an orphan's estate").

11. For these requests see Isae. 6.36.

12. Peter Rhodes kindly wrote me in a letter: "David Whitehead thinks that, when the *phasis* was brought to force Timandrus to have the estate leased, Timandrus prevented it by some improper means; I suspect that as in Dem. 38.23 Timandrus simply won the case when it came to court." Here I partly agree with Whitehead 2009: 139. Winning a *phasis* trial does not fit the list of Timandrus's illegal behavior: he prevented (*ekōlusen*, l. 17)—though with good reason, I think—the *phasis*, not the *misthōsis* ("leasing").

13. Hyp. Against *Timandrus*, lines 3–5 (Netz et al. vol. 2, Fol. 138R + 135V): αὐτοῖς δὲ τοὺς ἐπιτρόπους ἀπαγορεύουσιν οἱ νόμοι μὴ ἐξεῖναι τὸν οἶκον μισθώσασθαι. For the translation "on their own authority," see Thür 2010: 13–14. Cf. Maehler in Horváth 2014: 167: "Aber dass die Vormünder den Besitz für sich pachten" ("leasing the estate for themselves").

14. Wolff 1953 convincingly demonstrated that the guardian also was allowed to lease his ward's estate.

15. On the basis of Dem. 27.58 I suggest restoring the beginning of the fragment: [ἐξῆν δὲ τοῖς ἐπιτρόποις μισθῶσαι τὸν οἶκον | κατὰ τοὺς νόμους, ὥστε τὸ κεφάλαιον τὸ διαχειρισθὲν] | τοῦ μὲν . . . ("The guardians could have let the property in accordance with the laws, so that the capital managed . . .").

16. I agree with Rubinstein 2009 (and Rhodes, see above n. 12) that the law quoted in line 53 specified only that "wards should be brought up wherever was best for them," and the notion that they should not be separated from one another is not, despite the speaker's insinuation, likely to have been included in the law.

17. For details, see Thür 1972.

18. Text quoted in Dem. 29.31; most probably Demosthenes had produced this witness deposition in 27.22.

19. See the brief remarks in Harrison 1968: 183.

20. MacDowell 2004: 25 n. 24 (commentary on Dem. 27.14), contra Cox 1998: 147.

21. See Foxhall 1996: 146.

22. *Pace* Foxhall 1996: 144 (incorrectly referring to Hunter 1989: 40), and 147, "Demochares was her 'alternative' *kurios*" (beside Aphobus).

23. Hunter 1989: 43–44 correctly remarks that Aphobus was not Cleobule's *kurios* (*pace* Harrison 1968: 59); she probably also had no *kurios* in her father's family.

24. See also Foxhall 1996: 144, asserting Cleobule was the "real heroine of this social drama."

25. On slandering women, see Foxhall 1996: 141–142.

26. See also Dem. 29.43.

27. For the ideological background, see Thür 1992: 127.

28. Thür 1975: 184–186 with further literature; see also n. 5. Today in the world of business, the method of "limbic presentation" is based on the classical technique of "complex associations" that combine sober facts with emotions.

29. This might have been important also in the different ways of controlling summary fines. See the paper of Lene Rubinstein in this volume.

30. Thür 1977: 252–254. Theophemus's opponent retorted by filing a *dikē pseudomarturiōn* against two witnesses, Euergus and Mnesibulus; his speech is preserved as Dem. 47.

31. In an admirable way, without using the term "isolation," Steel 2004 deconstructs the "Lampsakos episode" in Cic. *Verr.* 2.1.63–86.

32. In 2005 Adriaan Lanni performed this trial at Harvard, and I did the same in Graz, Austria, and Mostar, Bosnia (see the speeches in Thür 2006: 215–232 [in German]). In 2007 I performed the trial of Socrates in Graz and Freiburg, Germany (fig. 11.3). The idea of performing Athenian trials, from Isaeus's speeches, originated with Sima Avramović and his Belgrade students. For his "clinicum," see Avramović 2003.

33. The video was prepared by my colleague, Gernot Kocher, from Graz.

34. For this reason in the "Athenian style" of moot courts I dismiss copious oral depositions of witnesses and cross-examining them. See Thür 2006: 194–195; 2014: 745 (*pace* Avramović 2003). The performances of the Belgrade teams are doubtlessly more colorful.

35. For the difference between the two "counterparts" (*antistrophē*) dialectic and rhetoric, see Arist. *Rh.* 1354a.

36. Fully specified in [Arist.] *Ath. Pol.* 63–69.

REFERENCES

Avramović, Sima. 2003. "Simulation of Athenian Court: A New Teaching Method." *Balkans Law Review* 16: 47–50.

Cox, Cheryl Anne. 1998. *Household Interests: Property, Marriage Strategies, and Family Dynamics in Ancient Athens*. Princeton: Princeton University Press.

Dostoyevsky, Fyodor. 1978. *Crime and Punishment*. Translated by Constance Garnett. New York: Modern Library.

Foxhall, Lin. 1996. "The Law and the Lady: Women and Legal Proceedings in Classical Athens." In *Greek Law in Its Political Setting: Justifications not Justice*, edited by Lin Foxhall and A. D. E. Lewis, 133–152. Oxford: Clarendon Press.

Harrison, A. R. W. 1968. *The Law of Athens*. Vol. 1, *The Family and Property*. Oxford: Clarendon Press.

Horváth, László. 2014. *Der "Neue Hypereides": Textedition, Studien und Erläuterungen*. Berlin: De Gruyter.

Hunter, Virginia J. 1989. "Women's Authority in Classical Athens: The Example of Kleoboule and Her Son." *Échos du monde classique/Classical Views* 33: 39–48.

MacDowell, Douglas M., trans. 2004. *Demosthenes, Speeches 27–38*. Austin: University of Texas Press.

Netz, Reviel, William Noel, Nigel Wilson, and Natalie Tchernetska. 2011. *The Archimedes Palimpsest*. 2 vols. Cambridge: Cambridge University Press for the Walters Art Museum.

Proust, Marcel. 1919/1946. *À la recherche du temps perdu*. Vol. 2, *Du côté de chez Swann*, Pt.2, *Un amour de Swann*. Paris: Editions Gallimard.

Rubinstein, Lene. 2009. "Legal Argumentation in Hypereides *Against Timandros*." *Bulletin of the Institute of Classical Studies* 52: 149–159.

Steel, Catherine. 2004. "Being Economical with the Truth: What Really Happened at Lampsakos." In *Cicero the Advocate*, edited by Jonathan Powell and Jeremy Paterson, 233–251. Oxford: Oxford University Press.

Tchernetska, Natalie, Eric W. Handley, Colin F. L. Austin, and László Horváth. 2007. "New Readings in the Fragment of Hyperides' *Against Timandros* from the Archimedes Palimpsest." *Zeitschrift für Papyrologie und Epigraphik* 162: 1–4.

Thür, Gerhard. 1972. "Der Streit über den Status des Werkstättenleiters Milyas (Dem. *Or.* 29)." *Revue internationale des droits de l'Antiquité*, ser. 3, 19: 151–177.

———. 1975. "Komplexe Prozeßführung: Dargestellt am Beispiel des Trapezitikos (Isokr. 17)." In *Symposion 1971: Vorträge zur griechischen und hellenistischen Rechtsgeschichte*, edited by Hans Julius Wolff, Joseph Mélèze Modrzejewski, and Dieter Nörr, 157–188. Cologne: Böhlau.

———. 1977. *Beweisführung vor den Schwurgerichtshöfen Athens: Die Proklesis zur Basanos*. Vienna: Verlag der Österreichischen Akademie der Wissenschaften.

———. 1992. "Armut: Gedanken zu Ehegüterrecht und Familienvermögen in der griechischen Polis." In *Eherecht und Familiengut in Antike und Mittelalter*, edited by Dieter Simon, 121–132. Munich: R. Oldenbourg.

———. 2006. "Clinicum Antike Rechtsgeschichte. Forensische Rhetorik." In *Imperium und Provinzen (Zentrale und Regionen): Internationales Sommerseminar in Antiker Rechtsgeschichte, Sarajevo, 30 April–04 Mai 2005*, edited by Gerhard Thür and Zdravko Lučić, 191–232. Sarajevo: Pravni fakultet univerziteta u Sarajevu.

———. 2007. "Rhetorik im Rechtsunterricht: Clinicum Antike Rechtsgeschichte." In *Zur Geschichte des Rechts: Festschrift für Gernot Kocher zum 65. Geburtstag*, edited by Helmut Gebhardt and Markus Steppan, 461–472. Graz: Graz Universitätsverlag, Leykam.

———. 2008. "The Principle of Fairness in Athenian Legal Procedure: Thoughts on the '*Echinos*' and '*Enklema*.'" *Dike* 11: 51–73.

———. 2010. "How to Lease an Orphan's Estate in Classical Athens." *Annals of the Faculty of Law in Belgrade–Belgrade Law Review* 58: 7–19.

———. 2014. "Antike Streitfälle im Rechtsunterricht." In *Inter cives necnon peregrinos: Essays in Honour of Boudewijn Sirks*, edited by Jan Hallebeek, Martin Schermaier, Roberto Fiori, Ernest Metzger, and Jean-Pierre Coriat, 741–750. Göttingen: Vandenhoeck and Ruprecht.

———. *Opera Omnia*. ‹http://epub.oeaw.ac.at/gerhard-thuer› will be on open access in 2017.

Whitehead, David. 2009. "Hypereides' *Timandros*: Observations and Suggestions." *Bulletin of the Institute of Classical Studies* 52: 135–148.

Wolff, Hans Julius. 1953. "Verpachtung von Mündelvermögen in Attika." In *Festschrift Hans Lewald*, 201–208. Basel: Helbing and Lichtenhahn.

Zanker, Paul. 2003. *Augustus und die Macht der Bilder*. 4th ed. Munich: C. H. Beck.

CONTRIBUTORS

EVA CANTARELLA, now retired, was professor of ancient Greek law in the School of Law, Università di Milano. She is co-founder and editor (with Alberto Maffi) of *Dike*, a journal of ancient Greek law and legal history. Her work has focused largely on the history of women and sexuality, archaic Greek law, and criminal law. Her books include *Pandora's Daughters: The Role and Status of Women in Greek and Roman Antiquity* (1987), *Bisexuality in the Ancient World* (2002), *I supplizi capitali in Grecia e a Roma* (2005), *Il ritorno della vendetta* (2007), and (with Andrew Lear) *Images of Pederasty: Boys Were Their Gods* (2008).

EDWARD E. COHEN is professor of ancient history and classical studies (adjunct) at the University of Pennsylvania. His books include *Athenian Economy and Society: A Banking Perspective* (1992), *The Athenian Nation* (2000), and *Athenian Prostitution: The Business of Sex* (2015). He is presently preparing for publication *Roman Economy and Society: Slaves' Perspective*.

MARTIN DREHER is professor of ancient history at Otto-von-Guericke-University, Magdeburg, Germany. His books on Greek history include *Athen und Sparta* (2001, with a 2nd ed. in 2011) and *Sizilien in der Antike: Geschichte und Archäologie* (2008), and he has published many articles on Greek history and Greek legal history, particularly on the Greek sophists, Athenian democracy, asylum, amnesty, and curse tablets.

MICHAEL GAGARIN is James R. Dougherty, Jr. Professor of Classics Emeritus at the University of Texas. His books on Greek law include *Drakon and Early Athenian Homicide Law* (1981), *Early Greek Law* (1986), *Writing Greek Law* (2008), and (with Paula Perlman) *The Laws of Ancient Crete, c. 650–400 BCE* (2016). He is also series editor of *The Oratory of Classical Greece* (1998–) and editor in chief of the *Oxford Encyclopedia of Ancient Greece and Rome* (2010).

MOGENS HERMAN HANSEN is emeritus reader in classics in the Saxo-Institute at the University of Copenhagen. From 1993 to 2005 he was director of the Copenhagen Polis Centre. He has written numerous books and articles on ancient Greek history. His books include *The Athenian Democracy in the Age of Demosthenes* (1991, 2nd ed. 1999), *Polis and City-State: An Ancient Concept and its Modern Equivalent* (1998), *The Shotgun Method: The Demography of the Ancient Greek City-State Culture* (2006), and *Polis: An Introduction to the Ancient Greek City-State* (2006).

ADRIAAN LANNI is the Touroff-Glueck Professor of Law at Harvard Law School, where she teaches criminal law, criminal adjudication, and the criminal justice workshop, as well as a variety of legal history courses on ancient Greek and Roman law. Her publications include *Law and Justice in the Courts of Classical Athens* (2006), *Law and Order in Ancient Athens* (2016), and articles on ancient law and the modern criminal jury.

ALBERTO MAFFI, now retired, was professor of Roman law and ancient Greek law at Milano-Bicocca State University. He has written numerous books and articles on Greek and Roman Law, including *Studi di epigrafia giuridica greca* (1983). He is co-founder and editor (with Eva Cantarella) of *Dike*, a journal of ancient Greek law and legal history.

LENE RUBINSTEIN is professor of ancient history, Royal Holloway, University of London. She is the author of *Adoption in IV. Century Athens* (1993), *Litigation and Co-operation: The Use of Supporting Speakers in the Courts of Classical Athens* (2000), and numerous articles and chapters on ancient Greek law, oratory, and history.

GERHARD THÜR is emeritus professor of Roman law and ancient legal history at the University of Graz, Austria, and chairman of the Kommission für Antike Rechtsgeschichte at the Austrian Academy of Science. He has written numerous articles on ancient Greek law, especially Greek procedural law, and (with Hans Taeuber) published *Prozessrechtliche Inschriften Arkadiens* (1994). A second edition (in English) of his first book on evidence in Athenian law, *Beweisführung vor den Schwurgerichtshöfen Athens: Die Proklesis zur Basanos* (1977), is in preparation.

JULIE VELISSAROPOULOS-KARAKOSTAS is emeritus professor of the history of law (ancient Greek and Roman law) in the School of Law, Athens University. Her publications include *Les nauclères grecs: Recherches sur les institutions maritimes en Grèce et dans l'Orient hellénisé* (1980), *Droit grec d'Alexandre a Auguste: Personnes, biens, justice* (2011), and numerous articles on ancient law, economy, and society.

ROBERT W. WALLACE is professor of classics at Northwestern University. He is the author of numerous articles on Greek law, history, intellectual history, literature, numismatics, and music theory. His books include *The Areopagos Council, to 307 BC* (1989) and *Reconstructing Damon: Music, Wisdom Teaching, and Politics in Perikles' Athens* (2015), and (with Josiah Ober and Kurt Raaflaub) *Origins of Democracy in Ancient Greece* (2007) and (with Chloe Balla) *Aristotle's Constitution of the Athenians* (2015). Current projects include books on Sophocles, Thucydides, and Plato's Socrates.

INDEX LOCORUM

Demosthenes
    9.3: 166–167
    18.275: 153n29
    19.123–127: 140n63
    20.219–225: 18
    21.32–33: 141n73
    21.47: 16, 66
    21.74–76: 29
    21.76: 29–30
    21.103: 16
    22.25–26: 19
    22.25–29: 80
    23.29: 27
    23.32: 29–30
    24.20–23: 190n75
    24.33: 190n75
    24.39–40: 190n75
    24.42: 190n75
    24.45: 190n75
    24.50: 190n75
    24.54: 190n75
    24.56: 190n75
    24.59: 190n75
    24.149: 12, 19
    [25].71: 74
    [25].76: 18
    [26].24: 17
    27.5: 199
    27.13–18: 200
    27.14: 205n20
    27.15–17: 199
    27.19–23: 198
    27.22: 205n18
    27.50–52: 198
    27.58: 205n15
    27.65: 200
    27.69: 200
    28.12: 198
    29.9: 199
    29.22: 199
    29.26: 200
    29.31: 205n18
    29.43: 205n26

    29.50: 198
    30.27: 41
    34.37: 42
    35.11: 152n13
    35.13: 44, 52n34, 78, 154n35
    35.39: 52n33, 154n35
    35.50–51: 42
    36: 57–58
    36.12: 57
    36.13: 64n26
    36.13–14: 57–58, 63n19
    36.14: 58
    36.37: 57
    37.22: 64n33
    37.25: 64n33
    37.51: 59, 64n34
    38.23: 205n12
    39.40: 19
    42.12: 51nn23–24, 204n6
    [43].62: 12
    [43].71: 13
    45: 57–58
    46.10: 204n6
    47: 206n30
    47.39: 200
    47.45: 200
    47.77–78: 39, 50nn10–11
    48: 40
    48.11: 50n12, 51n24
    51.13: 78
    53.20: 64n27
    54: 19
    55: 59
    55.31–32: 64n36
    56.2: 42, 51n24
    57.7: 18
    57.34: 63n23
    57.59–60: 18
    [59].16: 13
Diodorus Siculus
    12.19: 12
Diogenes Laertius
    2.40: 14

Ephorus *ap.* Strabo
    6.1.8: 12, 14
Euripides
    Ion 855–856: 167
    Supp. 429–434: 12, 186

Herodotus
    6.57.4: 189n61
Hesiod
    Op. 11–12: 13
    Op. 38–39: 20
    Op. 255–285: 90
    Theog. 84–92: 90
    Theog. 901–903: 90
Homer
    Il. 9.96–99: 90
    Il. 18.499–504: 27
    Od. 11.568–571: 90
Hyperides
    3: 35–49, 55–57
    3.3: 62
    3.6: 63n13, 63n23
    3.8: 49n1
    3.9–11: 65n55
    3.10: 56
    3.11: 63n17
    3.13: 45, 65n56
    3.19: 63n17
    3.22: 63n14
    3.26: 65n56
    c. Timandrum: 197–198, 205n13

Isaeus
    6.36: 204n11
    10.2: 22n30, 22n42
Isocrates
    7.33–44: 18
    11.20–21: 51n31
    15.314: 18
    20: 19

Lycurgus
    1.3–4: 80

1.4: 12
1.129: 189n62
Lysias
    1: 49, 51n51, 202
    1.29–34: 30–31
    1.30–34: 12
    1.49: 12
    6.10: 185
    9: 74, 129–130
    9.6: 140n66
    9.7: 140n66
    9.10: 140n66
    12.38: 18
    17: 74
    20.31: 169n36
    23: 59
    24: 18, 74
    25.13: 169n36
    30.1: 18

Plato
    Ap. 24b: 14
    Ap. 34c: 19
    Grg. 483b: 64n27
    Leg. 762b: 136n42
    Leg. 793a: 153n27
    Leg. 933a–e: 99n38
    Phdr. 275a: 180
    Plt. 295a–b: 14
    Resp. 364b: 99n38
    Resp. 400a: 14
    Resp. 563b: 167
Plutarch
    Agis 5.2: 189n62
    Agis 9.1: 189n62
    Lyc. 6.1: 189n61
    Lyc. 6.4: 189n61
    Lyc. 13.1: 189n62
    Lyc. 13.3: 189n62
    [*Mor.*] 227b: 189n62
    Solon 18: 17
    Solon 20.3: 12
    Solon 24.1: 13

INDEX

Note: Some terms that a reader might expect to find in the index of a volume on ancient Greek law are not included here because they are pervasive, occurring either explicitly or implicitly multiple times in many of the chapters. Among these are "Athens," "citizen," "court," and "justice." Readers are advised to consult the Introduction, pp. 3–7, for guidance on which chapters focus on, for example, "Athenian law." For specific types of legal proceedings (e.g., *dikē pseudomarturiōn*, "prosecution for false witness") and various public officials (e.g., *thesmothetai*, "judicial officials"), see the *Index of Greek Terms*.

Adkeme Milga, 176
admission, pre-trial, 41
Aeschylus, 26–29, 31. *See also* Aeschylus in *Index Locorum*
agreements, law on, 4, 35–49; maritime, 44, 51n24; with slaves, 54–62; unjust/unlawful, 4, 42–47; voluntary, 42, 44, 47; written, 35, 38, 43, 55, 147. *See also* contracts; *homologia* in *Index of Greek Terms*
Albanian Kanun, 177–178
amautas. *See* Inca
Andocides, 185–186. *See also* Andocides in *Index Locorum*
anger, 4, 25–33
anthropology, 2, 157–160; legal, 165
antidemocratic, 18. *See also* democratic; non-democratic
Aphobus, 41, 193, 196, 198–200
appeal. *See* verdict

Areopagus, 12, 16, 19, 27–29, 31, 184
aristocracy, 104–105, 130
Aristotle, 14, 21n18, 36, 141n73, 148. *See also* Aristotle in *Index Locorum*
asebeia. *See* impiety
asylum, 93–94, 97

Blas Valera, 176–177

canon law, 89
Charondas, 12, 91, 181
Cleisthenes, 184
cleruch, 198
coinage, 63n16, 136n38, 194
commerce, 4, 54–62; maritime, 44, 58–59, 146–147
community, 10–20, 73, 77, 96–97, 126–127, 166
confiscation of property, 78–79

constitutional reform, 20, 184; rule, 183–185

contracts, 4, 12, 36, 56–59, 70, 74–75, 78, 86, 92, 113, 121, 123–125, 145–146, 149–150; consensual, 4, 39–40; real, 4, 39–40; specific performance, 39–40

cooperation, 31

curse, 13, 85, 88–89, 91–92, 96; curse tablet, 6, 97

custom, 6–7, 98n15, 146–149, 151, 175–176, 178

Damon, 14

definition of terms, 3, 13–14

Delphic amphictyony, 94, 147, 152n19

democratic, 4, 6, 16–19, 72–77, 105–107, 126, 128, 131. *See also* anti-democratic; non-democratic

demos, 12, 18, 31, 75

Demosthenes, 7, 29–30, 39–41, 43, 57–59, 146, 148, 198–200. *See also* Demosthenes in *Index Locorum*

Denmark, 182–183

depositions, 39, 199, 202–203

dicast, 15, 17–20, 29–31, 79, 131n1; oath of, 12, 19, 29, 31, 49, 147. *See also* jury

Dikē (goddess), 90

Draco, 181, 184–185; law on homicide, 11, 13, 26–27, 38, 179; punishments of, 12

economics: law and, 161–165; new institutional, 161. *See also* transaction costs

egalitarianism, 25, 27, 31–32

emotions, 4, 17, 25–33, 145

enforcement: of contracts, 42–43, 47; of laws, 6–7, 10, 13, 36, 94–96, 104–131, 147, 164–165. *See also* contracts: specific performance; verdicts

enmity, 4, 18, 26–27, 30–31, 127

Ephialtes, 31; laws of, 184

Ephorus, 12, 14

Erinyes, 28

Eritrea, 7, 175–176, 181

estate, 15–16, 40, 43, 197–198

evidence, 164–165, 197

expressive function of law, 166–167

fines, 6, 96; summary, 104–131

feud, 3–4, 19, 26, 30; blood feud, 162, 178; feuding society, 26, 72, 158, 162

Foucault, Michel, 25–26

gods, 14, 87, 89, 90–91, 93, 96–97. *See also* priests; religion; sacred law

gossip, 160, 165

Hawaiian chants, 181

homicide, 11–12, 27–28, 30, 89, 92, 178. *See also* Draco

hubris, 11, 14–15, 29, 166; law on *hubris*, 13, 16, 19, 166–167

Hundertwasser, Friedensreich, 194–196

Hyperides, 7, 35–49, 55–57, 61, 197–198, 201. *See also* Hyperides in *Index Locorum*

Iceland (medieval), 7, 26, 173–174; laws of, 173–175, 180–182

Iliad, 180, 186

impiety, 5, 11, 14, 16, 89, 92–93, 96, 185; law against impiety, 11

Inca: *amautas*, 177, 180; empire, 7, 176–177, 180–182; laws, 177, 180

indictment, 14–16, 97; counterindictment, 37, 72

inheritance, 38, 43, 162. *See also* estate; orphans

"isolate the facts," 193–204

judge, 17–18, 27–30, 72, 91–92, 104–105, 120, 123, 130–131, 147–148, 173,

175–177, 194, 199–200, 202–203;
foreign judges, 6, 97, 107, 151
judgment, 121–122, 174, 203; collective,
19–20; execution of, 110, 163–164;
most just, 147–148. *See also* dicast;
judge; jury; verdict
jury, 30–31, 41–43, 45–49, 201. *See also*
dicast; judge; verdict

Koran, 180

law: above the, 43–44; administrative, 5,
74–77; and economy, 161–165; code,
17; international, 144–151; interpretation of, 46–49; meaning of, 46–
49; organization of, 17; primitive, 11,
16; private, 70–81; procedural, 2–4,
10–20, 86, 158, 162, 173, 176; public, 5, 70–81, 86–88, 145; rule of, 4,
25–33, 72–77, 165; substantive, 10–
16, 158; unity of Athenian law, 44–
45; unity of Greek law, 104–107,
120, 122, 128–131, 149, 151. *See also*
canon law; economics: law; expressive function of law; oral law; sacred
law; sharia law; soft law; torts; unwritten law
laws: on agreements, 35–49; on concealment of slave's physical defects, 45;
against *hubris*, 11, 13, 16, 166–167;
on influencing someone drawing
up a will, 45–46; on lying in the agora, 45; on misrepresentation of facts
in a betrothal agreement, 45–46;
Rhodian maritime, 146. *See also* hubris; impiety
lawspeaker, 173–174, 180–182, 187n7
leases, 57–58, 75, 126
legal koinē, 107, 149, 151
litigants, 4, 17–18, 27, 29–30, 37–38,
41–42, 47–49, 56, 58–59, 91–92, 130,
159, 163–164, 194, 196–197, 200,
202–203

loans, 57, 59, 61, 78, 146, 149, 163
logographer/logography, 18, 30–31, 35,
196–197
Lombard laws, 174–175, 179, 182
Luria, Alexander, 180
Lycurgus (of Athens), 12, 80–81, 181
Lycurgus (of Sparta), 91, 176, 181
Lysias, 18, 30–31, 202. *See also* Lysias in
Index Locorum

MacDowell, Douglas, 1, 11, 13, 16,
58–59, 71, 185, 199
magic, 5, 85, 92, 97–98
magistrates, 73–80, 87, 91, 96–
97, 154n37, 163, 184–186, 198,
202
Maine, Henry Sumner, 10–11, 16
manumission, 58, 91–92, 99n36,
107, 199
memory, 172–192
Milyas, 198–199
mining, 58–59
moot court, 193, 201–204
murder. *See* homicide

New Testament, 180
Njal's Saga, 174
non-democratic, 126, 128. *See also* antidemocratic; democratic
Norway, law of Gulating, 182

oaths, 48, 50n20, 82n33, 88–89, 91–92,
96, 115–117, 123–126, 147–148. *See
also* dicast
Odyssey, 180, 186
oligarchic, 6, 78, 97, 104–105, 130–131,
183. *See also* non-democratic
oral law. *See* unwritten law
oral procedure, 72, 158, 186
oratory, 2, 31–32, 105, 193–204. *See
also* Aeschines; Andocides; Demosthenes; Hyperides; Lysias;
rhetoric

INDEX OF GREEK TERMS

adikein ("wrong doing"), 14, 40
agōgimos ("liable to seizure"), 29
agōnothetai ("overseers of contests"),
120, 133n21, 137n42
agoraios ("commercially savvy"), 62
agoranomos ("overseers of the marketplace"), 75, 110–111, 114, 129, 133,
141n69
agrapha nomima ("unwritten rules"),
148
agraphoi nomoi ("unwritten laws"),
99n31, 185
aikeia ("assault"), 200
anagrapheis nomōn ("promulgators of
laws"), 185
anakrisis ("preliminary hearing"), 17,
197, 201–202
andreia ("manliness"), 54, 62
androlepsia ("seizure of foreigners"), 77
androphonia ("manslaughter"), 29
androphonos ("one convicted of manslaughter"), 29
anēr eleutheros ("free man"), 54
antigraphē ("defendant's plea"), 202
anupeuthynoi ("immunity from auditing"), 119
anupodikoi ("immunity from prosecution"), 114, 119
apeleutheroi ("freed slaves"), 62n3

apellaia ("type of sacrifice"), 121
aphanēs ousia ("invisible economy"), 61
apographē ("catalogue of a debtor's
property"), 79
apologoi ("auditors"), 120, 138n50
apophainein ("to report"), 15–16
apophora ("sharing arrangement"), 58
aporrhēta ("unmentionables"), 21n27
ara ("curse"), 88, 92
archon ([chief] "magistrate"), 13, 17, 75,
77, 118, 129, 135n32, 136n42, 197–198
asebeia ("impiety"), 5, 11, 89, 92–93, 96
astunomoi ("overseers of the city"), 75
asulia ("inviolability"), 85, 94, 97
atechnoi pisteis ("artless proofs"),
193–194
atelēs ("tax exempt"), 141n69
atimia ("disenfranchisement"), 16, 109,
119–120, 162
axones ("rotating boards"), 185

basileus ("high-ranking official"), 11, 17,
90, 129
blabē ("damages"), 35, 145
boulē ("Council of 500"), 16, 185
boulē ("council"), 115, 118, 123, 133n21,
135n29, 136n35, 137n42
(ho) boulomenos. *See* prosecutors: volunteer in *Index*

225

chiliastus ("division of citizens"), 137n42

damosios ("public servant"), 115–116
dēmarchos ("chairman of a deme"), 112–113
(ta) dēmosia ("[the] public interest"), 73
diadikasia ("suit to decide between claimants"), 79
diaita ("arbitration"), 197
dikai emporikai ("commercial maritime suits"), 58–59
dikai metallikai ("commercial mining suits"), 59
dikaios ("just"), 30, 36
dikai trapezitikai ("commercial banking suits"), 59
dikastērion ("people's court"), 17, 19, 97, 106, 114–115, 201
dikē ("private lawsuit"), 19, 32, 197
dikē blabēs ("suit for damages"), 37, 40
dikē epitropēs (prosecution for mismanagement of an orphan's estate"), 197, 199–200
dikē pseudomarturiōn ("prosecution for false witness"), 200
diorizein ("to define"), 12, 14
dogma ("resolution"), 150
douloi chōris oikountes ("slaves living independently"), 54, 60–61
doulos ("slave"), 55–56, 57, 59, 61

echthra ("enmity"), 4, 26, 27, 30
echthros ("enemy"), 30
ekklēsia ("citizen assembly"), 31, 80
ekphora ("carrying out the corpse"), 118
eleutherous apheisan ("set them free"), 57–58
enklēma ("complaint"), 201–202
epexelthein ("to follow through"), 15–16, 79
ephetai (?), 11
epidekaton ("court deposit of 10%"), 137n43

epieikeia ("decency"), 18
epikleros ("heiress"), 12, 162
epikrisis ("judgment"), 112, 121
epimeletai ("overseers"), 134
epipempton ("court deposit of 20%"), 137n43
epistatai ("board of officials"), 120–121
eranoi ("friendly loans"), 61
ergasia ("business"), 54, 57
ergastērion ("workshop"), 59
esdotēres ("offfficials in charge of letting public contracts"), 112–113
ethismos ("accustoming"), 153n26
ēthopoiia ("character representation"), 18
ethos ("custom"), 153n26
euexia ("bodily vigor"), 123
euthunai ("auditing"), 119
euthunos ("public examiner"), 77
exetastai ("examiners"), 114–115, 138n50
exōmosia ("oath of disclaimer"), 123–126

gerea ("perquisites"), 123
gerontes ("elders"), 27
gnomē dikaiotatē ("most just opinion"), 147
gnomē te heautou ("own and true opinion"), 147
graphē ("public lawsuit"), 11, 13–14, 19, 32, 79
graphē paranomon ("indictment for an illegal proposal"), 22n39
grapta nomima ("written rules"), 148
gumnasiarchos ("official in charge of gymnasiums"), 114, 135n31, 140n64, 141n74
gunaikonomoi ("overseers of women"), 117–118

halia ("assembly"), 121
hellanodikai ("chief judges at games"), 120, 136n42

hemiolion ("50 percent surcharge"), 113, 119, 122, 128, 136n42, 137n43

hiereus ("priest"), 135n29

hieroi ("sacred judges"), 97

hieromnēmones ("rememberers of sacred matters"), 182

hieronomoi ("overseers of sanctuaries"), 114, 133n22

hieropoioi ("temple officials"), 118, 133n21, 134n29

hieros ("sacred"), 92, 98n11, 98n17

hieros nomos ("sacred law"), 86

hierosulia ("theft of sacred property"), 89, 92–93, 99n26

hierotamiai ("treasurers of sacred funds"), 115–116

hierothutēs ("sacrificing priest"), 115–116

hikesia ("supplication"), 94

hiketai ("suppliants"), 94

homologia ("agreement"), 41–42, 147, 199, 204n6

horoi ("mortgage markers"), 61

horophylakēs ("overseers of boundaries"), 109–110

hosios ("profane"), 98n11

idiotēs ("private citizen"), 75, 77–79

kakourgos ("offender"), 106

katēgoros ("accuser"), 80

(ta) koina ("[the] public interest"), 73

koinoi prosodoi ("public revenue"), 78

(to) koinon ("public treasury"), 78

koinon poleos ("official acting on behalf of the polis"), 78

kosmos ("chief magistrate"), 183

kotos ("grudge"), 31

kurios ("authoritative"), 19, 36, 39, 43–44, 116–117, 119–120, 150

kurios ("woman's guardian"), 199

lampadarchēs ("leader of the torch race"), 123, 125–126

lampadistai ("participants in the torch race"), 138n55

leukoma ("white-washed board"), 140n66

lipotaxion ("battlefield desertion"), 16

metapemptoi dikastai ("foreign judge/arbitrators"), 151

mnēmones ("rememberers"), 182

moichos ("adulterer"), 13

monarchos ("high-ranking official"), 133n20

naopoiai/neopoiai ("temple officials"), 133n21, 137n43

nomos ("law"), 36, 138n46, 148, 150

oikou orphanikou kakōseōs ("impeachment for mismanagement of an orphan's estate"), 204n10

orphanōn kakōseōs ("impeachment for mistreatment of an orphan"), 204n10

oxuthumon ("keen to punish"), 28

paidotribai ("gymnastic trainers"), 148

paragraphē ("counter-indictment"), 37, 72, 200

parakatathēkai ("lease of deposits"), 58

patrios nomos ("ancestral law"), 185

patrios politeia ("ancestral constitution"), 183–184

phainein ("to show"), 15

phasis ("denunciation"), 15, 197–198

phularchoi ("tribal officials"), 121

poinē ("blood money"), 27

polemarchoi ("board of high-ranking officials"), 118

(hoi) politeuomenoi ("professional politicians"), 80

politikoi nomoi ("civic laws"), 148

politikos praktōr ("exactor of public debts"), 114

praktōr ("exactor of public debts"), 113–115

praxis ("exacting of the penalty"), 108–109, 112, 114–115, 119, 133n21, 136n40, 138n47, 138n55

probouloi ("magistrates"), 153n22

proix ("dowry"), 200

prokatabolē ("installment"), 133n21

proklēsis eis basanōn ("challenge to torture a slave"), 196–199

pronoia ("premeditation"), 11

prutaneis ("public officials"), 111, 135n29, 136n35, 137n43

psēphisma ("decree"), 147, 150, 152n15

rhabdos ("whip"), 129

rhetra ("pronouncement"), 187n2

sōphrōn ("temperate"), 26

strategoi ("military commanders"), 16, 76, 78, 140n68

sulān ("seizure"), 78

sulē ("right of seizure"), 78

sunēgoros ("co-speaker"), 197

synthēkē ("treaty"), 150

tagos ("official"), 121

tamiai ("treasurers"), 113, 136n42, 140n66

thesmoi ("ordinances"), 184

thesmothetai ("judicial officials"), 13, 29

thetes ("lowest census group"), 105

thorubos ("hubbub"), 19

timoria ("punishment"), 30

trapeza ("bank"), 57